Non-Traditional Aspects of the Mexican Financial Crisis of 1994/95

European University Studies

Europäische Hochschulschriften
Publications Universitaires Européennes

Series V
Economics and Management

Reihe V   Série V
Volks- und Betriebswirtschaft
Sciences économiques, gestion d'entreprise

Vol./Bd. 3406

PETER LANG
Frankfurt am Main · Berlin · Bern · Bruxelles · New York · Oxford · Wien

Roxana Xonalí Orozco de Plesnar

Non-Traditional Aspects
of the Mexican Financial Crisis
# of 1994/95

Structural Weaknesses in the Real Sector
and the Role of Domestic Investors,
OTC Derivatives & Synthetic Capital Flows

PETER LANG
Internationaler Verlag der Wissenschaften

Bibliographic Information published by the Deutsche Nationalbibliothek
The Deutsche Nationalbibliothek lists this publication in the Deutsche Nationalbibliografie; detailed bibliographic data is available in the internet at http://dnb.d-nb.de.

Zugl.: Eichstätt, Kath. Univ., Diss., 2011

Printed with the support
of Friedrich Naumann Foundation for Freedom
with funds of the German Federal Foreign Office.

ISSN 0531-7339
ISBN 978-3-631-61942-1

© Peter Lang GmbH
Internationaler Verlag der Wissenschaften
Frankfurt am Main 2012
All rights reserved.

www.peterlang.de

I dedicate this work to my loving mother, Ma. Minerva García, for teaching me with your example courage and spirit, to my daughters Anna-Valentina and Lena-Sofía for inspiring me continuously and to my husband Christian Plesnar and my brother Dr. Héctor Fabiel Orozco García, for supporting me, not only to reach this goal but always. Thank you Lord for showing me that nothing is impossible.

Foreword

Financial crises have been recurrent after the nineties all over the world, with the 2008 Global Crisis outstanding. The Mexican crisis of 1994/5 was the first of various episodes that followed a common pattern. Destabilizing capital inflows financed both imbalances in the real sector, specifically a large current account and a credit boom associated to credit deterioration, until capital reversals triggered off a crisis. The appreciation of the domestic currency, aggravated in earlier shocks by a pegged exchange rate management, supported the large and growing current account deficit. These similar chains of events were up to 2008 associated to most previous crises in the developing world, including the Mexican case.

However, the research in this thesis provides some evidence of *derivative trading*, an aspect highlighted by the Global Crisis of 2008-2009 also present in Mexico's financial crisis of 1994-1995. As first discussed by Garber (1998), given regulatory loopholes, Mexican banks negotiated significant amounts of OTC (over the counter) derivatives with foreign banks, which reached their peak in 1994 at 4.9% of GDP. This practice caused capital inflows associated to leveraged Tesobono buys (dollar-denominated government bonds), which were themselves largely purchased only as a result of derivative trading and hedging. Evidence suggests that the existence and magnitude of the bubble, which burst in late 1994, was determined by the massive availability of *synthetic capital inflows*, defined as the mere result of derivative trading. In the absence of leveraged derivative trading and the resulting capital inflows, Mexico would likely not have been able to finance the large current account deficit of over 7% of GDP in 1994. A softer landing might have been possible despite the necessary exchange rate correction that occurred after December 1994.

The prolongation of the pegged exchange rate regime contributed partially to the development of the crisis. However, even if certain macroeconomic misbalances are a precondition for a crisis, capital flows are at the core, since they influence the emergence and magnitude of a bubble. *Synthetic capital inflows*, through their leverage effect, artificially "inflate" the bubble and therefore magnify the burst effects on the economy. Mexico was able to improve its financial regulation after the 1994/5 crisis, as evidenced by the resilience of the domestic financial markets to financial spillovers in 2008-2009. The international challenge ahead is to establish financial regulations that restrict excessive risk-taking behaviour to avoid systemic risks and recurring crises. The scope and features of leveraging and the increase of the equity ratios should be reconsidered in the redesign of an international financial system geared to promote, not to hinder, economic growth.

Acknowledgments

I would like to thank the **Friedrich Naumann Foundation for Freedom** for the generous financial support to the present research project provided by the **German Federal Foreign Office** Funds. But above all, I would like to heartily thank the German liberal family for deepening my liberal convictions and for their excellent Scholarship Program Group. I also want to express my deep gratitude to Prof. Dr. Joachim Genosko, Prof. Dr. Johannes Schneider, PD Dr. Reinhard Weber and their teams for their guidance and help along the rough way. I am indebted to Manuela Schieck-Konjaev for the reading of a previous manuscript. A key person from the beginning on was Prof. Dr. Jörg Clostermann. Hearty thanks for being a liberal example to follow and a great contribution to this thesis. I thank God for giving me so many opportunities in life and dedicate this work to the loving memory of our colleagues Adolf Zöpfl and Michael Gold.

I owe my deepest gratitude to my loving husband, Christian Plesnar for his time and support in these long years and to my children Anna-Valentina and Lena-Sofia for-challenging and motivating me continuously. My brother and sisters in law, Héctor, Leyme and Claudia, thank you for being a light on my way. To my family in law, Dr. Albin and Helene Plesnar, thank you for your permanent support. I am also grateful to my nephews Héctor, Erick and particularly Lineth. Especially to my mother, I want to thank you for being an example of courage and spirit.

I also wish to thank the staff of the Ingolstadt University of Applied Sciences, which helped in one way or the other to the completion of this thesis, mainly the supportive Business Administration Faculty, the helpful library team and the friendly cafeteria employees.

I also thank my inspiration and friend Dr. Ing. Efstratia Zafeiriou for the partial lecture of this thesis. Carlos Villarreal, Neeta Shetty, Erika Paredes and Jens Wengorz thank you for reading previous sections of this document. My deep appreciation is to be expressed to all my good friends who took care of my beloved children in these years of efforts. I am also very grateful to Getrud and Heinz Reim and my other neighbours for supporting this research project by assuming some of my domestic duties.

I would like to express gratitude to my former colleagues in the Mexican public sector, especially to Ricardo Vargas, not only for his contribution to this project but also for revealing me the fervour of working for the sake of public policy. I also would like to take the opportunity to thank Lions Club, Presbyterian Pan American School, and ITESM Campus Monterrey for the scholarships they granted me in the past. These were decisive pillars of my academic formation and a great motivation to continue my path.

Last but not least I want to thank Mr. Peter Garber and Ms. Benu Schneider for your willingness to support this cause, Prof. Albert Britton and Dr. José de Jesús Salazar for your useful literature hints, Dr. Leonardo Torre for your helpful interviews and Aquico Wen, Carlos Perez Verdía, Dr. Ricardo Basurto and Dr. Klender Cortez for your collaboration.

Table of Contents

Figure Index

Table Index

Abbreviations List

APEC: Asian-Pacific Economic Cooperation
Banxico: Banco de México
BIS: Bank of International Settlements
CEO: Chief Executive Officer
CETES: Mexican Federal Treasury Certificates
FDI: Foreign Direct Investment
Forex: foreign exchange
GDP: Gross Domestic Product.
IMF: International Monetary Fund.
INEGI: Instituto Nacional de Estadística, Geografía e Informática
IOSCO: International Organization of Securities Commissions
MexDer: Mercado Mexicano de Derivados
NAFTA: North American Free Trade Agreement
NAV: Net Asset Values.
OECD: Organisation for Economic Cooperation and Development.
OTC: Over the Counter
SEC: Securities and Exchange Commission
SECOFI: Secretaría de Comercio y Fomento Industrial
STIC: Standard International Trade Classification
TESOBONOS: Mexican Federal Treasury Bonds denominated in U.S. dollars
UNAM: Universidad Nacional Autónoma de México
UNCTAD: United Nations Conference on Trade and Development
US-GAAP: United States Generally Accepted Accounting Principles

"For one of the things that does already seem clear is that Mexico was the first of a new style of crisis" (Naím/Edwards 1998)

1 Introduction and Structure

1.1 Introduction

From 1985-1994 the Mexican government was committed to the development and implementation of market-oriented structural reforms. Success was achieved on many fronts and Mexico became "a splendid example of successful economic policy reform" (Krueger/Tornell 1998: 9). As a result, before the crisis, Mexico received the largest portfolio capital inflows among developing countries. However, in 1994 endogenous and exogenous factors caused capital reversals which led to the Mexican crisis of 1994/1995.

Various literature strands have been developed to try to explain the Mexican crisis. Some relate the crisis to the implemented pegged-exchange rate and the overvaluation resulting from the extension of this type of currency regime (Dornbusch/ Werner 1994). Others associate the crisis to capital outflows, political instability and reserve losses (Krueger/Tornell 1999 and Gil-Diaz/Carstens 1996). Some claim that sequencing and pacing were not adequate. Liberalization was too prompt and trade opening should have preceded financial liberalization (Sitglitz 2002). The introduction of Tesobonos, dollar-denominated government securities, as a response to nervousness in the financial markets in 1994, is also typically related to the crisis. Poor macroeconomic management in 1994 regarding the loosening of monetary and fiscal policy is also frequently associated to the crisis (Meltzer 1996, Dornbusch /Goldfajn/Valdés 1995, Krugman 1995). Some others claim the existence of asymmetric information (Mishkin 1991). Finally, over-borrowing (McKinnon/Pill 1995), also linked to moral hazard performed by local banks (Calvo/Mendoza 1995), has also been related to the eruption of the crisis.

Conventional literature on the Mexican Crisis of 1994 is mainly associated to macro imbalances, volatility of the international financial markets or excessive practices of the domestic banking sector. Nevertheless, no single approach seems to offer an integral answer to explain this shock. The in this thesis performed research on the Mexican experience complements and expands the prevailing literature by specifically exploring three unconventional research strands, which can be summarized as follows.

The first is the assessment of the Mexican trade structure to evaluate possible impulses from the real to the monetary sector via a sudden drop in exports. Although this thesis can be discarded, the trade structure revealed by this effort describes the opposite side of what Sinn (2007) calls a "Bazaar Economy"[1]. Mexican exports are based largely on pre-imported inputs and dependant on the U.S. economy. Therefore, these are relative insensitive to currency changes. Favouring stabilization goals in the early nineties, the authorities strived for exchange rate stability through a peso peg and tolerated a prolonged appreciation, which turned out to be a major policy

---

[1] Originally coined to describe a trend in German (and global) trade. The term describes an economy successful in terms of exports based on a growing portion of their aggregate value in a foreign

error. Basic econometric analysis indicates that Mexico's imports react much faster than exports to appreciation. Therefore, the currency appreciation and the current account deficit associated to the crisis can be related to this structural weakness in the real sector.

The second is the triggering role played by domestic investors in the financial stampede that elicited the crisis. Different information sources gathered in this document evidence this behavior, traditionally associated to foreign investors.

The last research strand highlights the role of financial derivatives behind the Mexican crisis. The abnormal capital inflows in 1994, generally considered as rational investment, were largely the mere result of derivatives transactions as described by Garber (1998). To circumvent the existing regulation, domestic banks leveraged through their off-shore subsidiaries the purchase of dollar denominated government securities (Tesobonos) using derivatives. The flows resulting from these relatively unknown operations[2], which reached 4.9 % of the GDP in 1994, were crucial to underpin currency appreciation and in the development of a credit boom, external imbalances and crisis' dynamics.

1.2 Structure of the Thesis

This thesis is structured as follows. Chapter 2 compares the actual liberalization efforts with a previously introduced theoretical rationale. Mexico followed the policy prescription only partially, giving more weight to stabilization goals. Actually, currency appreciation, a faux-pas in trade liberalization manuals, underpinned the enlargement of current account deficits and impeded growth. This policy was at the core of the Mexican problematic. Further, this chapter presents selected macroeconomic indicators and briefly sketches the reform program. Despite an impressive fiscal adjustment and inflation control, growth was modest due to currency overvaluation. Private credit expansion supported a consumption boom. The imbalances were driven, as opposed to in 1982, by the private sector.

Chapter 3 reviews different theoretical frameworks to analyze the origins of the Mexican crisis. These concepts vary from traditional such as the Mundell-Fleming model to more recent work such as third generation crisis models. The Mundell-Fleming model shows how in a domestic boom interest rates increase, attract capital inflows, which appreciate the currency and worsen the balance of trade (Mundell 2002: 7, 9). However, while it sketches relevant dynamics, the model can explain neither the magnitude nor the origins of the 1995 crisis.

The introduction of crisis models of different so-called generations shed light on various elements that might partially explain the crisis. While fiscal expansion was absent, current account deficits and overvaluation are fundamentals of the first generation models which seem to have some explanatory power for the Mexican crisis. The second generation models contribute with speculative attacks and self-fulfilling mechanisms in open financial markets. Third generation models, rather diverse in

---

2   Further discussed in chapter 7.

nature, complement the explanations with structural distortions of domestic markets. Schneider/Tornell (2000) consider that deficient financial markets and asymmetric credit patterns of tradables and non tradables are behind significant credit booms and currency mismatches in a boom-bust cycle. In their view, the contractionary outcomes of a sudden and large devaluation are due to balance-sheet effects and the resulting credit crunch. A lending boom associated to a distorted domestic financial market, as suggested by this model, were key elements to the Mexican crisis.

However it seems that there is no paradigm, rather a diversity of approaches. Pluralism and the persistence of pluralism incidence are "inevitable in any case" (Phelps 1990: x).

Chapter 4 examines the trade structure. The exporting sector is largely composed of oil and pre-imported inputs. Based on elementary econometric assessment, it is safe to affirm that for Mexico imports react much faster to real currency appreciation than exports. These trends, supported by an official import-assembly-reexport Program (Maquila), have two relevant implications. The first refers to an export sector which only deficiently reacts to exchange rate overvaluation. The second sheds light on the vicious cycle of overvaluation and current account deficit behind the 1994 crisis.

A factor which is barely found in the literature is the detonating role played by domestic investors in the absence of institutional asymmetric information. In the Mexican case, as discussed in chapter 5, the expectations of domestic residents shifted long before those of foreigners did. This change was confronted with procrastination to depreciate the currency in early 1994 and policy mismanagement in Dec. 1994.

Chapter 6 focuses on distortions of the domestic financial markets in the early nineties. A swift credit expansion by the newly privatized banks was associated to inefficient credit allocation. The credit boom was self-reinforcing as a result of diverse factors: an increased availability of capital inflows, an improved economic perspective, the need to cover the financial costs of the leveraged buyout of the re-privatized banks, corruption practices and the lack of a solid regulation. After the eruption of the crisis, the banking sector in Mexico was confronted with a large amount of non-performing loans within a few months, significant currency mismatches and large passives. Two unusual factors behind the abrupt credit growth can be highlighted. Related lending, forbidden by regulation, was relevant in practical terms. The second factor refers to the engagement of banks in derivatives and currency mismatches in a lax regulatory framework, which increased the vulnerability of the sector.

The last chapter preceding the conclusions elaborates on the latter and confirms the estimations suggested by Garber (1998). A large portion of the abnormal portfolio capital inflows to Mexico in 1993 and 1994 were not traditional, rather the mere result of leveraged financial derivative-trading. These funds drove and financed most of the current account deficit and underpinned the depletion of the currency reserves prior to the crisis. A specific type of OTC financial derivative, with Tesobonos (dollar-denominated government bonds) at the heart of the transactions, magnified destabilizing flows, which were exacerbated by inadequate exchange rate policy and a distorted domestic financial market.

I. Macroeconomic Aspects: Stylized Facts and Literature Review

2 Liberalization and Macroeconomic Developments

Mexico's path towards liberalization started with an ambitious reform program after the 1982 Debt Crisis[3], which was formalized as Mexico joined the GATT. The fiscal expansion and import-substitution policies pursued in the early eighties were replaced by fiscal discipline and an export-led growth strategy. Pillars of the new adopted scheme were trade liberalization, capital account liberalization and regional integration. The country carried out profound changes in a relative short-period of time to integrate to the world markets.

This chapter reviews some aspects of the theoretical background, mainly of macroeconomic nature, behind the comprehensive liberalization effort. Further, it compares selected expected outcomes with the actual effects seen in Mexico and is organized as follows. First, an introductory section reviews the stand of selected theoretical aspects of trade liberalization as of 1994. Theory highlighted the benefits of the opening of the goods markets. However, it also stressed the key role of a competitive and depreciated currency to avoid an import surge and a balance of payments crisis.

The following section presents selected effects of Mexico's actual liberalization patterns. The overall process can be summarized as comprehensive and rash. Additionally, it can be safely stated that the exchange rate management favored inflation targets over the conventional wisdom on trade liberalization. A large and growing current account deficit was an outcome of the currency appreciation which was induced by significant capital inflows. In the presence of an overvalued currency, as suggested by Dornbusch/Werner 1994, some by theory expected results such as growth were not able to capitalize.

The last parts of the chapter highlight the scope of the fiscal adjustment and the challenges faced by monetary policy considering a consumption boom and capital inflows. Finally, a brief description of the eruption of the crisis concludes the chapter.

2.1 Liberalization Theory: Rationale, Expected Results and Policy Recommendations

The benefits of trade for a country are associated to traditional trade theories: the Ricardian and Hecksher-Ohlin models. These theories, based on classic and neoclassic economics, conclude that all countries benefit if international trade takes place. The range of benefits varies from efficiency gains, growth, technological spillovers, to Samuelson's expansion of economic choices. The Ricardian single factor model defines productivity differences among countries as the cause of product spe-

---

3   For an introduction on the 1982 debt crisis see Appendix 1.

cialization. The more productive country will have higher wage rates, regardless of on which sector it specializes (Krugman 1996: 122[4]).

The Heckscher-Ohlin trade theory implies that countries would trade those goods that use its most abundant factor (either capital or labor). For developing countries, since their most abundant factor is (low-skilled) labor, an expected effect of trade liberalization is that increased (low-skilled) labor demand through exports using this factor would imply a raise on its price (wage) [5] and some convergence towards wage levels of developed countries[6].

Basic trade theory indicates that trade liberalization should result in reallocation of resources into more productive sectors and a decline in imported goods prices. Additionally, as soon as negative effective rates of protection and overvalued exchange rates are eradicated, exports would grow rapidly and diversify.

> "From a growth perspective the fundamental objective of trade reforms is to transform international trade into the engine of growth….Although different empirical models have yielded different results[7], the general thrust of this line of research is that indeed countries with less distorted external sectors appear to grow faster. As Dornbusch (1991) has pointed out recently, openness possibly affects growth not only through one channel, but through a combination of channels, including the introduction of new goods, the adoption of new methods of production, the new organization of industries, the expansion in the number of intermediate goods available, and the conquest of new markets that permit the expansion of exports" (Edwards 1994: 12).

Moreover, literature concerning liberalization strategies emphasized the role of exchange rate policy during a trade reform effort. Edwards (1994) highlights the importance of an early large devaluation in a trade reform process. The author references work on Bhagwati (1978) and Krueger (1978), which indicates that quotas and import

---

4   The first translation of their work is found in Ellis/Metzler (1949), however, Krugman's textbook version offers a useful summary.

5   The argument of the positive trend towards labor demand-led income redistribution appears to be particularly relevant for countries with a tradition of income inequality.

6   How far it factually occurs and which factors affect the wage convergence of developed vs. developing countries is a matter of discrepancy in economics. However, according to Lederman et al. (2003): "At least since the publication of Barro (1991), the economics profession has been aware that convergence might be conditioned by convergence in certain fundamentals that are believed to cause economic growth". The problematic lays on determining which fundamentals should converge to foster growth. This question is, however, outside the scope of this document.

7   The author refers to different models of "endogenous" growth, contemporary at the time of elaboration, which highlight the role of openness. For example, in the Romer's model (1989) larger markets— the world market— enables an open economy to specialize in the production of a relatively larger number of intermediate goods and, therefore, grow faster. Other authors analyzed the relationship between openness, technological progress, and productivity growth. Grossman/Helpman (1991) and Edwards (1992) suggested that openness influences the speed and efficiency with which small countries can absorb technological innovations developed in the industrial world. Therefore, countries with a lower level of trade distortions will grow faster in terms of total factor productivity and will grow faster than countries that deter international competition.

licenses and real exchange rate depreciation diminish the rents received by importers and shifts relative prices towards export-oriented activities.

In the early nineties, the view that a gradual trade reform would be advisable was replaced with the notion that a prompt reform would be more credible and therefore persistent (Edwards 1994 ref. Stockman 1982). A World Bank study by Michaley et al. (1991) indicated that the costs of the reform in employment terms can be small (Edwards 1994: 14).

Another aspect related to liberalization is the sequencing[8] of the reform (Edwards: 1984). Consensus ruled regarding the concept that stabilization and macroeconomic reforms should precede a structural reform. Subsequently, trade liberalization should take place before the capital account is liberalized. A "financial reform cannot be implemented before a modern and efficient supervisory framework is in place" (Edwards 1994: 14). The logic behind this sequencing is the behavior of the key variable real exchange rate.

As explained by the author, the main concern is that if the capital account is liberalized, large capital inflows might materialize. As a result, the real exchange rate would appreciate and "send the "wrong' signal to the real sector, frustrating the reallocation of resources called for by the trade reform" (Edwards 1994:15, also ref. McKinnon, 1982; Edwards, 1984; Harberger 1985). In the presence of unusually large capital inflows that cause temporary appreciations, the outcomes would be critical as suggested by McKinnon (1982) and Edwards (1984). Nevertheless, if the reform foresees delaying financial account liberalization, the real sector could adapt to the new resource allocation (Edwards 1994:15)[9].

Ffrench-Davis (1992) also expressed concerned with the destabilizing influence of the growing capital inflows to the real sector, mainly through the misbalancing effects on exchange rate and aggregate demand. In his view, the policy choice lies between regulating the exchange rate and short-term capital flows to achieve macroeconomic stability or to fully liberalize the capital account with the effect of outlier exchange rate and radical shifts in balance of payments and macroeconomic cycles.

Edwards (1994) further argued that the "conventional wisdom" on how to liberalize trade suggests a large initial devaluation. The main factor during a trade liberalization process is the real exchange rate behavior in order to avoid a balance of payments crisis:

"Maintaining a *depreciated and competitive real exchange rate* during a trade liberalization process is also important in order to avoid an explosion in imports growth and a balance of payments crisis. Under most circums-

---

8 Sitglitz (2002) favors a gradual reform. Sequencing and pacing should in his view be key factors in the engineering of liberalization programs and privatization efforts.

9 An argument against the sequence recommended by Edwards (1982, 1994) is related to net capital import. A current account deficit also reflects the import of foreign savings. If both accounts are liberalized at the same time, moderate capital account deficits could finance the technology adoption or capital goods associated to know-how transfer. This argument, however, is conditioned to the size, the type and the final use of the capital inflows.

tances a reduction in the extent of protection will tend to generate a rapid and immediate surge in imports. On the other hand, the expansion of exports usually takes some time. Consequently, there is a danger that a trade liberalization reform will generate a large trade balance disequilibrium in the short run. This, however, will not happen if there is a depreciated real exchange rate that encourages exports and helps maintain imports in check" (Edwards 1994:5).

As a conclusion, it can be stated that trade liberalization to improve growth prospects was a contemporary and adequate policy prescription for developing countries. This strategy was also useful tool to correct the abundant distortions resulting from previous import-substitution phases. Nevertheless, the exchange rate was crucial to achieve the above mentioned goals. A depreciated and competitive currency would avoid a surge in imports and the formation of distortions in the exporting sector. Therefore, the postponement of financial liberalization was also suggested, in order to prevent pressure on the currency stemming from large capital inflows.

2.2 Liberalization in Mexico and Selected Effects

The ideological origin of Latin American import-substitution prior to the nineties was based on Prebisch's (1950) work. In his view, outward orientation did not capture all growth potential and therefore called for a growth strategy, which could be "stimulated by moderate and selective protection policy" (Prebisch 1984:179, ref. in Edwards 1994). However, the notion, related to infant-industry protection actually supported a huge inefficient productive system, a small, non-traditional export sector facing an overvalued domestic currency (Edwards 1994:5). Accordingly, Mexico had some of the most distorted foreign trade sectors in the world as corroborated by Balassa (1971). His conclusions are in line with Little et al.'s (1970) findings on trade policy and industrialization in the developing world:

"These authors persuasively argued that the high degree of protection granted to manufacturing in Latin American resulted in a serious discrimination against exports, in resource misallocation, inefficient investment and deteriorating income distribution" (Edwards 1994:5).

The distortions in the productive sector and the debt crisis of 1982 forced Mexico to abandon the import-substitution regime. Selected liberalization efforts and their effects are subjects of the remaining sections of the chapter.

2.2.1 Trade Liberalization

As an attempt to reverse the negative effects of protectionism, Mexico started formally its path of trade liberalization as it joined in 1986 the GATT. The import-substitution policy followed prior to this date was substituted by an export-led growth strategy. The trade liberalization can be regarded as prompt. Mexico was as early as

1990 one of the most open developing countries of the world. Table 1 shows the rash reduction of average tariffs in the eighties[10] compared to less developed and industrialized countries in relative terms. The average tariff fell more than 50% within a decade. Krugman (1996: 141) considers liberalization to be significant between 1985 and 1989. The fractions of imports subjects to licenses fell from 90 to 25, where the maximum tariffs were decreased by ¾.

Table 1 Trends in Tariff Rates Mexico and Developing Countries

Unweighted averages, %	1982	1990	1999
Mexico	27.0	11.1	10.1
Average less developed countries (129 countries)	30.0	23.2	11.3
Average industrialized countries (23 countries)	11.0	7.9	4.0

Source: World Bank in: Ledermann et al. (2003: 315).

A key instrument to trade liberalization was the North American Free Trade Agreement (NAFTA) with the U.S. and Canada, which came into force in 1994. Full liberalization was progressive and scheduled to be completed within 10 years for most products. However, both imports and exports rose immediately and continuously after the implementation of the treaty.[11]

2.2.2 Financial Liberalization

A full liberalization of the financial sector, both of the capital account and the stock market took place in 1991. Liberalization on different fronts was undertaken in 1988-9: interest rates, credit controls, lending restrictions, reserve requirements and liquidity ratios were freed or removed. Another major movement in this direction was the re-privatization of Mexico's banks (discussed in section 6.2).

Large capital inflows followed the opening of the capital account. Mexico became in 1993 a top recipient of portfolio capital inflows in the world. Relevant for this section is the large and abrupt net capital import which started roughly two years before the

---

10 However, Ernst (2005) points out that at sectoral level, OECD countries have high protection – direct or indirect- for products that have undergone a competitiveness loss while establishing low protection for competitive high-tech branches. The author affirms that the observed trend in Mexico is the opposite: "low protection for primary products and higher protection for industrial products" despite the fact that the comparative advantage is generally located in low-value-sectors (Ernst 2005:2).

11 An innovative aspect of NAFTA was the disparity in terms of development of the partners, both economical and regarding the institutional frame (Ledermann et al. 2003: 5). NAFTA also represented the commitment of the U.S. towards the economic reforms being pursued (Tornell/Esquivel 1997:26). However, it was in fact a free trade agreement that fostered intra-block trade in the mid-term. See Ledermann et al. (2003) for a comprehensive report on NAFTA and its effects for Mexico.

crisis erupted. These "abnormal" capital inflows were caused by various exogenous and endogenous factors. These subjects are discussed in chapter 5. The rash and simultaneous trade and financial liberalization were cornerstones which made the capital surge possible.

2.2.3 The Pegged- Exchange Rate Management

Exchange rate management in Mexico has a history of tradition. Different regimes have been adopted throughout history. Table 2 summarizes the different exchange rate systems pursued, which share the common characteristic of being state-intervened through different mechanisms.

Table 2 Exchange Rate Systems since 1955

Period	Exchange Rate Regime
1955-1976	Fixed.
1976-1982	Flexible through crawling.
1982-1983	Controlled.
1983-1987	Minimal crawling with undervaluation goals.
1987-1991	Predetermined crawling decided by the Pacts, used as nominal anchor.
1991-1994	Crawling Bands.
Since 1995	Managed floating.

Data source: Cortez (2004)

Mexico had different reasons for Mexico to strive exchange rate stability. Exchange rate fluctuations were a supporting factor to the inflationary phenomenon that had plagued the country since 1973. Further, speculation and capital outflows were encouraged by currency volatility. Exchange rate variations dampened as well numerous productive investments. Finally, the currency instability in the eighties had a negative impact on growth, since credit and foreign investment were quasi deterred due to the extreme volatility and the prevailing conditions (Cortez 2004: 40).

As a main element of the anti-inflationary process, a hard exchange rate peg was implemented from December 1987 until 1989. Thereafter, the government set up a preannounced rate of crawl that suffered only minor changes. In November 1991, a band was created with a fixed floor and a daily rate of crawl ("desliz") of the upper band[12]. This system remained in place until the crisis in December 1994 (Sachs et al. 1996: 39).

The pegging of the peso to the dollar posed two main conflicts to the central bank: trying to control both the peso dollar exchange rate in the presence of liberalized capital markets while maintaining a non-inflationary growth of the monetary base. This inconsistency, called the open economy trilemma, was formalized by Obstfeld (1998). Mexico pursued stabilization goals with a pegged currency regime and open

---

12   The automatic daily "desliz" was 0.0002 pesos. On October 1992, the ceiling of the band widened 0.0004 pesos per day.

financial markets. As it will be discussed in the next section, the difficulties started to arise as capital inflows resumed after 1993.

2.2.4 Selected Effect of Liberalization: Real Exchange Appreciation

Structural reforms and exogenous factors resulted in improved international reviews[13] and abnormal capital inflows in 1993-1994. Nevertheless, as suggested by Cline (1995) signs of appreciation were present as early of 1991:

"By 1991 there were already signs that the pendulum had begun to swing too far in the use of the exchange rate as an anti-inflationary nominal anchor rather as the signal to trade performance" (Cline 1995).

Table 3 presents a triennial real overvaluation[14] average and supports Cline's (1995) after the surge in capital inflows in 1993.

Table 3 Triennial Overvaluation Average

Triennium	Average Overvaluation*
1986-1988	-15.5
1989-1991	9.1
1992-1994	32.3

Data source: Centro de Estudios de las Finanzas Públicas de la H. Cámara de Diputados, with Banco de México and Federal Reserve Bank of St. Louis data.
* Traditional calculation

The level of the overvaluation and its implications were controversial both a priori and a posteriori. Certain was, regardless of the calculation approach used, that the currency had appreciated through due to the lack of flexibility of the peg. Corrective action was necessary after 1992. Policy makers were convinced that the existing appreciation of the currency was first of all difficult to evaluate and second of all a "natu-

---

13 Krueger/Tornell (1999: 2) stated to this regard: "many pointed to Mexico as a splendid example of successful economic policy reform".

14 In the long term the traditional, though controversial, approach to measure the real exchange disparities is using the differential in price levels versus a reference country:

$$e = \eta \, (P'/ P)$$

Where :

P'= foreign price level, P =domestic price level and η = domestic/foreign nominal exchange rate
This expression shows that a real exchange rate equals nominal exchange rate once adjusted for the differential in foreign and domestic price index level, the so-called purchasing parity theory. The idea behind the simplest exchange rate theory is based on the law of one price. This means that a currency should be able to acquire the same quantity of goods and services. Therefore, the nominal exchange rate between two countries would indicate the differential in the price levels of both countries. This concept reflects the influence of monetary policy on real exchange rate through price levels. The theory can be applied in the long term (see for example, Mankiw 2007: 133 ff.).

ral and not necessarily a negative consequence of the reform process in Mexico" (Dornbusch/ Werner (1994: 255) reference Ortiz (1994))[15]. Salinas (2000) recognized a posteriori the fact that the exchange rate peg had already accomplished its (stabilization) goal and that a transition towards a managed float was necessary in 1994.[16]

Most academics, investors and institutional evaluations were confident in Mexico's currency since: "by 1992-1994 the Mexican record looked extremely impressive in terms of structural reform and emergence from the debt crisis" (Cline 1995: 301). However, as reviewed in Meigs (1997: 36), not all economists failed to perceive the possibility and need of devaluation. The author reports that as early as of May 1992, Milton Friedman visited Banco de México. Friedman's conclusion[17] was that Mexico's quasi-fixed exchange rate policy was no longer sustainable and that the peso had to be freed or otherwise the rate of monetary growth had to be controlled (Friedman 1992 ref. in Meigs 1997).

In a later comment[18] on his reaction to the Mexican figures, Friedman declared:

"I must record that I did not regard it as anything special at the time. It seemed to me that anybody who looked at those same numbers had to come to the same conclusion" (quoted in: Meigs 1997:36).[19]

In Friedman's opinion, the problems were associated to the consideration and interpretation of the available information (Meigs 1997: 36). Dornbusch/Werner (1994) joined Friedman and during 1994 repeatedly expressed their ex-ante concerns about Mexico. Considering the traditional approach, the data showed according to the au-

---

15 Gil/Carstens (1996), former executives of the Ministry of Finance, argue that some issues in connection with the comparative price index measurements of the real exchange rate point to the inaccurate results of the value obtained. The authors mention some of the topics of their concern:
    A) The vulnerability of the value obtained if data sources or dates are modified;
    B) The index does not allow a proper inference of the level of competitiveness of the economy (1988 vs. 1994) given that the ability to export and substitute imports depends on other factors;
    C) Prices do not measure costs;
    D) Different productivity trends in tradables versus non-tradables may cumulate real differences in the real exchange rate over time, etc.
    Gil/Carstens (1996: 11) also argue that it is not possible to identify a significant yardstick for the equilibrium real exchange rate. The authors affirm that in the case that the equilibrium rate exists, "it very likely presents a moving target". Mankiw's textbook (2007) agrees with the limitations of the traditional calculation, however, he affirms that it is still a useful yardstick to follow the development of real exchange movements.
16 However, the outgoing president does not explain the reasons why his government refrained from modifying the exchange rate policy before leaving office in November 1994. Smith (1996) explains that for symbolic, political and economic motives the devaluation of the currency had an annihilating effect for outgoing presidents. The departing president in 1994 was not willing to "take that step" (1996: 39).
17 Friedman's comments were published in the national press such as Morales (1992).
18 Friedman's comments were drawn from letters to the author (James Meigs) on March 4th and May 23rd, 1996.
19 In the first of the letters to James Meigs regarding the exchange rate problematic in Mexico, Friedman declared: that he had not quite realized "the extent to which in practice the approach via quantity theory (monetarist) and the approach via international trade and financial movements had become nearly exclusive ways of looking at things rather than components of an integrated view."

thors that the bilateral[20] exchange rate (U.S. vs. Mexico) had appreciated in the 1991-1994 period, approximately 20-25%. (Sachs et al. 1995:5). Kildegaard's (2005) more current estimates of the real exchange rate considering econometric relevant fundamental factors brought about the following results. In the period between 1990 and 1994, the fundamentals seem to play an important role (as opposed to the prior half-decade). The author calculated an overvaluation in 1993 of 23%, similar to Werner's (1996) and Dornbusch/Werner's (1994), which were estimated by 20% and 25% respectively. Accumulated overvaluation between 1990 and 1994 was calculated by Kildegaard (2005) to round up to 26%.

In Meigs' (1997) opinion, the pegged exchange rate system was at the core of the crisis:

"I believe that if Mexico had adopted market-determined exchange rates in 1988 or soon thereafter, instead of trying to control the peso/dollar exchange rate, there would have been no peso crisis in 1994-95".

Figure 1 displays the interbank and bank exchange rates. The spreads of the bank rates started to widen after 1991 and were exacerbated in 1994. This increase reveals the exchange rate pressure and risks associated to the exchange rate. This development matches the above discussed real exchange appreciation.

Figure 1 Interbank* and Bank Exchange Rate and Spreads

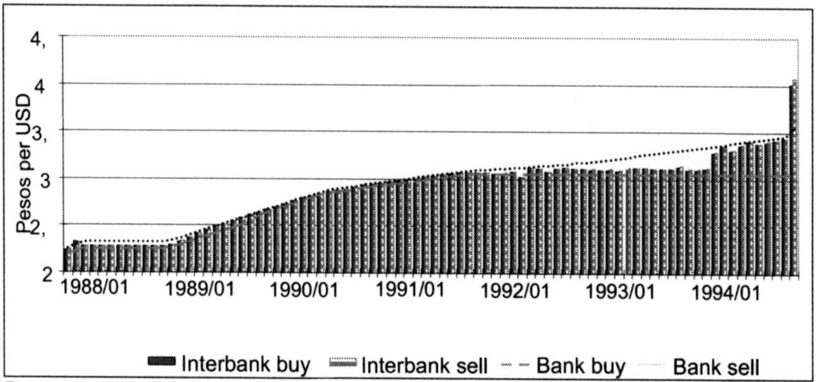

Data source: INEGI (Indicadores Económicos del Banco de México online: 2008)
* Monthly average, interbank exchange rate is the standard used among banks, exchange brokers and private wholesalers.

The substantial appreciation observed in 1994 was considered, in domestic policy terms as a win-win situation. The central bank was able to control inflation through

---

20 The authors recall that inflation had been controlled as the pace of overvaluation had slowed down. Further, the U.S. dollar was depreciating against the European and Japanese currencies. Therefore, Mexico's multilateral exchange rate was less depreciated than the bilateral exchange rate.

the nominal anchor, the real sector massively imported relatively cheaply for domestic production and exports and the domestic households could maintain a consumption boom (Figure 9). This trend was strengthened by capital inflows. The dangers of such a vulnerable position were practically ignored by policy makers before the eruption of the crisis. Frenkel/Razin (1996: 555) affirm, that although overvaluation was a consensus, "there is less agreement on what would have been the appropriate way to unwind the devaluation".

The Mexican crisis elicited a literature strand blaming the peg or its chronological extension. However, prior to the crisis, pegging currencies to the dollar had met wide approval in governments, international financial institutions, financial markets, and academic economics departments (Meigs 1997: 36).

The peg and the resulting appreciation are considered a key policy error, since they hindered the positive effects of trade liberalization suggested by theory and it supported the widening of the current account deficit. In this thesis, the adoption and prolongation of the peg currency regime is also considered critical to the accrual of macroeconomic imbalances. However, as it will be discussed in the last two chapters, it exacerbated the difficulties caused by large capital inflows by conditioning monetary policy, known as the policy trilemma[21]. Further, it seems plausible that the actual massive capital inflows in 1993 and 1994 might have not materialized in the absence of the inflation control achieved by the peg. Finally, the peg proved useful in bringing inflation down but its effects were underestimated by far by the monetary authorities, which did not to opportunely abandon the peg, as suggested by Friedman, as early as of 1992.

2.2.5 Selected Effect of Liberalization: Current Account Deficits

The real appreciation of the peso, as expected by theory, caused a rash increase in imports after 1991. As Dornbusch (1994: 11) affirmed: "The combined evidence would suggest that demand has shifted to foreign goods". The effects of the appreciation on the current account started to become noticeable long before 1994. Krugman (1995) supports this line of opinion and linked it to stagnation by stating that the lack of growth (see Figure 7) was directly related to the appreciation of the peso after 1990: "which discouraged any rapid growth in exports and caused the growing demand to be spent primarily on imports rather than domestic goods" (Krugman 1995: 41-42)

The current account deficits in the early nineties increased abruptly (Figure 2). The chart presents the decomposition of the current account deficits between 1988 and 1994. The manageable deficit in the first year of the period, 1.4% of GDP, almost doubled within one year in 1991 to reach 4.6% of GDP. Three years later this deficit reached 7.7% of GDP. Public finances were balanced as a result of the stabilization goal pursued by the authorities. Sachs et al. (1995) also highlight the fact that the Mexican public debt levels were low and decreased from 67% of GDP in 1989 to

---

21 See Obstfeld et. al (2004) for a contemporary discussion on the trade off of open capital markets, exchange rate stability and monetary policy.

30% in 1993. Private savings continuously decreased in the period and private investment increased. Their difference reflects the enlarging current account.

Figure 2 Decomposition of the Current Account

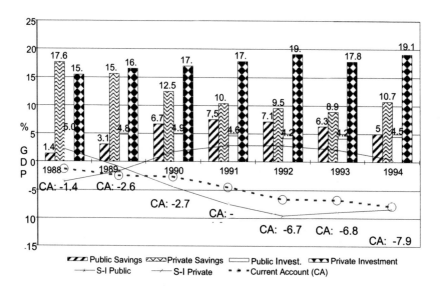

EZZ Public Savings   **ESSS** Private Savings   ⊏⊐ Public Invest.   **CXX** Private Investment
—✦— S-I Public   —✦— S-I Private   ▪ ▪ ▪ Current Account (CA)

Data source: Sachs at al. (1995) with Banco de México data.

Public Savings are defined as the operational balance.
Private Savings are defined as S-I Private plus private investment
Private S-I are defined as the current account deficit minus S-I public

Producers and consumers adapted in Mexico during the early nineties to a level of overall expenditure that surpassed the potential GDP. "What is extremely important is that the disequilibrium was lead and encouraged by capital flows"(Ffrench-Davis 2000: 204). The mismatches were caused, as opposed to 1982, in the private sector. The unsustainability of a current account deficit is a debatable issue in the literature[22]. Reisen (1998) affirms that this indicator, in the absence of reliable theory, should be evaluated by policy makers along other "empirical hard evidence". Current account deficits linked to consumption booms and surges in credit allocation can be considered as excessive and can lead to a banking crisis (Reisen 1998: 26 ref. Gavin/Hausmann 1996). Their conservative view of excessive current account deficits fits well the Mexican data in 1994.

"Procrastination---the period of financing a balance of payments deficit rather than adjusting---had serious consequences in some cases" (Frankel/Wei 2004). Mexico's

---

22 The level is also a matter of controversy in the economic profession. Obstfeld/Rogoff (2008) considered, for example, for the U.S. deficits of over 4% of GDP to be historic high.

current account seems to have more explanatory power than previously considered by earlier literature contributions. Relevant is their association to large capital inflows, to currency appreciation and the resulting credit and consumption booms. A current account deficit is by definition financed by capital inflows, which might be of volatile nature. A further key effect is that these large inflows flood the domestic credit market. Therefore, the foreign financing of a large current account deficit is behind the emergence of a bubble in a boom-bust cycle.

Both aspects, the through the peg exacerbated currency appreciation and large and growing current account deficits were significant indicators of Mexico's dangerous macro imbalances.

2.3 The Structural Reform and Macroeconomic Policy

The first stage[23] after the 1982 crisis focused on stabilization. As Cline (1995) explains, Mexico was confronted with one of the largest challenges in Latin America given the second oil shock in 1986 and thereafter. Fiscal discipline was the cornerstone of México's adjustment. The primary fiscal deficit was eradicated in a short period of time and shifted from a deficit of over seven percent of GDP in 1981 into a surplus of eight percent in 1988 (despite a five percent of GDP oil revenue losses). The ambitious reform[24] program also included: the privatization of state-owned companies, fiscal reform, economic deregulation[25], the liberalization of trade and financial account and the renegotiation of external debt.

2.3.1 Introduction: The Persistent Inflation

Inflation in the eighties was a fundamental problem in Mexico, which was triggered by fiscal looseness in the oil bonanza era (Figure 3). Up to the mid eighties, credit aggregates were mainly regulated through quantitative controls. They took the form of reserve requirements, selective credit quotas and predetermined interest rates. Through the reforms introduced since 1988, the Central Bank started targeting on the level of inflation[26] and international reserves, allowing the interest rate to be determined in the market (Aspe 1993: 79).

---

23 During the presidential term from 1982-1988.
24 For a detailed discussion on Mexico's reform see the document drafted by policy makers: http://www.fias.net/ifcext/fias.nsf/AttachmentsByTitle/FIAS_Casestudies_MexicocaseDec08/$FILE /mexicocase.pdf
25 An extensive deregulation and a detailed revision of the existing legal framework for business activities were performed at national level. A numerous "deregulation team" was in charge not only of the revision of the existing legal framework but also of negotiating with the corresponding authorities improvements and reductions of red tape at all levels. Additionally, an (economic) manifest of regulatory impact became a compulsory requirement for approving all new laws and regulations.
26 As by advocated Aspe26 (1993) from the policy-maker view (Finance Minister 1988-1994), Mexico had to conceive and implement a program considering, not only the conventional aggregate demand adjustment aspects, but also the sources of inflationary momentum and the weaknesses of economic systems in developing countries. The author refers to different stabilization conditions for developing countries such as imperfect markets, budget rigidity and dynamics of price and

Figure 3 Inflation

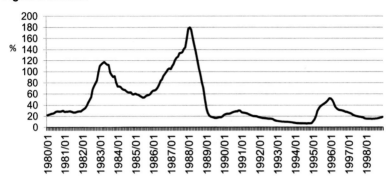

Data source: INEGI online (2010) and author's own calculations

*Calculated vs. same month in the previous year

Two main strategies were conceived to counteract the persisting inflation. The first was the decision to freeze the peso-dollar exchange rate at its February 29th, 1988 level, in the frame of the anti-inflationary pact. The second was the Pacto de Solidaridad Económica. The Pact was an agreement mechanism[27] signed by the president and labor, business and farming leaders on various fronts to trim the size of government, constrain monetary policy, correct the inflationary inertia and wage momentum, fix prices in selected (but changing) sectors and free trade (Meigs 1997: 39). The next sections present selected aspects of the macroeconomic management which made stabilization possible.

---

salary contracts. Mexico therefore designed under Aspe a "nonorthodox" type of stabilization program that combined "the principles of the neoclassical theory of aggregate demand with a more detailed study of the effect of market structure on the way in which fluctuations in nominal variables are divided into prices and quantities in the equilibrium". Under his point of view, inflation has an important inertial element and it can be a result of mismatches in the real sector or in monetary policy. Further, elements which explain the performance of aggregate demand like income distribution, market constitution and labor contracts, to name a few, constitute the inertial component of inflation. Inflation did not arise only from surpluses in the balance of payments. Negative changes in the terms of trade can cause inflationary pressure through devaluations. "The maladjustment of real wages sets off a vicious wages-prices-wages-cycle". Therefore, aggregate demand policy is able to significantly affect real variables in the short and mid-term. Inflation had two components: the initial surge and the propagation mechanism. "The initial surge can come from expansionary monetary and fiscal policies. Once the adjustments to the exchange rate and public finances have taken place, the remaining inflation was wholly inertial". Correcting fiscal and monetary policy and external strangulation would not allow to significantly deterring inflation. The sources of inflationary impetus had to be corrected as well (Aspe 1993: 9-10).

27 The Pacto de Solidaridad Económica included periodic revisions and amendments.

2.3.2 Fiscal Policy

Dornbusch/Werner (1994: 259) affirm that the fiscal strategy, main part of the reform and stabilization program had three core objectives:
- Major cut in government spending;
- Tax reform to increase the tax-base, efficiency and compliance[28], and
- Privatization of state owned enterprises[29].

Fiscal spending was the main factor behind budgetary discipline. The large fiscal deficit in 1987 was transformed into a surplus in the first triennium of the nineties (Figure 4). Between 1987 and 1994, fiscal expenses, measured as a percentage of GDP, fell from 44% to around 26% (Gil-Diaz/Carstens 1996: 8). Government investment was halved to 5% of GDP. [30] The average net debt of the public sector fell from 74.4% in 1987 to 22.5% of GDP in 1994 (Ibid.:8).

Figure 4 Fiscal Deficit/ Surplus

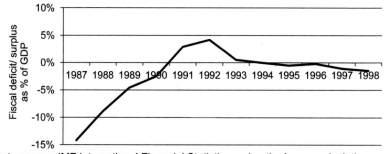

Data source: IMF International Financial Statistics and author's own calculations.

The negotiation of the Brady plan set a precedent for the transformation of the economy. In 1989 and early 1990 Mexico negotiated the above mentioned agreement, which reduced its public external debt by an equivalent of 15% of the total debt outstanding or 35% of the total long-term bank claims. Savings on interest rates were approximately two- thirds of one percent of GDP. While the direct effects on growth were only limited, considering the improved favorable expectations, the contribution

---

28 The success in this front was remarkable considering the complex initial conditions. See Aspe (1993) for first-hand references.
29 Privatization of around 1,000 corporations was a strategy that generated $25 billion U.S. dollars in revenues that were used to reduce government debt (Gil/Carstens 1996:7). The three main privatized branches were the telephone system, the domestic airlines and the in 1982 nationalized banks. The divestiture of governmental enterprises offered a two-fold benefit towards correcting fiscal imbalances: income generation and avoidance of recurrent losses. This approach was, in the view of the author of this thesis, valid and effective given the previous overexpansion of the government into economic activity.
30 According to Puyana/Romero (2006: 28) ideologically the observed fall in public investment supported the "private sector based strategy". However, the authors underline the convenience of this practice to balance the budget.

to growth was much larger (Cline 1995: 298).[31] The Brady Program that Mexico ne-gotiated was not only key to the reform process, but also served as a benchmark for debt-reduction schemes in 17 other countries (Cline 1995: 234).[32]

Two further aspects improved Mexico's fiscal position. Interest rates on Cetes (T-bills) halved (from around annual 50%) in the months after the signature of the Brady plan and the large exchange rate premium associated with the possibility of failure and a peso attack disappeared (Cline 1995: 298). Van Wijnbergen (1991) estimated that the Brady Plan induced a 2% annual growth between 1988 and 1994. This con-tribution derives half from the direct effect on the government's reduced cash-outflow and the other half indirectly from higher investment induced by lower interest rates (Cline 1995: 298).

The fiscal reforms supported a financial crowding-in: the percentage of financial re-sources absorbed by the government fell from 65 % in 1989 to 8% in 1994. (Gil-Diaz/Carstens 1996:8). The reduction in public investment had two implications ac-cording to Cline (1995): the private sector was leading investment and larger, tar-geted, social spending was crowded in.

The signature of the debt-relief Brady Plan and a sharp fiscal contraction were cor-nerstones to attain stabilization and solve the 1982 debt crisis and its aftermath. The country's fiscal efforts can be considered as outstanding:

> "Mexico thus carried out a fiscal adjustment equal to 16% of GDP. This ef-fort corresponded to five times the never achieved Gramm-Rudman-Hollings target for U.S. fiscal adjustment in the late 1980's" (Cline 1995).

2.3.3 Monetary Policy

A wide range of monetary reforms[33] were introduced after the 1982 crisis. These were designed to control inflation through the stabilization of the peso. Further goals were the development of the banking system and expanding the availability of bank credit to the private sector. A currency peg and partial sterilization of capital flows through government-issued bonds supported the efforts to keep the growth of the monetary base in accordance with nominal income increases and inflation targets (IMF 1995c).

Monetary aggregates grew between 1990 and 1994 at a different pace (Figure 5). M1 experienced a swift increase in the fall of 1991, to then grow continuously at a rela-tive stable rate. The holdings of financial assets by residents (M3) displayed more aggressive growth rates and picked up in the fall of 1991. M4, practically inexistent in

---

31 The author, despite his positive evaluation on this deal, considers that this agreement would not have been necessary in the absence of the oil shock of 1986 (Cline 1995: 246).

32 Philippines, Costa Rica, Venezuela, Uruguay, Niger, Mozambique, Nigeria, Guyana, Argentina, Brazil, Uganda, Dominican Republic, Bolivia, Jordan, Bulgaria, Poland, Ecuador. For more infor-mation see Cline (1995: 234 ff.).

33 In 1993 the Central Bank was granted autonomy for the first time in history. A new peso replaced the older peso and was equivalent to one thousand units of the latter one.

the eighties, expanded rapidly as well. International reserves in U.S. dollars increased largely starting in 1990, reflecting the intervention performed by Banxico in an attempt to sterilize large capital inflows until the end of 1993.

Figure 5 Monetary Aggregates* & Reserves　　**Figure 6 Selected Indicators**

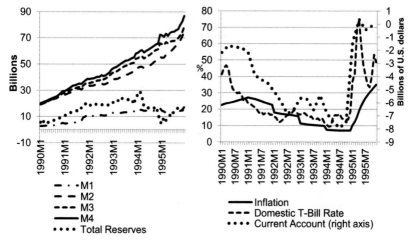

Data source: IMF Financial Statistics

*Ms in domestic currency, with the exception of total reserves of the central bank (excluding gold).

Monetary tightening was successful in bringing inflation to historical one-digit levels (Figure 6). Large capital inflows in the early nineties (see also Figure 41 and chapter 5) financed a growing capital account deficit and continuously put pressure on the domestic monetary aggregates and called for sterilization[34].

Mexican monetary authorities attempted to sterilize the capital inflows by increasing interest rates (Figure 6), up to early 1994 through bonds in local currency. One of the main advantages of sterilization through this means is that it limits the monetary-credit expansion without imposing other burdens on the domestic banking system or

---

34　The sterilization goals of monetary policy are to reduce pressure on the forex market and to avoid the monetary expansion in heavy capital inflows phases. The three main forms of sterilization are of open market operations, reserve requirements and management of public sector deposits. (Reinhart/Dunaway 1996). Cline (1995) reviews the literature regarding policy response to increased capital inflows. The author partially supports the view of Schadler et al. (1993) that differentiate between inflows motivated by improved domestic conditions and those reacting to higher interest rates. While the former are considered to be equilibrating, the latter should be confronted with sterilization and moderation of the interest rates to avoid self-correction. In their view, fiscal tightening is the main means to approach with excessive inflows and state that another possible choice such as high bank reserve requirement on foreign deposits achieves only transitory results.

overexposing[35] them to the intermediation of capital inflows. However, higher interest rates further attract capital inflows, which aggravates the original problem that is actually being fought (IMF 1995: 80 ff.).[36]

After studying the sterilization experiences of Chile, Colombia, Malaysia and Indonesia, the IMF (1995) reached the following conclusions. First, there was significant central bank intervention, as evidenced by reserve accumulation. Second, the revaluatory effects on the exchange rate are clear despite heavy intervention. The conjunction of both remarks suggests the limitations of sterilization coping with very large capital inflows. Third, Central bank securities issuance rose significantly in a relative short period of time. Fourth, domestic short-term interest rates rose as sterilization was carried out and sterilization might have brought involuntary tightening of monetary policy. A fifth conclusion is that sterilization policies might have kept away domestic interest rates from converging to international levels.

The conclusions reached by the case studies reviewed in IMF (1995) match the outcomes observed in Mexico. The main effect of the heavy sterilization, which was partially loosened in 1994, were the disappointing growth rates observed in the period, the persistence of high interest rates and the financing of a large and growing current account.

In Cline's (1995) opinion, policy response to capital inflows was still controversial: "fiscal tightening is less than a panacea- as suggested by the Mexican case, where by 1993 the growth rate was down to one percent partly because of this response". Krugman (1996) further states that the concept of tightening both fiscal and monetary policy was promptly rejected in industrial countries after the challenges of the German reunification.[37] The Mexican central bank, however, defended its pro-cyclical

---

35 Relevant, according to the referred document, if the financial system is not well developed or if the flows are considered to be temporary.

36 An increase in reserve requirements is another possibility to reduce the money multiplier, since it limits the monetary expansion that results from the intervention in the foreign exchange market. Mexico's policy was mixed and scanty. In 1989 compulsory reserve requirements of direct credits to the government were eliminated and replaced by a "liquidity requirement". The obligation was to hold 30% of the portfolio in interest-bearing government paper (APEC/Banco de México 2003: 206 ff.). In April 1992, as the privatization of banks was completed, a compulsory liquidity coefficient for dollar liabilities was set at 15 %, which had to be invested in liquid securities denominated in the same currency. However, as expressed in IMF (1995), evidence suggests that increasing reserve requirements to sterilize capital inflows might exacerbate the original problem. Reserve requirement is likely to be passed on to the customers and should result in lower levels of deposits or higher loan rates. If higher loan rates predominate, banks will tend to borrow abroad, further increasing capital inflows. Additionally, if disintermediation is considerable and resources are channeled into the non bank financial sector (which is not affected by reserve requirements) this would mean a deviation from original goal (IMF 1995: 82). As it will be discussed in the microeconomic section of this thesis, the divestiture of Mexican banks was deficient and buyers had to leverage heavily. Another possibility to sterilize capital inflows, which offers rather a limited scope, is the shifting deposits of public sector to the central bank. Mexico used this tool in 1991 and deposited the privatization income in the central bank to support sterilization efforts (IMF 1995: 83).

37 Krugman (1996.) describes how different factors in the mid-nineties challenged the "Washington View" that was almost indisputable in 1990. The success of the European Monetary System between 1982 and 1990 or the sound money part of the prosperity equation, worked according to Krugman (1996) because fixed exchange rates were convenient to stabilize France, Italy and

monetary policy and affirmed that "the benefits derived from stabilization and structural change; particularly regarding increases in general social welfare need time[38] to materialize" (Banco de México 1995:19).

2.3.4 Other Macroeconomic Performance

Economic growth between 1989 and 1994 was modest considering the 10% increase in population (Figure 7). Further, as pointed by different authors such as Krueger/Tornell (1999)[39], Sachs et al. (1996), Dornbusch (1997), Edwards (1997), it did not match the structural reforms and the large flows of foreign investments.

Figure 7 GDP Annual Rate of Growth (real)

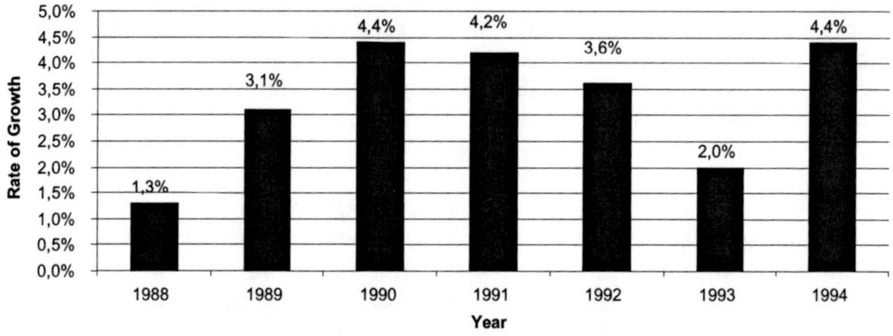

Data source: Banco de México online (2008)

Productivity growth stayed practically stable until 1993, real wages had only recovered their 1980 level, savings had declined sharply and poverty and income distribution posed a large challenge (Edwards 1997: 3). In 1993 a temporary halt in private investment that awaited the polemic final approval of NAFTA by the U.S. Congress caused the observed fall (Gil-Diaz/Carstens 1996: 8)

UK's persistent trend towards inflation. However, pegging their currency to the German mark left monetary control in the hands of the German Central Bank. However, with the reunification of Germany, the fiscal costs of rebuilding the East created important inflationary pressures that were contained through a very tight monetary policy. The other countries in Europe suffered the consequences of the loss of autonomy. They had to follow the tight monetary policy without having the fiscal expansion, which lead to a recession. Therefore, the application of the Washington Consensus was sooner rejected in advanced countries (Krugman 1996: 133 ff.).

38 Real growth rates were before 2008 disappointing, given the economic transformation that took place. The evidence might suggest policy omissions and/or mismanagement. Some of them, such as currency alignment and import propensity are a topic of this thesis. Others, such as oligopolic forces and reforms in the oil and refinery sector are outside of the scope of this thesis. All in all, over two decades after the initial reforms, growth prospects have not been able to materialize as expected.

39 Krueger/Tornell (1999) compare the low growth rates to population and labor force growth and the stagnation of the early 80's, to end up with a per capita income drop of over 15% compared to 1981.

Figure 8 displays the contribution of aggregate demand components to GDP growth. In 1993 and 1994, exports and private consumption were the main drivers of the output increase. Currency overvaluation, however, was behind a large increase in imports, both related to the production of exports (for further elaboration see 4.2.3) and an increase in consumption. Private investment played only a minor role, public investment rose only in 1994, a presidential election year.

Figure 8 Contribution of Aggregate Demand Components to GDP Growth

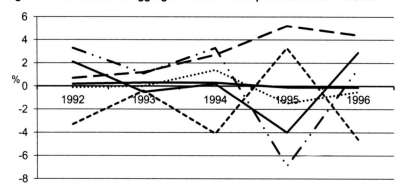

Data source: Anexo Estadístico del 2. Informe de Gobierno (State of the Nation Report) 2002 with INEGI data.

Private consumption, as a percentage of GDP, grew steadily after 1989 (Figure 9). According to APEC/Banco de México (2003: 210 ff.) different explanatory variables are held responsible for the observed growth in private consumption:

a) Financial liberalization. Deregulation and privatization in the banking sector promoted competition and allowed increased financial deepening (defined as M2 or 4/GDP). Therefore, more lending resources were available at the market.

b) Fiscal crowding-in. During the period, deficit reduction reached around 10% of the GDP. Through this means, more resources were assigned to the private sector.

c) Economic stabilization. Economic success in many fronts was achieved (e.g. inflation was controlled, positive international debt renegotiation, record capital flows).

d) Optimistic economic outlook. Mexico's performance seemed to be a splendid case of how economic policy could be conducted by an emerging economy (Krueger/Tornell 1998: 9).

e) Wealth effect resulting from a boom in the stock and real estate markets.

f) Recovery of durable consumer goods sales.

g) The appreciation of the peso in real terms.

Figure 9 Private Consumption / GDP

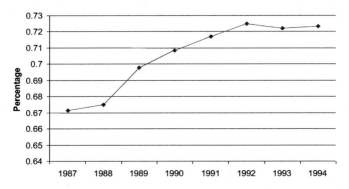

Data source: OECD National Accounts.

Crowding-in, via a stimulation of domestic demand, is a precedent condition to achieve full employment. Based on this line of reasoning, trade liberalization must have been linked to a real depreciation and not appreciation. A real depreciation was necessary to support the economy in the long term and to firmly fix the benefits of economic reform (Dornbusch/Werner 1994: 253).

Table 4 Domestic Savings as a Percentage of GDP

Domestic saving as a percentage of GDP			
Year	1983	1989	1994
Gross National Saving composed of: Public Sector Private Sector Total	 3.49 26.85 30.33	 1.74 19.50 21.24	 -0.07 18.48 18.4
Gross Domestic Saving	26.88	20.92	16.77
Private Domestic Saving	21.78	15.69	12.14

Data source: Gil-Diaz/Carstens (1996a :64) with INEGI, National Accounts data.

In the early nineties the country had a high propensity to consume, roughly 80% of disposable income, (Gil-Diaz/Carstens 1996a: 64). Table 4 displays domestic savings as a % of GDP. According to this data, private domestic savings almost halved in these terms compared to the decade prior to 1994. The overall level of savings fell steadily during the main reform years to reach a record low in 1994. Public savings showed a positive pattern as a result of the strict fiscal policy and numerous privatizations. However, this growth was not enough to compensate the expansion of private consumption. The financing of investment relied mainly on external savings.

Domestic credit, as seen in Figure 10, increased significantly in the period following the financial liberalization. Credit to the private sector increased over 450%[40] according to Torre (1999). In his opinion, this trend reflected the availability of capital, the bank privatization, the crowding-in of the public sector and the improved economic outlook. The swift credit expansion supported the consumption boom in the private sector.

Figure 10 Domestic Credit and Claims on the Private Sector

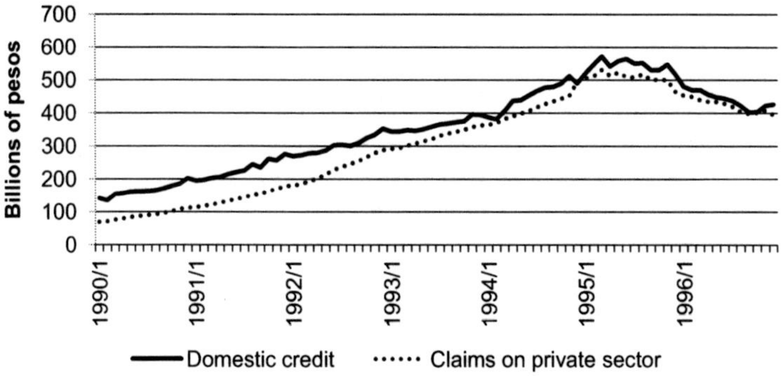

Data source: IMF International Financial Statistics

2.4 Eruption of the Crisis

In 1994, mainly in the late fall, turmoil both country-specific and in the international financial markets was intensified. Capital flight by domestic and foreign investors, discussed in Chapter 5, increased the pressure exerted on the already appreciated peso. After large losses of reserves[41], the authorities were forced to modify the peso's exchange rate band on 20th December 1994, effectively devaluing the floor by 13% (BIS: 1994). Two days later, as capital outflows persisted, the exchange rate was freed after over 6 years of control.

The devaluation triggered further capital outflows and left Mexico illiquid in the short term given large amounts of in U.S. dollar denominated government obligations (Tesobonos). The peso and the stock market plummeted until the early months of 1995. Credit lines authorized by the IMF and the U.S. government of $40 billion two months[42] after the eruption of the crisis helped to stop the peso fall. The currency had devalued over 100% in this period of time. Section 3.4 displays selected macroeconomic indicators and draws some conclusions using the traditional Mundell-Fleming

---

40 The effects of inflation, gradually decreasing, do not change the trend of this argument.
41 Reports on the level of international reserves were released only three times a year. This "tradition" dates back from the forties. Data was released in March, October and November.
42 Cavallo (2006) criticized the tardiness of the aid considering the information policies prevailing in the international financial markets.

model. Figures 4, Figure 6 and Figure 8 also display the contraction of the economy and the pro-cyclical fiscal and monetary policy pursued after the crisis. Net exports became after the devaluation became the motor of the economy. After a sharp contraction in 1995, economic recovery resumed after 1996.

This chapter presented some evidence on the magnitude of Mexico's reforms. The most tangible and remarkable was the fiscal adjustment carried out in a short period of time. Privatizations and a resolute foreign debt renegotiation were key factors that complemented fiscal discipline. Monetary changes were not less impressive, however, posed important challenges. Inflation control, the main goal, was achieved in the face of large capital inflows and a consumption boom, particularly after 1993. Sterilization supported both the inflationary goals and attracted further capital inflows. This scenario put the Mexican peso further under pressure and supported an import surge.

All in all, the structural program was successful on many fronts. The economic reforms fostered capital inflows and productivity growth. However, while domestic demand increased rapidly and the already low propensity to save fell[43], supply adjusted sluggishly. The resulting disequilibria were exposed in 1994 by the overvaluation of the peso by approx. 20% and the widening of the current account deficit (BIS 1995: 34 ff.). Credit to the private sector grew at a rapid pace. The privatization of the branch, the large availability of funds and the changes in the willingness to save were behind this development. A boom was driven by private consumption; however, given the large current account deficit, the impulses to growth were minimized. Growth was modest considering the scope of the reforms. External mismatches made the country vulnerable to capital reversals, which materialized in the late 1994.

As a conclusion on Mexico's liberalization's efforts, it can be stated that the country followed liberalization theory only partially, giving more weight to stabilization goals through the pegging of the peso. The prolongation of this regime led to imbalances in the external sector. The appreciation of the peso supported the import-encouraging behaviour suggested by theory. Therefore, imports neutralized much of the export contributions to growth.

The level of overvaluation and a strategy for a soft-landing were controversial both before and after the eruption of the crisis. Unambiguous was, whatsoever the need for correction and the perilous effects associated to a currency peg. Further, the deficits of the current account, driven by the private sector, reached in 1994 an unsustainable level and were de facto linked to vulnerability in the financial sector. As it will be scrutinized in the last chapters of this thesis, external and internal conditions in 1994 precipitated capital outflows, which caused an abrupt external sector adjustment.

The following chapter elaborates on the macroeconomic developments and selected aspects of the structural reform prior to the crisis. Further, it introduces traditional and more contemporary theoretical models to try to disentangle the origins of the crisis.

---

43 From 19%in 1990 to 15% in 1994 (BIS 1995: 34 ff.)

3 Theoretical Considerations: Mundell-Fleming Model & Selected Models

Following the Mexican crisis of 1994, particularly after the Asian Crises, numerous approaches to search for the origins of these phenomena have been originated. This chapter, far from being exhaustive, focuses on reviewing some traditional literature to then evaluate the macroeconomic performance in 1994.

This section begins by introducing the basic Mundell-Fleming standard model in an open economy. Key developments previous to the Mexican crisis, such as capital flight, devaluation and appreciation are analyzed in this simple, but still useful framework. An expansion of the model is attained by introducing a particularity of the Mexican economy: its high import-propensity. Import content indexes are calculated to determine the final impact of shifts on the curves, and refine the conclusions induced by the traditional model. This adapted model describes the occurrences in Mexico, however, does not explain the underlying causes and the magnitude of the crisis. These are of financial nature and are scrutinized in posterior chapters of this thesis.

The last parts of the chapter introduce the three different theoretical models' generations. As it is the case for the Mundell-Fleming model, while they present relevant insights, they cannot explain per se the Mexican Crisis of 1995.

3.1 Mundell-Fleming Model: Introduction

This model was the first systematic analysis of the open economy. While it was formalized by Fleming (1962) and by Mundell (1963)[44], different authors[45] contributed, directly or indirectly to its development. The Mundell-Fleming model, extension of the IS-LM model, explains the effects of monetary and fiscal policy to output in a small open economy considering a framework of either fixed or floating exchange rates[46]. Its main contribution, as expressed by Frenkel/Razin's (1987) review is the: "systematic analysis of the role played by international capital mobility in determining the effectiveness of macroeconomic policies under alternative exchange rate regimes".

The Mundell-Fleming model is widely considered as the "main "work horse" of traditional open economy macroeconomics" (Frenkel/ Razin: 1987 and Gärtner/Lutz 2004). Its "enduring importance can be attributed to its transparency and solidity to

---

44 The model, well known as the Mundell-Fleming model, was developed parallel, not conjunctly.

45 The study of open economics can be traced back to Hume (1752). However, formal mathematical models emerged mainly over the last half of the past century. Harrod/Meade published in the same year Keynes' General Theory appeared relevant works in this topic: "The Trade Cycle" and "Economic Analysis and Policy", respectively. Likewise, successive work by Meade and Metzler, to name a few, influenced the development of the IS-LM Model for the Open Economy (Young 2004).

46 The discussion on the validity and scope of Keynesian-style instruments is out of the scope of this thesis. Therefore, as expressed by Mankiw (2007:545): "increasingly, theories at the research frontier meld many of these elements (new Keynesian theory and real business cycle theory) to advance our understanding of economic fluctuations". Neither in basic textbooks nor in advanced research is there a consensus on business-cycle fluctuations in the short run.

describe the interrelationships of the short-term business cycle "[47] and to the fact that this model set a basis for later research trends (Gärtner/Lutz 2004: 27).

In this section, the Mundell-Fleming model textbook version for a small economy with fixed exchange rate is presented factually and diagrammatically. The model, despite the questionability of various assumptions and shortcomings, which will be discussed subsequently, is yet a useful basis to analyze short-term fluctuations.[48]

The Mundell-Fleming model explains the behaviour of real GDP and interest rates as the real and monetary markets interact. Several variables such as price level[49], exchange rate, economic policy instruments (government expenditure, taxes and monetary mass) and GDP abroad are considered as exogenous in this model (Burda/Wyplosz 1994).

A small open economy is assumed, implying that the country is not able to influence per se the world financial market conditions. In the IS-LM model for the open economy there is no graphic or structural difference between fixed or flexible exchange rates, rather the fact in a fixed rate regime the exchange rate is the exogenous variable controlled by the government and the monetary mass is the endogenous variable that adapts as required by the fixed rate. A key assumption of the IS-LM Model for an open economy is capital mobility. If perfect capital mobility exists, arbitrage ensures interest rate parity, once adapted to risk, between a country and the rest of the world. A fixed[50] exchange rate scenario and less than full employment condition are assumed throughout this section.

Equilibrium in the world economy (two countries) is reached if the goods, money and bonds[51] clear.

1-1 $Y = C\,(\Omega,\ Y^d) + I\,(q,\ i,\ \Delta Y) + G + NX\,(Y,\ Y^*,\ \lambda,\ e)$

Effect on Y: + +   + -   +   - + + -

1-2 $M = M\,(Y^d,\ i)$

Effect on M: + -

---

47 The authors consider it a significant lingua franca tool for the analysis and discussion with non-specialists. The Mundell-Fleming model, poses, as summarized by Gärtner/Lutz (2004) the same limitations assumed in the Keynesian literature:
•Output is only determined by the aggregate demand since the full employment condition is not fulfilled.
•The price level is fixed.
•The interest rate parity condition holds.

48 The data has been taken from Burda/Wyplosz (1994 and 2001), Mankiw (2007) and Gärtner/Lutz (2004). However, small variations in different textbooks are considered irrelevant for the pretended analysis.

49 This implies that the real and nominal interest rates are equal.

50 Recall that Mexico adopted an exchange rate peg that was kept up to the eve of the crisis.

51 Frenkel/Razin (1987) omit the bond market from the equilibrium specification of the two –country model of the world economy based on Walra's Law.

Where Y is GDP, * denotes foreign, G government purchases (exogenously determined), C the consumption function affected by consumption propensity (Ω)[52] and domestic disposable income (Y^d). I denotes investment, a positive function of q (incorporates Tobin's q elements regarding expected future marginal products of capital) and interest rate i. NX are exports minus imports, e is the real exchange rate and Y* foreign income. The import function is a function of domestic income and the terms of trade (λ), which reflect the price relation of domestic and foreign products, and the real exchange rate e. Exports show the reciprocal of the imports function given that they are imports in a foreign country. Output is positively related to investment (ΔY). Domestic money holding (M) is positively related to income and negatively to domestic interest rates.

The traditional IS Curve[53] shows the different equilibrium real income-nominal interest rate combinations in the goods market (equation 1-1). The negative slope of the curve is determined by the inverse relation between interest rate and consumption and investment. A rise both in interest and output create an excess of goods. The steepness of the curve is determined by the interest rate.

The LM curve plots the equilibrium combinations of income and interest rate in the money market, considering, as aforementioned, money supply of the central bank as endogenously determined through asset swaps (equation 1-2). The slope of the curve is positive since in the money market a higher output level raises demand for real money balances. The short-term equilibrium expressed by the model points out the importance of capital mobility in which exchanges of money for bonds take place to adjust money stocks and restore equilibria.

The foreign exchange market curve (FE) shows the combinations of income and interest rate that equilibrate the balance of payments. The balance of payments, composed of the current account and the capital account which offset each other, represents the connection of the economy to the rest of the world. The FE curve plots the forex market equilibrium that reflects interest rate parity and perfect capital mobility. In this scenario i=i* and the FE curve, also called financial integration line, is horizontal. If the exchange rate expectations are stationary[54], the capital and current account balance if the domestic interest rate equals (plus a risk-premium) the foreign interest rate.

Some of the above mentioned assumptions are relaxed in the rest of the chapter and result in a more pragmatic version of the model. The next sections examine the impact of selected policies and shocks on growth, focusing on those which are relevant to evaluate the Mexican experience.

---

52 Both consumption propensity and imports are affected by expectations.
53 See for example Gärtner/Lutz 2004: 30 ff., Burda/Wyplosz (2001: 258).
54 As pointed out by Mankiw (2007:352), considering the existence of a risk premium for the interest rates of a specific country, "expectations about the exchange rate are partially self-fulfilling." The assumption of stationary exchange rate expectations seems not realistic for a small open economy. This assumption is dealt with in section

3.2 Mundell-Fleming Model Policy and Exogenous Changes

3.2.1 Changes in Aggregate Demand Components

Variations in the demand components (C, I, G and/or NX) shift the IS schedule and cause, ceteris paribus and in a fixed exchange rate framework, modifications in the output levels in the short-term.

Consider the classic fiscal policy expansion (Figure 11). Additional demand for domestic products is created at the current level of output. The IS schedule shifts to the right (↗), which causes a temporary excess demand for money balances and an increase in domestic interest rates. The latter leads to capital import (attracted by the higher interest rates) and to exchange rate pressure. The monetary authorities have to react to the appreciating trend by reducing the interest rate and serving through monetary expansion the domestic currency excess demand to preserve the exchange rate level. The increase in the monetary mass takes place until the level of domestic interest rates move downward to the world level (↗) . As a result, the output level increases, up to point c, where equilibrium is restored. Increases in consumption, investment or exports and cause analogous a shift to the right of the IS schedule and a short term increase of output.

Figure 11 Effects of an Expansionary Fiscal Policy

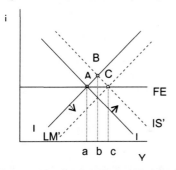

Source: Mundell (1962) and Fleming (1962)

However, the overall impact on output growth is determined by the levels of imports embedded in the aggregate demand components. Introducing this fact into the analysis, consider a rise in consumption, caused either by an increase in the propensity to consume (Ω) or in disposable income (Y^d). Such a change would shift the IS curve to the right (↗), as seen in Figure 12.

The increased demand for goods and services (domestic) causes a short-term excess demand for money balances and increases the interest rate. Higher capital gains attract capital into the country and domestic currency demand expands. The central bank has to neutralize the increased demand for domestic currency and increases the interest rate until the LM curve reaches the foreign level ($\nearrow$) and cross the FE line. Appreciation and further capital imports are collateral effects of the higher interest rates. However, imports act as a counteracting force, since they increase foreign exchange demand. Therefore, the central bank has to enlarge the supply of foreign currency to avoid a nominal devaluation of the fixed exchange rate.

In order to equilibrate the worsening of the current account, capital flows are necessary. The FE curve moves up, increasing the domestic interest rate to balance capital and flows of goods and services. The equilibrium shifts to point D ($\square$), with higher interest rates and, in the presence of imports, a lower impulse to output (d) than the original consumption stimulus (c). The dimension of this negative parameter depends on the import propensity, which will be analyzed for Mexico in section 3.3.

Figure 12 Effects of an Increase in Consumption

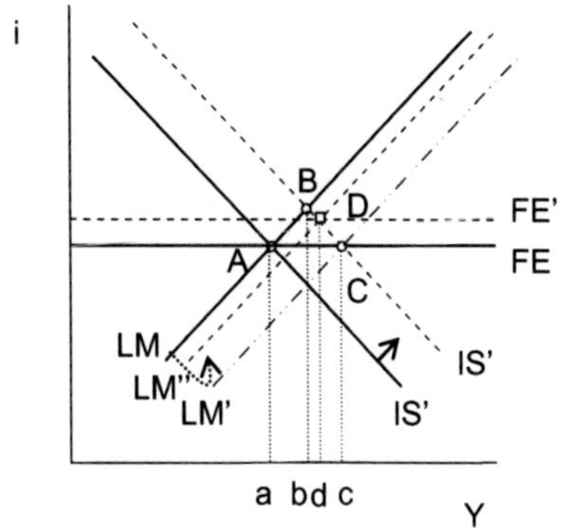

Adapted from: Mundell (1962) and Fleming (1962)

The counteracting effect of imports also applies for all other components of aggregate demand. Export growth as defined by this model, depends on the terms of trade, real exchange rate and foreign income. As it is the case for consumption increases (Figure 12), the extent to which exports can increase output is equally conditioned by their import contents. Imports lessen the expansionary effect of exports on growth and raise the interest rate, which further attracts capital (also see 3.3 and 4.2 and for implications on Mexico).

3.2.2 Changes in Monetary Supply

The effects of an expansive monetary policy are in the analyzed framework (fixed exchange rate) not on output. When the LM schedule shifts to the right, financial assets in foreign currency are more demanded due to the short-term interest rate differential (Figure 13).

Figure 13 Effects of an Expansive Monetary Policy

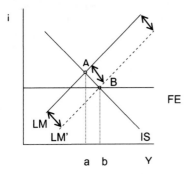

Source: Mundell (1962) and Fleming (1962)

Domestic investment, employment and output would rise due to the decrease of the interest rate[55]. However, since the central bank is committed to the exchange rate, the authorities are forced to sell foreign currency to maintain the fixed rate. This implies that the LM curve shifts back as a result of this accommodating policy. Therefore, no output changes are observed (from point a to b and back to a). The only effect is a decrease in the reserves of the central bank.

Although in the case of contractionary monetary policy, the shift of the LM curve would be in the opposite direction, the final effect is the same than in the above described diagram. Monetary policy has therefore no effect on output in a fixed rate regime. The only possibility to allow monetary policy to have an increased room for manoeuvre, by limiting capital outflows, would be the introduction of curfews[56].

Under the here described fixed exchange rate scenario, monetary authorities are required to adjust the money supply to maintain a fixed exchange rate. In this case, monetary policy, as it will be highlighted in the next section, only accommodates movements in the foreign exchange market.

3.2.3 Changes in the Foreign Exchange Markets

The position of the FE curve depends on parameters that affect import and export demand and the demand for domestic and foreign financial assets, since they affect the demand for the domestic currency. Changes in domestic or foreign income or price level, exchange rates and interest rate are examples where the FE curve must adapt to new conditions. Variations in the capital and current account shift the FE curve and modify the interest rates, which are necessary to equilibrate the capital

---

55 The decrease of the reference interest rate decreases the profitability line for the approval of investment projects. Therefore, investment is stimulated.

56 Such as those introduced in Chile, where financial assets had to be kept for a minimum of one year after purchase. In practice, however, this measure is disapproved by international and domestic investors, which in an open economy determine the financing of current account deficits.

and current account. This process links the performance of the real and financial economies, even though the dynamics, mechanism and incentives of both markets are different. An underlying difference, considering full capital mobility, is that changes in the current account develop relatively smoother in terms of time, whereas changes in the capital markets can occur quasi-immediately. Consequences in the real side of the economy caused by sudden-capital reversals can become very costly in terms of output.

Consider a real appreciation caused either by an increase in the domestic price level or through a nominal appreciation. In this case, domestic and foreign spending shifts from domestic to foreign goods, which shifts the IS curve to the left crossing the LM curve at point B (Figure 14). As a result of the increased foreign currency demand, the FE curve must shift up since the current account worsening must be compensated with a better position of the capital account through higher interest rates. Higher interest rates attract more capital and there is an increase in foreign currency supply. In a fixed exchange rate framework, this excess supply must be removed from the market to avoid a nominal revaluation. As a result, the monetary mass is reduced, shifting the LM curve to the left. Finally, all three curves equilibrate at point C, reflecting the contractionary effects (to point c) of the interest rise due to appreciation of the real exchange rate and the resulting increases in imports.

Figure 14 Effects of a Real Appreciation on Output and Interest Rates

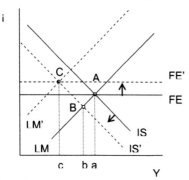

Based on: Mundell (1962) and Fleming (1962)

Other variations, which positively influence the domestic import demand, worsen the current account and are diagrammatically the same case as the one observed in Figure 14, since the negative effect on the current account via an import expansion follows the same track. Among the factors that worsen the primary current account are: increases in wealth, disposable income and Tobin's q[57], real growth or a decline in the interest rate, since they are positively related to domestic absorption and imports.

---

57 Tobin's q refers to the ratio of market valuation of a firm's stock market to the replacement costs of the installed capital. Firms tend to invest when the value of q is superior to the unity, since the market values firms by discounting future earnings using the real interest rate. The higher the

Figure 15 Effects of Capital Flight in the Presence of Large Current Account Deficits on GDP and Interest Rates

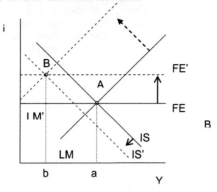

Adapted from: Mundell (1962) and Fleming (1962)

Consider a significant and sudden-capital reversal in the presence of a large current account deficit (Figure 15). The increase in domestic currency supply causes the FE curve to abruptly shift up. Both the LM and IS curves shift to the left, because of the higher interest rates and the resulting decrease in domestic absorption (total final spending by residents in investment, consumption and government expenditure). Large current account deficits (measured as a % of GDP) financed by capital account surpluses in the framework of full capital mobility are based on the optimistic expectation that no changes in investors' perceptions are to occur. However, as it is known, financial markets have periods of high volatility and herding behaviour. In this case, the abrupt changes in the financial markets severely affect the real economy (contraction to point b).

Increases in foreign interest rates imply some level of capital flight and a higher demand for foreign currency. This occurrence exerts pressure in the domestic currency market by increasing the sale of domestic currency and therefore, a depreciating trend (Figure 16). The monetary authorities, in order to maintain the exchange rate, are then forced to increase interest rates to re-attract capital, inducing a restrictive monetary policy and the shifting of the LM curve to the left.

While diagrammatically an increase in foreign exchange rates would only alter the sequence of the shifts, the effects for the small open economy with fixed rates are the same. Domestic monetary policy must follow a contractionary policy in a larger foreign country. The end effect is a loss of output (Figure 16 from a to b) due to the exogenous interest rate increase in the foreign country. This policy manoeuvre discourages both consumption and investment. Decisive to maintain a pegged exchange rate regime are the levels of both reserves available and of capital flight. Fur-

---

rate, the heavier the discounting and the lower the stock prices (see for example Burda/ Wyploz 2001: 138-9).

ther, if the exogenous interest rates increases are continuous and/ or large and sudden, the output loss would be magnified. A small open economy is forced to replicate to some extent an exogenous contractionary policy.

Figure 16 Effect of an Exogenous Increase in a Foreign Interest Rate on Interest Rates and GDP

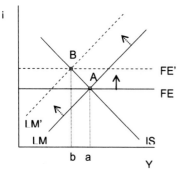

Based on: Mundell (1962) and Fleming (1962)

A devaluation (or revaluation) is certainly possible in a fixed-exchange rate scenario. The exchange rate demand and supply, associated to the capital and current account, determines the nominal exchange rate. The underlying difference compared to the floating regime is that the not the market but the authorities, based on their targets and possibilities, determine the nominal fluctuations. While the market determines the trend of nominal exchange rates, the availability of foreign currency reserves allows authorities to counteract market forces in order to maintain an exchange rate.

Devaluation stimulates domestic demand[58] due to the substitution effect of imports and the increase in exports, both caused by improved relative prices (Figure 17). This shifts the IS curve to the right. The excess demand for money balances is also compensated with a shift to the right of the LM curve. The FE curves moves downward due to changes in the demand for foreign currency (not illustrated). Output grows in the short-term to point c.

In a traditional framework, changes in the nominal exchange rate do not affect demand for money balances. They only affect the FE and IS curves. Consider, how-

---

58 Assuming that import demand elasticities satisfy the Marshall-Lerner Condition. The Marshall-Lerner condition refers to the increase of exports based on a real devaluation. The condition applies if the exchange rate elasticities of export and import demand, on absolute terms, add up to more than one. Only in this case the additional export revenues compensate the increase in the import prices caused by the devaluation. The original literature is found in Lerner (1944) and Marshall (1923) but it is subject of most textbooks.

ever, the case of exchange rate overshooting[59] triggered by devaluation and caused by capital flight (Figure 17). A monetary expansion to LM' due to excessive demand for foreign currency has to be equilibrated through a higher interest rate LM". Depending on the responsiveness of capitals to interest rates, point d can be in extreme cases lower than the departing GDP point (a). In general, output decreases are expected in the case of massive capital flight. Expansionary fiscal policy or consumption or increases in exports would stimulate domestic demand and subsequently shift the IS curve to the right and could return output to a growth path.

Figure 17 Effects of a Devaluation, Capital Flight and Exchange Rate Overshooting on GDP and Interest Rates

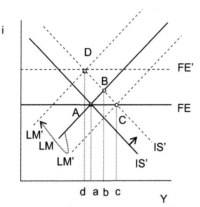

Adapted from: Mundell (1962) and Fleming (1962)

3.3 Policy Implications for Small Economies with High Levels of Imports in the Mundell-Fleming Model

3.3.1 Rationality and the Adjustment

General effects of imports in the Mundell-Fleming Model have been considered in the above developed framework. In this section, the goal is to develop policy implications based on the model considering the propensity to import of the economy and the import contents of the aggregate demand components, first intuitively and then empirically for the Mexican case.

If import contents in a small country are high in the different aggregate demand components, a significant portion of an aggregate demand increase (and the short-term

---

59 Dornbusch's (1976) seminal paper on exchange rate overshooting states that fluctuations are necessary in the presence of sticky prices and monetary instability to equilibrate the system (Rogoff 2002: 5).

output increase) will end up in the imports drainage. Any shifts of the IS curve will be linked in this case to a relatively strong countercyclical shift. Similar effects originate if the country presents an income elasticity[60] of demand for imports of over 1. The more output increases; an over-proportional increase in imports exacerbates the leakage problem within a growth path (Perrotini 2003, Pacheco 2005). Aggregate demand expansion is constrained then by imports.

In the literature, the balance-of-payments constrained growth model was introduced by Thirlwall[61] (1979), who analyzed in a relative simple manner the role of demand on the long-run growth performance of open countries. The author concludes that long-term economic growth is a function of output and capital inflow growth rate, the evolution of the terms of trade and of the import price and income elasticities of imports and exports. His findings were later extended by Krugman (1988) and are known as the 45° rule.

In this thesis, a relative simple but useful disaggregation of the aggregate demand components is applied to elaborate on the imports leakage argument in the Mundell-Fleming Model. This effort is an extension of Palley's (2009)[62] analysis of the effectiveness of tax cuts vs. fiscal expansion.

Palley (2009) splits the import function (1-3) into four different aggregate demand components. In this sense:

1-3 $M = MC + MI + MG + MX$

1-4 $M = M(Y^d, i)$

1-5 $MC = \alpha C \; 0 < \alpha < 1$

1-6 $MI = \beta I \; 0 < \beta < 1$

1-7 $MG = \gamma G \; 0 < \gamma < 1$

1-8 $MX = \varphi X \; 0 < \varphi < 1$

where MC = imports of consumption goods, M I = imports of investment goods, MG = imports by government, and MX = imports embodied in exports.

The coefficients α, β, γ, and φ determine the impact of imports on consumption, investment, government spending and exports, respectively. While the coefficients are not static, the author suggests that they only should change in the mid or long-term.

---

60 Income elasticity demand for imports relates to changes in import demand as income fluctuates.
61 According to Guerrero de Lizardi (2001), Thirlwall acknowledges in his 1995 paper the influence of Prebisch paper on immiserating growth.
62 Both Frenkel/Razin (1987) and Palley (2009) confirm the short-term positive output expansion caused by an increase in G. However, the latter does so by comparing it to tax-cuts focusing of imports leakages and the former highlights that debt-financed fiscal expansion has a straighter effect on output than tax-cuts. Frenkel/Razin's (1987), considered as a classic paper, included the effect of import on G and C, however, the impact on exports was excluded.

Particularly after liberalization, a country should have high coefficients for consumption and investment[63] that would tend stabilize after an initial surge. Intuitively, the coefficient with the lowest value should tend to be γ, since government expenditure tends toward domestic supply. The second-lower parameter would be then exports.

In the next sections some of the available data is presented to account for import elasticities and import contents in the Mexican case. As expected, imports surged after liberalization; however, they reached unprecedented levels. Surprisingly, by estimating an import-content coefficient of the aggregate demand components, exports and not investment and consumption are the driving force behind imports.

3.3.2 Existent Estimations of Mexico's Income Elasticity of Demand for Imports

Mexico is a country with high propensity to import, usual characteristic of developing countries. As calculated by Pacheco-López (2005), long-term income elasticities of imports increased significantly as a result of liberalization of trade (see Table 5). Imports reacted swiftly to the opening of the economy.

Table 5 Estimations of Long Run Income Elasticities of Demand for Imports

Period	π by Pacheco-López (2005)	Period	π by Moreno-Brid (2001)
1973-1987	1.21	1973-1988	1.55
1974-1988	1.50	1974-1989	1.46
1975-1989	1.85	1975-1990	1.5
1976-1990	2.09	1976-1991	1.6
1977-1991	2.31	1977-1992	1.46
1978-1992	2.20	1978-1993	1.60
1979-1993	2.04	1979-1994	1.65
1980-1994	2.47	1980-1995	1.55
1981-1995	3.34	1981-1996	2.66
1982-1996	4.56	1982-1997	3.53
1983-1997	4.43	1983-1998	3.10
1984-1998	3.12	1984-1999	3.14

Source: Pacheco-López (2005) and Moreno-Brid (2001)
Based on data from World Development Indicators (2002) and their own calculations.

Considering the sub-period starting after the crisis of 1982, both Pacheco-López (2005) and Moreno-Brid (2001), calculate long-term income elasticities of demand for imports[64] to be 3.5 and 4.6. In this case, imports have grown over-proportionally to income (and exports). Therefore, no substantial GDP growth has been able to mate-

---

63 Partially linked to technology transfers from foreign countries.
64 This term refers to the changes in the demand (of imports in this case) as a response to a variation in the income of the people. If elasticity equals one it implies that the import demand would move one-to-one vs. changes in income. If it is over one, then the demand for imports increases over proportionally to income.

60

rialize. The author's partial account for this outcome is "the increased dependence of the under-developed industrial sector on foreign inputs" (Pacheco-López 2005:22).

From the growth point of view, actually these findings question not liberalization in the view of the author of this thesis, but the policy framework. Pacheco-López/Thirlwall (2005) refer to sequencing of liberalization of trade to avoid a sudden import surge. The opening of trade took place in the absence of programs to support "exports with backward-forward linkages to the domestic economy" (Pacheco-López 2005:25). Further, policy makers supported and expanded an existent governmental program that practically banned domestic inputs (the effects of the Maquila[65] and similar official programs are analyzed in 4.2.3).

3.3.3 Estimation of Mexico's Import Contents of Aggregate Demand Components

The goal of this section is to examine Mexico's current account deficits to determine the import contents of the different aggregate demand components[66]. Subsequently, the conclusions in this regard are applied in the following section in a Mundell-Fleming extended framework for Mexico.

As the previous section indicates, Mexico presents high propensity to import, both due to structural factors and policy making. Figure 18 suggests that liberalization of trade has not contributed significantly to growth due to the import bias of national production, both for exports and the domestic market. While consumption and investment-associated goods have a non-negligible share of imports, the main problem lies in the dependence of the productive plant on pre-imported inputs. Almost forty percent of all imports in 1994 were linked to exports and an additional third to domestic production. Only less than one third of all imports were associated to investment and consumption together.

Actually, one of the arguments pro liberalization of trade, as found in Dornbusch (1992:74), is the possibility of importing technology and intermediate goods, that would be too expensive or not available and in their absence, the positive effect on employment of domestic production would not materialize . However, the author explicitly suggests that by freeing trade there is an: "opportunity to graduate over time from assembly to tasks with higher value-added". Figure 18 suggests that no tangible effects in this direction have been possible. The exceptions in 1995 and 1996 reflect the large devaluation after freeing the peso at the end of 1994. Imports associated to both domestic production and exports have increased significantly, without a matching development in exports.

---

65 *The Maquila program involves of the temporary introduction of duty and tariff free imported inputs to perform marginal activities (such as assembly) to then return them as exports to the country of origin, in most cases the U.S. Legally, the domestic content was limited for fiscal reasons. Chapter 4 examines this program and its effects on trade in detail.

66 Relevant data to estimate the import contents of aggregate demand components was available in the official statistic data banks, with the exception of exports. Official data regarding import content of exports was only found in the statistical annex of former president Zedillo's Report (1998) for the here displayed period.

Figure 18 Imports vs. Exports and their Destination

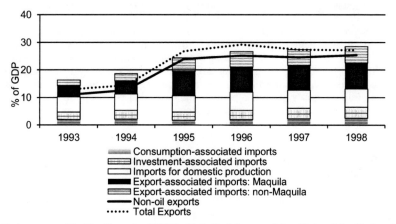

Data source: Zedillo, Ernesto: (1998), Statistical Annex of the State of the Nation Report and author's own calculations.

Figure 19 displays the estimated import contents of exports, investment and government expenditure. The behaviour of the analyzed import coefficients, excluding exports, was the one expected intuitively. Government expenditure's import content conveys to zero, investment shows a significant, as anticipated, share of imports. Consumption-associated imports, including both final products and pre-imported inputs, display a moderate share of the total with less than 15% for the whole period. Exports, however, showed already in 1993 high import contents, of roughly 50% and 60% if crude oil exports are excluded. Figures 18 and 19 provide evidence suggesting that exports are the main force behind imports.

Financial pressure at macro level is a further implication to this phenomenon. The non-Maquila imports[67] associated to exports are expectedly linked to capital flows and represented in 1994 with 2.6% a noteworthy fraction of the GDP.[68] Private consumption exerted further pressure on the capital flows position, since imports related to this variable increased in absolute and relative terms from 2.8% of GDP at the beginning of 1993 to 4.2% in the last quarter of 1994. The annual imports of non-maquila exports and production-associated imports summed up 10.7% of GDP in 1994. Both were important contributors to the current account deficit which reached 7.9% of GDP in 1994. These developments in the real sector influenced capital flows and contributed to magnify the current account deficit observed prior to the crisis.

---

67 Capital flows related to this development are for the Maquila related imports, approximately two thirds of the total, presumably not taking place. In the maquila framework, goods are temporarily imported duty-free to assemble or process, without cash-flows taking place for the input contents. Cash-flows in general only finance only the minimum "value added".

68 Further data disaggregation is not available. Data source: Zedillo (1998), INEGI online (2009) and author's own calculations.

Figure 19 Import Contents of Aggregate Demand Components

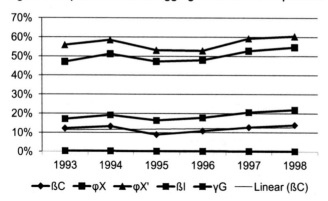

Data source: INEGI and Statistical Annex of President Zedillo's 4th State of the Nation Report (1998) and author's own calculations

*The data shows the percentage of imports embedded in each variable.

C=consumption, X=exports, X'=non-oil exports, I=investment and G=government expenditure.

All variables in 1993 constant pesos.

Note: The coefficients refer to their import share expressed in Zedillo (1998) divided by the total value of each component. The consumption coefficient includes imports of consumption goods plus the share of intermediate goods for domestic production minus the imports performed by the government. Investment includes capital goods regardless of the destination of the production. The addition of the here calculated coefficients total over 99% of total imports in every year.

3.3.4 Policy Implications

The in Mexico observed development of an export sector based mainly on pre-imported inputs also has important policy implications. Increases in domestic government expenditure, consumption and investment are clearly more effective to increase output than exports. Due to the high-import-contents, the impact of traditional exports on growth is roughly forty percent of its gross value. Mexico's difficulties with the current account deficit in 1994 were driven by the import-bias of Mexican exports. The challenges of Mexico's import propensity expressed in the last two sections are therefore scrutinized in Chapter 4.

Relevant for policy making is the consideration of this structural weakness while developing a growth strategy. The export-growth model as designed and implemented by the authorities in the view of Mexico's import bias appears paradox and points out to a policy omission and mismanagement to gradually correct this distortion. [69]

---

69 While an in-depth analysis of industrial policy and exports developments is out of the scope of the thesis, some general arguments are presented as subjects of further research. After high inflation periods, Mexico's government saw macroeconomic stability as its main assignment. The rash liberalization, the regionalization of trade and the lack of an effective industrial policy are presumably at the core of the problem. Economic policy can be described in presidential terms. During the

3.4 Macroeconomic Overview in 1994 and the Mundell-Fleming Model

The purpose of this section is to evaluate the macroeconomic settings in 1994 using the Mundell-Fleming Model. This section was elaborated attempting to take into account the challenging complexity of economic developments in a simple model. However, it generates straight forward reactions and policy recommendations considering exogenous shocks. The relative low growth is explained by the model, through the imports leakage (counteracting force for the expansionary IS curve). The need for sterilization in the presence of capital inflows, given the peg, explains the increases in interest rates and supports the above mentioned trend. Capital flight and exchange rate overshooting cannot be explained by the model, those are of financial nature. However, the model does explain the contraction of the economy once the exogenous financial reversals are integrated into it.

Table 6 summarizes the growth rates of key indicators of Mexico's economy. The observed variables in 1994 were the prolongation of the trend that started with the stabilization and liberalization of the economy. In 1994 a notable increase was observed in total domestic expenditure (4.6%), driven by an increase in private final consumption. Furthermore, a fiscal deficit after two years of surpluses was caused by a 2.5% increase in government consumption during the presidential election year. Investment increased 8.1% during the year.

Exports grew significantly, but by far not matching the rise in imports. The central bank sterilized partially the large capital inflows described in chapter 5. The turbulent development of the economy in 1994 was marked by different factors. Domestic political turmoil and volatility in the international financial market due to an astringent monetary policy in the U.S (Table 7) were among the most significant. M2 and M3 grew significantly as a result of large capital inflows to purchase government bonds, both by residents and non-residents.

---

mandate where these processes were consolidated (1988-1994) an active industrial policy was absent as it is reflected by former president Salinas' declaration: "This microeconomic transformation which is occurring in the countrY is not the responsibility of the State." The exceptions were the automotive and electronic sectors, which were addressed by specific official programs. As expressed by Moreno-Brid (2006), the horizontal programs were characterized by very limited economic resources. "In practice, the initiatives instrumented to strengthen the export potential were based on the premise that no subsidy should be given more than tariff reductions" (Moreno-Brid 2006: 101). Altex, a program that favours imported inputs for large exporters further supported (like Maquila and PITEX) this development. Additionally, the rule 303 of NAFTA, forced Mexico to offer third countries after eight years (starting in 2003) the same preferential treatment than to NAFTA partners. Considering the market distortions after the import-substitution period, a selective policy supporting the development of local suppliers would have probably been beneficial in terms of growth. In the last presidential term, according to Moreno-Brid (2006) a relative better financed strategy was implemented, however, since it was carried out almost 20 years after liberalization, it has not been able to replace imported inputs as the main industrial policy instrument.

Table 6 Growth Rates of Mexico's National Account Variables

Real Sector Variable	1994	Yearly Avg.	Accum.(87-94)
Government consumption expenditure	2.5%	1.86%	13.0%
Private consumption expenditure	3.7%	4.4%	30.6%
Increase in stocks	6.0%	12.6%	88.5%
Gross fixed capital formation	8.1%	9.0%	63.2%
Total domestic expenditure	4.6%	5.1%	36.0%
Exports	7.3%	4.7%	32.8%
Imports	12.9%	30.4%	212.5%
Trade deficit	28.6%	20.6%	144%
GDP	3.5 %	3.0%	21.2%
Priv. consumption/ GDP	0.19%	13.3%	92.8%
Terms of Trade*	11.6%	2.8%	19.73%
M1	4.7%		1264%
M2	18.5%		685%
M3	21.7%		803%

Data source: OECD National Accounts and author's own calculations.
Note: 1990 price levels/Changes are based on December data.
   * Changes in the index of terms of trade variations of goods show some level of volatility.

Capital flight was avoided during the year by exchanging government t-bills (Cetes) into dollar-denominated Tesobono bonds (Figure 20). An outstanding switch was seen after turbulence in March 1994, as a presidential candidate was murdered.

Table 7 U.S. Interest Rates　　　　**Figure 20 Domestic Financial Assets**

Date	3-month T-bill
3.Jan. 1994	3.39%
4. April 1994	4,19%
1. July 1994	4.84%
3.Oct. 1994	5.61%
22.Dec.1994	6.5%

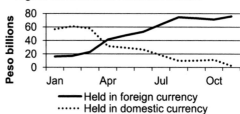

Data source: Fed online (2009)　　　　Data source: Banco de México online (2009)

The policy of supplying exchange risk free yields was very risky and costly, since by the end of the year there were enough open Tesobonos to totally finance the large current account deficit (Figure 43 and Table 29).

Figure 21 plots the contribution of private and public expenditure and net exports to GDP on a quarterly basis. The chart indicates that private spending drove GDP growth in the last three quarters of 1994. Public expenditure increased from a surplus into a deficit of roughly 1% per period. The large trade deficit slowed down growth during 1994. While fiscal expansion was large compared to the previous trend, there is no evidence to blame fiscal looseness in 1994. The main imbalances stemmed from the private sector and the high levels of imports.

Figure 21 Contribution of Aggregate Demand to Growth of GDP

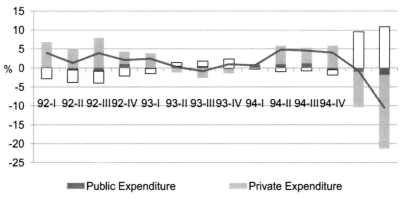

■■■Public Expenditure   ■■■Private Expenditure

Data source: Gil-Diaz/Carstens (1996:64)

Increases in the aggregate demand components: exports, consumption, investment and government spending, caused output growth (right shifts of the IS curve, see Figure 12). Nevertheless, a large increase of imports (12.9%) also took place, fuelled partially by the overvalued currency. The rise in imports caused a significant shift to the left of the IS curve (Figure 14). However, the predominating effect were right shifts of the IS curves, as evidenced by the 3.5% of GDP growth. Growth impulses stemming from IS shifts and the monetary authorities accommodating the monetary mass (Figure 13) to maintain the pegged exchange rate are correlated to increases in the interest rate. However, the required interest rates rises were lessened by increasing the supply of Tesobonos in foreign currency[70], as highlighted in Figure 20.

The relaxing of the fiscal policy[71] and a rise in consumption (right shifts of the IS curve) were complemented by monetary expansion and partial sterilization[72] during

---

70 Lower interest rates in foreign currency proved to be a risky strategy given the volatility and the magnitude of the offered bonds (see chapter 7 for an analysis of their nature). Tesobonos were held in earlier literature contributions as a cause for the crisis. See for example Lustig (1995).
71 Dornbusch/Werner (1994: 253) estimated in the spring of 1994 that any GDP growth would be caused by expansive fiscal policy.
72 Sachs et al. (1996) affirm that the insufficiently restrictive monetary policy during 1994 facilitated the decrease in international reserves. In their view, this strategy "may have put the economy where multiplicities exist and where a self-fulfilling attack was feasible". During the period, the authors consider that the authorities were able to ensure that no devaluation was to take place,

the first months of 1994, which followed the decrease in demand for peso assets. Credit expansion was very swift (Figure 10) and was fostered by the expansion of private expenditure and the sterilization, which caused interest rates to increase, given the credit expansion in foreign currency. Further, exogenous interest rates increased the pressure in the financial markets (Figure 16). The interest rate increases contributed to lower growth and intensified the vulnerability of the banking sector.

The policy mix that was implemented as a response further fostered the short-term capital inflows:

"A combination of little or no short-term exchange uncertainty (as it is the case when there is an implicit or explicit peg), sterilized intervention (which tends to prevent domestic short-term interest rates from converging towards international levels) and no capital controls. This policy mix in conjunction with a substantial stock of government debt characterizes reasonably well the Mexican experience." (Reinhart/Reinhart 1998: 122).

Credit expansion[73] supported investment and consumption and consequently growth. These movements caused right shifts of the IS and LM curve. However, capital imports shifted the FE curve and forced sterilization, which caused further capital inflows due to higher interest rates. A corrective devaluation would have relieved the accumulated pressure in 1994. However, it only took place in an abrupt manner and triggered capital flight[74] (Figure 17).

Summarizing, the movements displayed in Figures 11, 12, 14 and 16 preceded capital flight and the crisis of 1995, displayed in figure 17. Growth was constrained by imports, favoured by an overvalued currency. However, the magnitude of the Mexican crisis can only be explained by significant capital swings. The overshooting of the currency, followed by a very astringent monetary policy after the initial devaluation in Dec. 1994, can explain through this model the contraction of the economy in 1995. However, it has no explanatory power to determine the underlying causes of the crisis. The next sections of the chapter attempt to find pieces of evidence in this direction. Most of them, however, are found in the last two chapters of this thesis.

---

while increasing debt and using up reserves. This strategy in their view guaranteed, that if a devaluation would take place, would be then be significant (Sachs et al. 1996: 23).

73 Birdsall et al. (1996) consider that the fragile situation of the banks (see chapter 6) was a significant constraint on monetary policy in 1994. The continuous pressure in 1994 and the related capital outflows should have generated a more astringent monetary policy; however, given the weaknesses of the financial sector, such a policy was not pursued. The authors nevertheless point out, that a lending boom are also possible in the "best regulating financial systems of the world and a substantial responsibility for the financial fragilities must rest with the macroeconomic policies that made the boom possible" (Birdsall et al. 1996: 284).

74 Cavazos (2002) used Engle and Granger's methodology to calculate the sum of the absolute values of imports and export elasticities of goods and services. In the short run the value added up 1.05 and in the long run 1.36. Therefore the Marshall-Lerner condition is if barely, satisfied in both the short and long run. The methodology refers to Unit Root testing and Cointegration. Therefore, a currency devaluation would have import-correcting and expansionary effects as predicted in theory.

3.4.1 Final Considerations Regarding the Mundell-Fleming Model

In Mundell's recapitulation on the Mundell-Fleming Model the author summarizes:

> "One implication of the model is that a domestic boom would raise interest rates, attract capital inflows, appreciate the real exchange rate, and worsen the balance of trade, a conclusion that would hold under either fixed or flexible exchange rates... The critical assumption is complete capital mobility since capital flows were reactive to interest rates. Monetary policy had a comparative advantage in correcting the balance of payments. However, it proved that under fixed exchange rates and perfect capital mobility, monetary policy was ineffective... Sterilization policy is incompatible with fixed exchange rates, and leads to a "disequilibrium system." Here is the problem. With a stock of money constant, the increase in government expenditure will increase interest rates, which will check expenditure and lead to an increased net capital inflow. While the trade balance worsens, the capital account improves.... The money supply is an endogenous variable under fixed exchange rates...the balance of payments can be kept in disequilibrium under fixed exchange rates only if automatic effects of reserve changes on the money supply are sterilized, a *temporary* solution (Mundell 2002: 7, 9,10).[75]

The author's conclusions describe relevant implications for the Mexican economy in 1994. The domestic boom, driven by the private sector and supported by a swift credit expansion was financed through foreign capital, which appreciated the peso. Sterilizing the capital flows, which financed the current account deficit in a fixed-currency framework, should have been a temporary condition. Devaluation was required earlier in order to close the gap of the growing trade deficit. However, a sudden reversal of capitals did not enable a soft landing and caused the large output contraction in 1995. An overview of the macroeconomic variables indicates mismatches that had to be corrected. The in fact fixed exchange rate brought the country into significant difficulties. Nevertheless, the true culprits of the Mexican crisis are of financial nature. Therefore, the domestic financial sector, capital flows, their composition and behaviour are further analyzed in chapters 5, 6 and 7.

3.5 Crisis Models

Different theories have been developed to explain currency crises in the last three decades. They can be categorized into three groups (called generations). According to Frankel/Wei (2004) these efforts "attempt to answer the timing question" based on investors rational expectations. The main distinction among the three generations models, according to the authors, relate to the factors that originate the crisis. The

---

75 According to Mundell (2002) the Mundell-Fleming Model is best suitable for developed countries with well performing capital markets and convertible currencies. The author is sceptic in regard to the explanatory power of the model for developing countries. Die rationale delivered is that country risk factors broadly affect capital flows and that currencies interact in a chronic inflationary framework.

first generation models affirm that domestic macroeconomic policy is to be held responsible. Second generation models consider volatile financial markets as the cause. Finally, third generation models link crises to distortions and imperfections in financial markets. Table 8 presents a compact summary of selected models.

Table 8 Three Generation Models

Gen.	Description	Selected Models:
1st.	Fixed exchange rate is inconsistent with monetary/ fiscal policy.	Krugman(1979), Flood/ Garber (1984)
2nd	Governments considerations & speculators expectations interact/ Multiple equilibria (fixed ER might be abandoned to follow a goal).	Obstfeld (1994), Morris/ Shin (1998), Heinemann/Illing(2002)
3rd.*	Different kinds: Government's commitment causes moral hazard, which leads to overinvestment. Currency crisis occurs when the strategy is not longer plausible. Currency and banking crises are caused by illiquidity of the financial sector.	Krugman(1998), Corsetti et al. (1999)
	"Balance-sheet" problem if the private sector if it presents a high level of foreign debt. A pessimistic evaluation of the economic situation/ devaluation pressure might worsen the condition of the firms, then investments falls and a devaluation becomes unavoidable (eventually a fixed exchange rate system has to be given up).	Chang / Velasco (1998) Krugmann (1999) & Aghion/Bachetta /Banerjee (2000-2002)

Source: Gärtner/Lutz (2004)
* Other third generation models: Burnside/Eichenbaum/Rebelo (2000), Caballero/Krishnamurthy (1999), Calvo (1998), McKinnon/ Pill (1998) and Schneider/Tornell (2000).

As it was the case for the Mundell-Fleming model, it seems that no model offers an integral approach to explain and describe currency crises. Nevertheless, a brief overview of the different generation models facilitates the identification of relevant factors which contributed to the Mexican crisis.

3.5.1 First Generation Models

This strand of literature is distinguished by the contribution of Krugman (1979) and Flood/Garber (1984). Fiscal deficits are financed by borrowing or monetary growth. These fiscal imbalances lead to a current account deficit and an overvalued currency. Overvaluation is maintained until reserves are depleted according to the original Krugman (1979) model, in Flood/Garber's (1984) until the reserves equals the semi-elasticity of money demand and the rate of expansion of domestic credit.

The mechanisms of the first generation models accurately describe the observed path of the 1982 debt crisis in Mexico. Yet given the fiscal discipline starting at the end of the eighties, they do not seem to offer a plausible explanation of the Mexican crisis. Nevertheless, there are relevant common factors to the Mexican crisis of 1995 suggested by these models. These are unsustainable current account deficits and the preservation of an overvalued currency until the reserves of the central banks are depleted. These developments, however, were in 1994 driven by the private sector and the capital which financed them was not composed of syndicated loans to the public sector, as in the early eighties, but of voluntary financial inflows.[76]

3.5.2 Second Generation Models

Second generation models were introduced by Obstfeld (1994) after the European Exchange Rate Mechanism Crises in 1992-1993. In this model, economic fundamentals do not play the main role. Frankel/Wei (2004) relate this approach to the prisoner's dilemma and describe the problematic in an intermediate range of vulnerability. In the absence of strong fundamentals that do not justify a crisis, both a currency attack and non-attack are possible (multiple equilibria). A run would take place if and only if investors expect that others investors might flee too and reserves are not high enough to counteract capital flight. Some models suggest that unemployment is a key fundamental variable to determine if a country is in the intermediate range, others consider the level of debt (Obstfeld 1996). Relevant is the fact that multiple equilibria are caused by the circularity composed of the expectations of speculators and government policy, which influence each other (Gärtner/Lutz 2004: 342).

Figure 22 depicts the different equilibria possible in Obstfeld's (1994) second generation model. In the right side of the chart the equilibrium in the monetary market expressed by the LM curve and on the left the equilibrium in the international capital markets through the FE curve. The initial exchange rate e is fixed at $e= e_0$, the corresponding money mass is m_0 and the domestic interest rate i_0, equals i^*. Suddenly, the expectations of speculators change and they expect a devaluation. This shifts the FE curve to FE'. If the central bank is willing to maintain the fixed rate, i must increase to i' and therefore reduce the monetary mass to m'. Otherwise, a devaluation to e' becomes imminent, with the consequence of an rise in the price level, which shifts the LM' and m to m''. In this case, multiple equilibria is possible because given the initial positions A and B, the final outcomes depend on the expectations of the speculators and of policy makers and their interaction.

The Mexican crisis did not seem to be expected by the agents, as interest rates in the eve of the massive did not reflect any changes in expectations. The speculative attack hypothesis is therefore not satisfactory. Two aspects related to the second generation models have some explanatory power for the Mexican case: a sudden capital flight once the agents started to flee, which materialized the panic and the fact that central bank reserves were not enough to offset them.

---

76 Large international financial groups which offered syndicated lending to the governments before the oil shock in the early eighties might be related to the capital inflows observed in the nineties. However, this subject is out of the scope of this thesis.

Figure 22 Different Equilibria in a Monetary Focused Model

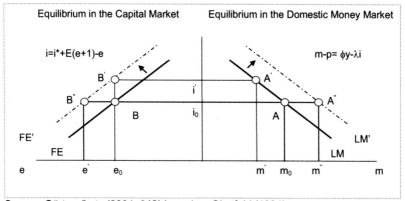

Source: Gärtner/Lutz (2004: 342) based on Obstfeld (1994).

Variables: Greek letters stand for positive parameters in the model. i = domestic interest rate, i* foreign interest rate, E= expectations, e= exchange rate, y= aggregate demand, p= price level and m= monetary demand

3.5.3 Third Generation Models

Third generation models attempt to link financial weaknesses to currency and/or banking crises (in combination known as twin crises):

> "In light of the judgment that most of these countries had relatively good macroeconomic policies, diagnoses have placed new emphasis on a different sort of fundamentals: structural distortions in the financial structures of emerging economies. "Crony capitalism," defined more formally as implicit government guarantees for poorly regulated banks and corporate debtors, has been the inspiration behind a "third generation" approach to currency crises (for some, the phrase "third generation" refers to the problems of balance sheet mismatch, particularly among banks. The two sets of issues are closely related)." (Frankel/ Wei 2004: 7).

The authors elaborate on the issue by adding moral hazard at national level and related lending into the crises explanation. Chang /Velasco (1998) cover relevant aspects to the Mexican crisis. The crises are in their view unexpected and related to domestic financial illiquidity. Larger capital inflows with short-term maturity increase the vulnerability of the banking sector, as it also does lowering its reserve requirements. Additionally, the crises are preceded by a period of "sharp increases in inelastically supplied assets –such as real state" (Chang/Velasco 1998:25).

Schneider/Tornell (2000)[77] developed a model which captures two important aspects associated to distortions in the international financial markets in the third generation models: bad policy and bad markets. The authors consider that the emergence of twin crises results from the interaction of balance-sheet effects and bailout guarantees in a specific scenario. In their view, their interaction generates conditions that characterize the boom in a boom-bust cycle. During a boom the relaxing of borrowing constraints to the non-tradable sector (N) leads to asymmetric growth dynamics (as broadly suggested by Chang/Velasco 1998) vs. tradables (T). The increase in credit to N is linked to a larger exposure of the banking system to currency mismatch, which is implicitly backed by the government.

As expressed by the authors: "many problems in the banking sector originated in the loans to that (N) sector". If many banks engage in such conditions, a real depreciation implies a systemic crisis. A credit boom and real appreciation typically precede a crisis. Exchange rate risks become endogenous and the economy is then vulnerable to a self-fulfilling meltdown of the banking system. A "sunspot"[78] can initiate twin crises, implying here both in the currency market and the banking system. This crisis mechanism is possible when banks are highly indebted in foreign currency.

In this model, the timing is exogenous, attributed to a sunspot, the likeliness, is however, determined by the specific factors mentioned above. Another implication is that the crisis is not merely financial but is then transferred to the real sector, through an investment crunch in the non-tradable sector.

Key findings of the paper are that guarantees[79] and contract enforceability problems generate the vulnerability situation required for self-fulfilling crises. However, improved expectations detonated, for example, by a far reaching liberalization program or the discovery of natural resources are required as well.

3.5.3.1 Selected Issues and Schneider/Tornell's (2000) Model

This model was conceived to explain the Mexican crisis of 1994. This section presents selected issues that find support for the arguments offered by Schneider/ Tornell (2000). Between 1992 lending from the banking system to the private sector increased by more than 50% in real terms and the real exchange rate appreciated by some 20% as suggested by Chang/Velasco (1998) and Schneider/Tornell (2000).

Alegría (2004) calculated an index (in pesos) of diverse firms in the Mexican Stock Exchange measuring passives in foreign currency against total capital. According to the author, in 1994 the ratio of foreign liabilities to capital was 15% (measured in pesos) and jumped to 64% in 1995. Further, the author calculated, supposing that the aforementioned group did not undertake any hedging, either in the financial markets or through income, that a 10% devaluation would have generated a 10% operative

---

77 This section is based on the original version of the paper and on the compact version presented in Tornell /Westermann (2004).
78 Referring to extrinsic uncertainty or an extrinsic random variable.
79 Bail out guarantees according to the authors, might have positive collateral effects such as a growth inducing effect due to the relaxing of borrowing constraints.

profit loss in 1994[80]. That implies, that every 1% depreciation translated into a 1% operative loss. Therefore the massive devaluation after Dec. 1994 (of nearly 100%) had dramatic balance sheet effects. In this sense, it appears that only companies in tradable sectors and with relative low import inputs were able to cope with the crisis.

The behaviour of tradables and non-tradables before and after the crisis was also predicted by the model. Between 1989 and 1993 the relative prices index of tradables grew slower than that of non-tradables (Table 9). Through liberalization of trade and the availability of funds, a greater import supply dampened increases in prices[81]. Reflecting the boom, the relative index of tradables vs. non-tradables almost halved in the above mentioned period (Gurria 1995: 272 ff.).

Table 9 Tradable and Non-tradable Price Index (1980=100)

Year	Tradables		Non-tradables		Tradables vs. Non-tradables Index
	Index	Growth rate	Index	Growth rate	
1980	100.0	--	100.0	--	100.0
1981	146.2	46.2	149.1	49.1	98.1
1982	286.1	95.7	278.4	86.7	102.8
1983	551.0	92.6	457.7	64.4	120.4
1984	908.9	65.0	684.7	49.6	132.7
1985	1484.6	63.3	1115.7	62.9	133.1
1986	3029.0	104.0	2050.7	83.8	147.7
1987	8248.4	172.3	4793.6	133.8	172.1
1988	12167.6	47.5	8638.0	80.2	140.9
1989	13680.2	12.4	12650.9	46.5	108.1
1990	15989.3	16.9	18470.9	46.0	86.6
1991	18591.6	16.3	22563.3	22.2	82.4
1992	20290.5	9.1	26059.4	15.5	77.9
1993	21453.9	5.7	28858.2	10.7	74.3

Data source: Gurría (1995) with data from the SHCP (Finance Ministry), México.

---

80 Foreign liabilities amounted 180 billion pesos.

81 Krugman/Obstfeld (2003: 409) present the argument that research on international price differences reveals an empirical paradox: if expressed in terms of a single currency, countries price levels are positively related to the level of real income per capita and that non tradables tend to be more expensive relative to tradables in richer countries. The authors present two explaining theories: Balassa/Samuelson's theory which assumes that the labor of less developed countries is less productive than that of developed countries in tradables as opposed as in non-tradables (where differences are minimal). Lower productivity in tradables reflects lower wages both in the tradable and non tradable sector and therefore lower prices in the non-tradable sector as well. The second possible explanation is the Bhagwati (1984)-Kravis-Lipsey (1983) view that supports the notion that differences in capital endowments of capital and labor in developing countries rather than productivity differences cause non tradables to be relative cheaper than in developed countries. The marginal productivity of labor is greater in the latter than in the former and therefore, wages are lower in developing countries. Since nontradables are labor intensive, they tend to be, less expensive in terms of tradables than in developing countries, where wages are higher. Both explanations according to Krugman/Obstfeld (2003) give empirical support to the argument that nontradables tend to be less expensive relative to tradables in developing countries and that price levels are positively related to the level of real income per capita.

After the crisis, as predicted by the model, the T sector picked up rapidly, the N sector collapsed and experienced only a sluggish recovery. This development is associated to the credit crunch in the N sector. Schneider/Tornell (2000) used manufactures and exports to proxy the path of the T sector and the construction sector to proxy the T sector. Non-oil exports were not affected by the crisis due to the depreciation and the booming US economy. The construction[82] sector followed the pattern described above.

3.5.3.2 Evaluation of the Model

The model seems to be the most fitting option of the third generation models to analyze financial distortions behind the Mexican crisis of 1994. It offers both valuable insights and challenging aspects.

Some of the significant aspects to explain the Mexican crisis are straight-forward. These include a lending boom, original sin, the lack of a prudential regulation and asymmetric sectorial performance. Other conclusions, such as the unfeasibility of the occurrence of a crisis after one already took place or the consideration that lending booms "only" increase crisis vulnerability are less evident but not less useful.

The bottom line is that lending booms financing growth in non-tradables, based on currency mismatch in the banking sector and related to a real appreciation phase put a state in a vulnerable condition. If a severe depreciation takes place, twin crises are imminent at this point of time.

Other relevant aspects such as unsustainable current account deficits, ineffective credit allocation, the role of abrupt capital inflows or asymmetric behaviour of agents are ignored or only partially explained. An extension of the model could include the balance sheet effects of financial institutions and macro-aspects linked to the boom such as significant current account deficits. Similar to their predecessors, this model is useful to disentangle relevant microeconomic aspects but does not offer an integral approach to explain the Mexican crisis

3.5.3.3 Commented Evaluation of Crises Models

The main problematic of using a currency crisis model to analyze the Mexican crisis is that they offer important elements but not comprehensive approaches. All three generation models offer valuable pieces of evidence which conform the puzzle observed in Mexico 1994. From the first generation models, overvaluation and current account deficits were present; nevertheless these were not originated by excessive expansionary fiscal or monetary policy. The second generation models contribute with the facts associated to volatility and herding in open financial markets.

---

82 However, regulatory changes regarding building credits available to workers introduced after the model boosted the sector. A deregulation in the use of credits, which gave workers the choice of using their available credits in private real state, is a good example how industrial policy and liberalization can be beneficial and not mutually exclusive.

Third generation models complement the explanation with the structural distortions of the domestic financial markets. Lending booms, currency appreciation and asymmetric sectorial performance are characteristic of twin crises. Banks in emerging economies are exposed to currency mismatch since they lend to firms in the non-tradable sector in local and borrow in foreign currency. The contractionary effect of a sudden and large devaluation is attributable to balance-sheet effects and the resulting credit crunch.

The conclusions of this section are in line with Frankel/Wei's (2004) systematic study of both empirics and theory of currency crises, where they find both examples for and against different theories and models:

"It does not seem possible to categorize the country experiences into first generation, second generation and third generation type crises. In each historical episode, some observers blame macroeconomic fundamentals, some volatile financial markets, and some structural flaws. In truth, all these factors play a role." (Frankel/Wei 2004: 15).

The here performed recapitulation, shares the authors' view and complements the traditional literature by scrutinizing non-traditional factors (see chapters 4, 5 and 7) which could lead to an improved understanding of the Mexican crisis.

3.6 Macroeconomic Conclusions

Literature on the Mexican crisis was very prolific. This chapter reviewed and extended some traditional arguments brought about by selected the contributions.

A domestic boom, which started after 1993, had some susceptibilies. Large capital inflows, linked to high interest rates, were not only financing investment, but private consumption. Further, intermediate goods and a large external deficit were offsetting demand for domestic products. Gil-Diaz/ Carstens(1996) referred to Krugman's (1995) conclusion:

"This growth slowdown was in a direct sense due to the rise in Mexico's real exchange rate after 1990, which discouraged any rapid growth in exports and caused growing demand to be spent primarily on imports rather than domestic goods" (Krugman 1995:41-2).

Dornbusch[83] (1994: 11) also stated: "The combined evidence would suggest that demand has shifted to foreign goods" and that the growth reducing impact of real appreciation has been reinforced by a high real cost of credit.

In this section, a structural weakness of Mexico's exporting sector was introduced. The estimation of import-contents coefficients of the aggregate demand components revealed that exports make the largest contribution to imports. While having imports embedded in exports is not exclusive of Mexico, the scope of the problem is signifi-

---

83 Defined by Gil/Carstens (1996) as "the most vocal critic of Mexico's former exchange rate policy"

cant with over 60% in 1994 for non-oil exports. Some of the implications of this phenomenon were the viability of an export-growth model in a fixed exchange rate scenario and the proneness to incur within this framework in current account deficits. The next chapter attempts to find some microeconomic evidence in this direction.

The pegged currency regime limited the room for manoeuvre for monetary policy, which was itself under continuous sterilization and stabilization pressure. The disorderly growth of credit to the private sector added vulnerability to the already volatile periods in 1994. Fiscal policy was relaxed in 1994 but far from being a matter of concern. The exogenously and endogenously induced interest rate hikes in 1994 were mitigated partially by the massive introduction of dollar-denominated Tesobonos. These increases endangered the growing credit allocation and slowed down growth. Tesobonos reached unprecedented levels, which as it will be further studied in the financial section of this thesis, can be considered as a major policy error. The appreciation of the peso favoured a large current account deficit in 1994, which was financed by abnormal capital inflows.

An indicator which seems to have more explanatory power than in the literature suggested is the large current account deficit. This argument stems from the fact that it links the financial and the real sectors. A large current account deficit is per definition financed by large capital imports. It might be financed by liquid funds which could impede a soft-landing in case of capital reversals. Further, in Mexico it was associated to a prolonged currency overvaluation, a pre-condition to the crisis' course.

Certainly, there was in 1994 the need for correction of imbalances in the real sector and the realignment of the currency. However, the exchange rate overshooting and the severe crisis afterwards cannot be explained by the indicators presented in this chapter.

This chapter's conclusions are in line with Tobin's (1996: 68):

> "The example of Mexico, which is suffering painful and cruel punishments for crimes of fiscal and monetary policy it did not commit, should suffice to raise doubts about the "markets-know-best" proposition".

Chang and Velasco (1998: 2) equally supported this argument for Mexico by stating that: "the punishment is larger than the crime".

Therefore, the next chapters explore microeconomic aspects of trade and financial to disentangle various factors and triggering effects of such a considerable event, which cannot be fully explained by macro and real variables.

II. Microeconomic Aspects of Mexico's Trade

4 The Trade Structure Revisited

The ambitious reform program undertaken in Mexico in the early nineties had significant effects not only in the financial markets, but also in the real sector of the economy. Structural changes in the export pattern were underpinned by the signature of
NAFTA, the rash liberalization and public policy. In this sense, a trend towards assembly and low value added was self-reinforcing as a result of the counteraction of
the above mentioned factors.

This section approaches microeconomic effects associated to the liberalization of
trade. The analysis of the exports patterns was originally meant to discard the possibility of catalyst effects to the crisis, such as the export growth slowdown seen in Asia
in the pre-crisis period. The thesis was, as expected, abandoned. However, it led to a
central fact of the Mexican economic reality in the last two decades. A backward link-
age of a main fundamental of the crisis: the rationality of the overvaluation trend, explained in terms of the export structure. The fact is that once reassessed the actual
exporting sectors are only moderately, in contrast to conventional wisdom, sensitive
to overvaluation.

The first section of the chapter reviews traditional trade theory to establish a theoretical framework to compare the expected vs. the actual export structure. Theory suggests that Mexican trade should be based on natural resources and comparative advantage. The next section includes a detailed taxonomy of exports from different an-
gles. The first is an empirical task related to the Life Cycle theory. Using an existing
classification, exports were categorized according to the applicability of three traditional trade theories: Ricardo, Heckscher-Ohlin and Schumpeter.

In line with the theory, Mexican exports mainly reflect their natural resources (oil) and
labor abundance. However, if these findings were adapted to include the balance of
trade per group, prior to the crisis all of them but the oil related fraction showed a
deficit. Mexico was in these terms a net importer of labor intensive products. This
deficit in 1994, as expected by theory, did not tend to be lower than the deficit in capital intensive goods, but roughly as large as the latter. A further implication of this disaggregated trade balance was the fact that the Schumpeterian and capital fractions
immediately exhibited a surplus following the drastic devaluations after 1994. Further,
geography plays a crucial role, since trade with the U.S dominates the trade transactions.

The further study of exports, encouraged by the import contents of aggregate demand components indexes[84], generated some further conclusions. Most exports are
either per se real exchange rate inelastic, such as oil, or include a large proportion of
pre-imported inputs. As a result, the authorities had only a feeble incentive to keep
the currency at its real value[85]. A biased structure towards pre-imported inputs was

---

84 See section 3.3.
85 While the exchange rate policy abandoned the pegged system, different exogenous factors such
    as the rise of oil prices, a main export fraction and the increase in FDI and transfers flows that

promoted by regulation. The Maquila-"export", program, which offered fiscal benefits if the national contents were kept low, was a cornerstone of an exchange rate irresponsive, low value added and vulnerable exporting sector.

To shed light on the explanatory variables of the export and import developments previous to the crisis, a basic regression analysis was performed in the penultimate section. To deal the distortions of the oil market, only non-oil exports were used. The results suggest that imports react much faster than exports to currency overvaluation. Mexican exports are highly associated to the U.S. business cycle. These conclusions explain, at least partially, the rationale behind macroeconomic policy. The appreciation of the peso was useful for stabilization goals and did not hurt the exporting sector given that they are relative exchange rate inelastic. The most influential factor on exports is still the performance of the U.S. economy. The last section reviews the contribution of Mexico's structural weaknesses of trade to the accrual of external imbalances behind the crisis.

4.1 Theoretical Framework

4.1.1 Expected Trade Pattern

This section presents fundamental theory to explain the international trade structure of a developing country. This compact outline highlights some important expected trends, which are useful in the next sections to compare Mexico's expected vs. actual trade path and performance.

Trade was mainly explained, prior to Krugman (1992), by Ricardo's comparative advantage. If a country is relatively less skilled labor abundant, then liberalization would imply that the country would tend to export goods intensive in less-skilled labor. Therefore, the relative return of less-skilled labor should increase in the long run. Comparative advantage was simple to model since constant returns and perfect competition and no transportation costs are assumed. Further, full employment, capital immobility and compensating mechanisms are assumed.

However, according to Krugman (1991) increasing returns if "analytically awkward and empirically elusive are evidently important in shaping economic relations across boundaries". International trade allows countries to concentrate in the production of a limited range of goods, taking advantage of economies of scale without giving up variety in consumption. Nevertheless, due to increasing returns[86], large firms possess an advantage over small firms. Therefore, markets tend to be dominated by a small number of large firms, implying imperfect competition. The new geography economy also sketches a model of regional economic divergence. In this model, the interaction of a strong demand, increasing returns and transportation costs, and therefore dis-

---

U.S. immigrants send into Mexico have, with the exception of the post crisis years, further supported a market led overvaluation trend.

86 Increasing returns affect economic geography at different levels according to Krugman (1992):
- Location of particular industries, which reflects the "lock in" of transitory advantages.
- Cities evidence the increasing returns phenomenon.
- Asymmetrical development of national regions in a country.

tance, account for economic differences and trade liberalization (Krugman 1991:11). In this sense, trade should be more localized than globalized. Frankel/Romer (1999) whilst analyzing the relationship and causality of trade and growth[87] found that: "countries geographic characteristics have important effects on trade".

Krugman/Obstfeld (2006) schematize a trade pattern between two countries facing increasing returns, different factor endowment and competition schemes (a monopolistically competitive sector[88] and a competitive industry). In the absence of increasing returns, there would be no predicted trade pattern. However, in their presence there is a differentiation of trade. The length of the arrows in Figure 23 indicates the value of trade on each direction. Interindustry trade is based on comparative advantage. The latter still plays a major role in shaping trade. Therefore, the labor-abundant country is expected to be a net exporter of labor intensive goods and vice-versa. Intraindustry trade, however, does not reflect comparative advantage. Demand provides the incentive for firms to produce differentiated goods, as well as home as abroad, and generates intraindustry trade. Increasing returns prevent countries from producing a full range of varieties and therefore represents a source of international trade.

Figure 23 Expected Trade Pattern of Two Sector Countries with Differing Factor Endowment, Increasing Returns and Monopolistic Competition

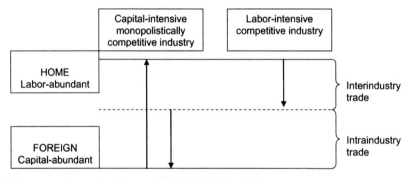

Data source: based on Krugman/Obstfeld (2006: 127).

The precise pattern of intraindustry trade, according to the authors, cannot be specified based on theory, since history and accident are significant components. However, country factor endowment shapes the expected direction. For countries with strongly differing factors trade will dominantly be interindustry, defined by compara-

---

87 In their view, only a modest positive relationship was observed, but the causality was not statistically determined.
88 Krugman/Obstfeld (2006) pick monopolistic competition as a form of oligopoly/ imperfect competition that is relatively practical to analyze. Monopolistic competition assumes an oligopoly where products are differentiated (no homogeneous product) and each firm assumes that the prices of competitors are given and ignores the impact of its own price in the market.

tive advantage and to a lesser extent by intraindustry trade due to economies of scale.

Intraindustry trade generates additional gains from trade since it allows countries to profit from larger markets, producing fewer varieties and therefore profiting from economies of scale while increasing consumer's choices. These gains will be larger if products are differentiated and economies of scale are strong. However, the income distribution effects of trade tend to be minor. On the other side, interindustry trade affects relative prices which have substantial effects on income distribution (Krugman/Obstfeld 2006: 129).

Krugman (1996: 125-6) expresses how essential the insights of Hume and Ricardo regarding international trade are. In his opinion: "the benefits of trade do not depend on a country having absolute advantage over its rivals".

Moreover, Krugman/Helpman (1996) developed an approach based on the factor proportions theory. The authors affirm:

> "one of our major purposes is to show that many of the insights gained from traditional trade theory continue to be useful even in a world where increasing returns and perfect competition are important" (Krugman/Helpman 1996:1).

4.1.2 Factor Intensity and the Product Life Cycle Hypothesis

Vernon (1966) was the first to conduct empirical work on the relationship between international trade and the product life cycle. The author departs from the premises of high average income in developed countries and their factor endowment (capital abundant) which condition demand for products. Accordingly, R & D takes place to develop labor-saving or high-income-based products. Companies are subject to temporary factors: input flexibility, low price elasticity on demand, critical need for communication with customers, suppliers and competitors. Therefore, facility location remains in developed countries. However, as product demand expands, standardization occurs and firms begin to focus on their cost structures. The locational effect is that production facilities would be moved to less developed country with low cost of labor. In Vernon (1979) the author recognizes that the time interval of the relocation to a foreign country had been rapidly reduced. According to An/Iyigun (2004) different empirical contributions suggest that with increased production experience developing countries were enabled to export products in earlier stages of the product life cycle[89].

This section synthesizes Hirsch's work (1975). The author, in the search for hypotheses to explain trade between developing and industrialized countries, creates a classification of traded goods. Hirsch (1975) developed some hypotheses to explain trade flows between developed and more developed countries. Using a 22 country

---

89 The authors cite work on Arpan/Kim (1973), Hobday (1995), Lall (1998, 2000), Narayan/Wah (2000).

sample of both kinds, the author finds empirical support for the product life cycle model.

Even as the author believes that trade flows might not be explained in terms of a single theory, he considers that the universe of traded goods can be classified into three categories to which existing trade theories apply: Ricardo goods, Heckscher-Ohlin goods and Schumpeter goods. This classification based on the factors determining the location of production sites is shortly introduced.

4.1.2.1 Ricardo Goods

Ricardo associated comparative advantage with the differing production conditions (nature-related) of countries. Hirsch defines Ricardo goods to be those whose comparative advantage is linked to the natural endowment of a nation[90]. The comparative advantage in Ricardo goods might erode over time due to demand changes, availability of substitutes, supply increases, better technologies or improvements in transportation. The trade pattern for Ricardo goods can be summarized as follows: supply mainly from developing countries as their availability in industrial countries is used up, demand seemingly affected by the business cycle and positively correlated to GDP. The expected direction of trade is from South (developing countries) to North (developed countries).

4.1.2.2 Heckscher-Ohlin Goods

Heckscher-Ohlin goods are mainly manufactured products whose comparative advantage is determined by the relative factor endowment of countries. Countries have a comparative advantage in products that utilize their most abundant factor of production (land, labor, capital)[91]. Distinctive among them is the availability of the stable manufacturing technology for those wishing to enter the industry.

The expected trade flow based on this model implies industrial countries export capital intensive goods, since their most abundant production factor is capital and developing countries to export labor intensive goods.

4.1.2.3 Schumpeter Goods

The remaining type of traded goods could be grouped in a category with specific characteristics. Products based on recent innovations and R & D efforts with a non-established hard to imitate technology. The Product Cycle Model defines three production factors: capital, skilled and unskilled manpower. Products typically undergo through a cycle. In the early phase skilled manpower is required to carry out R & D

---

90 Minerals, agricultural products and manufactures mainly composed of available resources are a few examples cited by the author.
91 The following assumptions apply: the production function is assumed to be the same in all countries and there are no economies of scale and factor reversals are excluded. Hirsch while recognizing that "the assumptions are quite heroic" finds diverse cases where the model fits.

and initial manufacturing. The production function at this stage varies along different countries; technology transfer is costly and hardly available for other firms. Once products advance in the life cycle skilled-manpower plays a secondary role and the other factors determine the comparative advantage. Mature goods have a similar profile to Heckscher-Ohlin goods, since their relative factor costs determine comparative advantage.

Theoretical work on the evolution on trade over the product life cycle (as reviewed An/Iyigun 2004) includes Krugman (1979) who develops a general-equilibrium model in which the North innovates and the South imitates. This piece of evidence shapes the trade structure: the North exports products in early stages of the life cycle and the South in later stages. Grossman/Helpman (1991) present a quality ladder model. The implication is that firms in the North invest resources to upgrade quality and those in the sound imitate technologies. The steady- state equilibrium can be described in a migration of production facilities first from North to South to then move from South to the North.

Schumpeter goods' comparative advantage is shaped by the availability of capital, skilled and unskilled manpower and by the costs of technology transfers[92]. Hirsch refers to Burenstam Linder (1961) to predict the trade flows in N goods. The authors propose that "products are designed to satisfy the needs of the market where the manufacturer resides" and since tastes are, according to them, are highly correlated with per capita income, trade for Schumpeter goods should take place among countries with similar income levels.

Hirsch (1975) used three different models to explain trade among industrialized and developing countries. Figure 24 shows the expected shares of different types of goods of the total exports of both. According to the author, the comparative advantage of industrialized countries lie on capital-intensive mature and Schumpeter goods and of developing nations on Ricardo and labor-intensive goods. Therefore, countries would mainly export those goods in which they have a comparative advantage. As a result, developed countries would concentrate in the export of capital intensive and Schumpeter products and developing countries in Ricardo and labor intensive goods.

Empirical results on the influence of the dynamic product life cycle on trade seem to be mixed. Hirsch (1975) develops some hypotheses to explain trade flows between developed and more developed countries. Using a 22 country sample of both kinds he finds empirical support for the product life cycle model. His work is presented in the next section. Gagnon/Rose (1995) use multilateral trade data disaggregated at the four-digit STIC level to test the dynamic product life cycle theory. The authors conclude that at this level of disaggregation "there is little evidence of dynamic patterns of reasonably frequency". Their findings support a more sluggish behaviour (in terms of time) of trade balances in most type of goods as foreseen by the Heckscher-Ohlin Model, while they accept that important (not majoritarian) sectors of the economy might be shaped by the product life cycle dynamics.

---

92 According to Hirsch, the technology transfer cost is positively correlated to the share of skilled labor to the production function.

Figure 24 Expected Export per Type of Product and Country

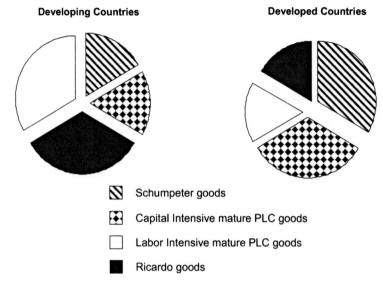

Developing Countries   Developed Countries

⧄ Schumpeter goods

⊞ Capital Intensive mature PLC goods

☐ Labor Intensive mature PLC goods

■ Ricardo goods

Based on: Hirsch (1975)

4.1.2.4 Relevance and Conclusions

Empirical results on the influence of the dynamic product life cycle on trade (Hirsch 1975) are mixed. Gagnon/Rose (1995) use multilateral trade data disaggregated at the four-digit STIC level to test the dynamic product life cycle theory. The authors conclude that at this level of disaggregation "there is little evidence of dynamic patterns of reasonably frequency". Their findings support a more sluggish behaviour (in terms of time) of trade balances in most type of goods as foreseen by the Heckscher-Ohlin Model, while they accept that important (not majoritarian) sectors of the economy might be shaped by the product life cycle dynamics.

Hirsch's empirical findings reflect a complementary approach between classic trade and the Schumpeterian (1975) innovation approach. The rather pragmatic methodology splits up the export palette into different classical theories to explain trade. They therefore serve as a departure point to analyze trade patterns in Mexico.

Summarizing, Mexico's expected trade should be influenced by geography as suggested by Krugman (1991) and Frankel/Romer (1999). The country, labor abundant, should be a net exporter of labor intensive goods, reflecting interindustry trade. Moreover, the export of Ricardo goods should prevail. The export of Schumpeter and capital-intensive goods should be less predominant. In the next sections, first the nominal data is presented which is subsequently revised and adjusted to Mexico's peculiarities to deepen and enhance the analysis.

4.2 Empirics of Mexican Exports

4.2.1 An Introduction to Nominal Data

Both nominal exports and imports show significant increases in the period. However, imports reacted more dynamically to the liberalization than exports did. Figure 25 shows their explosive growth in the years previous to the crisis. The data also shows a large and growing trade deficit.

Prior to liberalization, Mexican exports were concentrated. Traditionally, oil has been the most important export product by far. While export diversification took place during the reform period, exports were still strongly vulnerable to two variables: the exchange rate and economic growth of USA (World Bank 2004: 3).

Figure 25 Imports and Exports

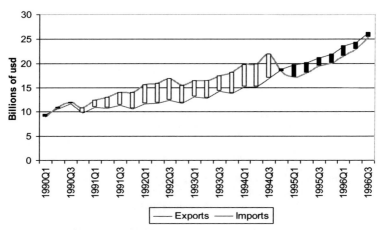

Data source: INEGI online (2008)

An expected outcome of an expedite trade liberalization following an import-substitution policy in a developing country is a sudden increase in imports. In Mexico, imports of consumer and capital goods increased significantly in the nineties in relative terms. The behavior of imports follows the arguments suggested by Dornbusch/Werner (1994) and Pacheco-López/Thirwall (2006).[93] Their finding suggests that imports largely exceeded the income growth.

---

93 The latter calculated income elasticity demand for imports to be 4.1 between 1982-1995.

Figure 26 plots different types of imports and exports based on the type of goods. The most straightforward development is the over-proportional growth of intermediate goods[94], intended both for domestic production and exports. While data disaggregation does not distinguish if their final destination is for re-export or for the domestic market, their value has been moving along and quite close to that of the total exports.

The alarming level of intermediate goods imports reveals the reliance of the Mexican producing plant on pre-imported inputs. Furthermore, the country's exports are linked to an almost parallel rise in imports[95]. The large increase of this type of imports is associated to a governmental program created in the import-substitution phase to promote employment, the Maquila program, discussed in section 4.2.3.

Figure 26 Exports and Imports Types

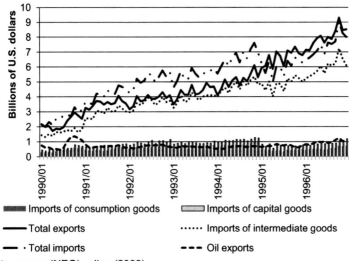

Imports of consumption goods — Imports of capital goods
— Total exports — Imports of intermediate goods
— · Total imports — — — Oil exports

Data source: INEGI online (2008)

The Mexican exports palette (displayed in Figure 27) has been traditionally led by the export of raw oil of the state-owned monopoly (Petróleos Mexicanos). Oil has not only been the most important export but also a large source of governmental income[96]. Their significance in overall terms has yet decreased noticeably.[97]

---

94 Intermediate goods are defined as those used in the production of a manufactured good or service.
95 Section 3.3.2 elaborates on the import contents of exports in macroeconomic terms.
96 The combination of this fact, the oil bonanza and fiscal indiscipline at the end of the seventies led Mexico to an "acute form of the dutch disease" which ended up in the Debt Crisis of 1982 (Cronin 2003).
97 Export diversification has been a public goal followed since the late eighties. Therefore, this "fact" has been publicly widespread by policy makers to show tangible benefits of the ongoing trade liberalization: exports diversification and less vulnerability on oil price. Oil as a percentage of total

Outstanding growth rates have been observed in the car, electronic and telecommunication industries (see also Figure 27). Roughly sixty percents of all exports in 1994 were oil or originated in these high-tech branches. The concentration of exports in a few branches indicates the vulnerability of the economy to fluctuations in these sectors.

Figure 27 Exports Palette

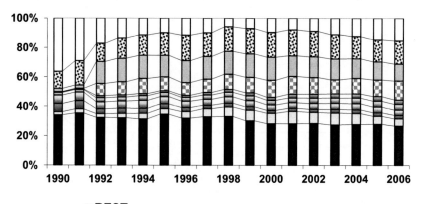

- ■ REST
- ▫ 75 - Office & data-processing machines
- ▣ 05 Fruits and Vegetables
- ▣ 71 - Power-generating machinery
- ▣ 74 - General industrial machinery
- ▣ 87 - Professional & scientific instruments
- ▣ 76 - Telecommunications & sound equipment
- ▫ 77 - Electrical machinery
- ▣ 78 - Road vehicles
- ▫ 33 - Petroleum and derivates

Data source: ECLAC/Badecel online (2007) using the SITC 2-Digit Classification and author's own calculations.

However, the dissection of nominal export data does not reveal any signs of a significant decline of exports. The leading industries (accounting for over 55% of total exports), as well most of them show a clear upwards trend (Figure 28)[98]. Triggering impulses of the real economy to the Mexican crisis can be rejected.

---

exports has decreased significantly. However, in this figure the large import content of both exports and oil products has been omitted.

98 In an attempt to partially dissipate the maquila effect, a trade balance in each of the groups was calculated. Interestingly, there is only group (776) that is amongst the most important exporters (12th place) and at the same time shows the most important inter-chapter trade deficit. This group comprises t.v. tubes. electrocircuits, diods and other electronic components .

Figure 28 Exports of Largest Groups

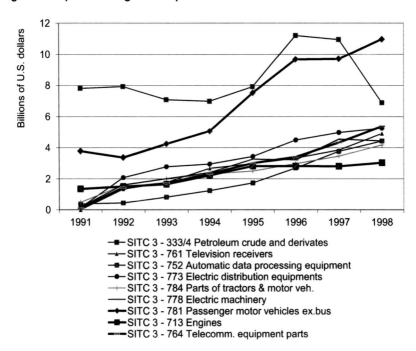

—■— SITC 3 - 333/4 Petroleum crude and derivates
—▲— SITC 3 - 761 Television receivers
—■— SITC 3 - 752 Automatic data processing equipment
—◆— SITC 3 - 773 Electric distribution equipments
—+— SITC 3 - 784 Parts of tractors & motor veh.
——— SITC 3 - 778 Electric machinery
—◆— SITC 3 - 781 Passenger motor vehicles ex.bus
—■— SITC 3 - 713 Engines
—— SITC 3 - 764 Telecomm. equipment parts

Data source: U.N. Economic Commission on Latin America and the Caribbean (ECLAC) / Foreign Trade Data Bank for Latin America and the Caribbean (Badecel) online (2006)

Mexican exports are risk prone also in geographical terms. As suggested by Krugman's (1991) geography and trade theory, Mexican exports are strongly shaped by geography. The United States has been historically its most important partner. The majority of overall exports and of the leading industries head to the United States with roughly eighty percent heading this market (Figure 29). This geographic situation represents a large chance, but also a challenge, since the Mexican real economy depends largely on that of its neighbour. Market diversification has not materialized despite numerous attempts.

Diverse trade agreements signed after NAFTA has allowed Mexico to have the most comprehensive network of preferential trade treaties in the world. This included 31 countries with a market of 850 million consumers. However, according to Bracho (2003) "those trade agreements have been more successful in promoting imports than exports". Part of the story is the perennial overvaluation of the peso as it is discussed in this thesis.

Figure 29 Mexican Exports Heading the U.S. (Total & Leading Industries)[99]

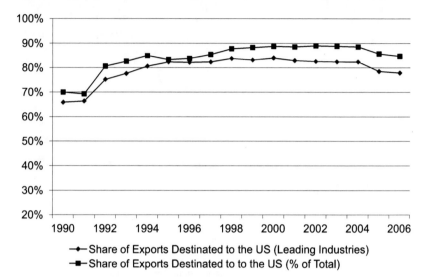

→ Share of Exports Destinated to the US (Leading Industries)
■ Share of Exports Destinated to to the US (% of Total)

Data source: ECLAC/Badecel online (2007)

To summarize, the nominal data of the pre-crisis period reflects significant imbalances in the external sector and a vulnerable exporting segment mainly concentrated in a few branches and a single market. Nevertheless, there were not negative impulses to the 1995 crisis from the real side of the economy that either justified or detonated the shock.

---

99 The leading industries include the following categories (SITC Rev. 2)
   33 - Petroleum, petroleum products and related materials
   71 - Power-generating machinery and equipment
   74 -General industrial machinery and equipment, and machine parts.
   75 - Office machines and automatic data-processing machines.
   76 - Telecommunications and sound-recording and reproducing apparatus and equipment
   77 - Electrical machinery, apparatus and appliances, and electrical parts thereof.
   78 - Road vehicles (including air-cushion vehicles)

4.2.2 Factor Intensity of Exports

Despite the trend towards exports' growth and relative diversification, in the period of 1990-1994 only four chapters, namely oil, road vehicles, electrical machinery and telecommunications equipment accounted for over half of all exports. These preliminary results seem to indicate that Mexico's trade pattern was not in line with the expected export pattern defined in 4.1. Recall that theory suggests that the country, labor abundant, should be a net exporter of labor intensive and natural resources goods

Therefore, data was arranged to reclassify exports based on their factor intensity concept derived from the Product Life Cycle Thesis. This endeavour was based on a methodology developed by Schrader/Laaser/Sichelschmidt (2006): The main goal was to shed light on this apparently paradox export structure.

Conventional trade theory states that developing countries have a comparative advantage and should tend to specialize in the production of "Ricardo and Heckscher-Ohlin" products, intensive in natural resources and labor, respectively. The production of Schumpeterian goods, intensive in research and development (R & D) and skilled-labor intensive should constitute the main export portion of developed countries.

The authors distinguish between mobile and immobile Schumpeterian goods, from which the distinguishing characteristic is if R&D can be geographically separated from production. The authors define mobile Schumpeterian products if R&D takes place in a different location than production and immobile Schumpeterian goods those were both activities, based on their level of specialization and complementarities, occur in a same region. Table 10 displays the specific categorization of export chapters based on an international U.N. product classification (STIC).

Table 10 Classification of Export Goods.

Industries	SITC Rev. 2 Classification
Natural Ressources Intensive Industries	0, 2 without 26, 3 without 35, 4, 56 and 57
Labor Intensive Industries	26, 6 without 62, 7, 68, 8 without 87
Capital Intensive Industries	1, 35, 53, 55, 62, 67, 68, 793
Production of Mobile Schumpeter Industries	51, 52, 58,59, 75, 76,77
Production of Immobile Schumpeter Industries	54,71,72,73,74,78,791, 792, 87

Source: Schrader/Laaser/Sichelschmidt (2006) referencing Schrader (1999), Klodt (1987) and Heitger et al. (1992) and their own compilation.

Mexican exports using this methodology are in line with the expected results (Figure 30). A large, but decreasing share of exports is natural-resource-based. As discussed in the last section, oil predominates. The export share of goods in labor- intensive sectors seems to be relative low. Nevertheless, significant and growing levels of mobile Schumpeterian exports (about one third of the total), include most of the electronic and chemical branches. These reflect Mexico's comparative advantage on labor. The country has specialized in the manufacture of high-tech products, such as those electronic-related. However, R & D takes place in foreign countries and the value added is in most cases the result of assembly and packaging.

In 1994, labor-intensive export products rounded only up to a sixth of all exports. In total, over sixty percent of Mexico's exports reflected the abundance of cheap labor and about twenty percent Mexico's oil. Most of the remaining fraction is outweighed by the transport vehicle and related sectors (immobile Schumpeterian). These results fit the expected trade pattern suggested by theory, since roughly eighty percent all exports are either Ricardo goods or products that reflect Mexico's comparative advantage, its labor force.

Figure 30 Factor Intensity of Mexican Exports

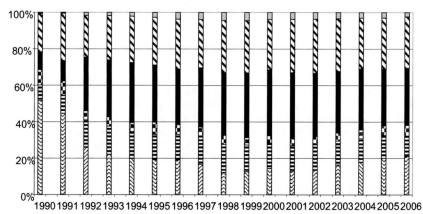

☑ Natural resources intensive industries ▫ Labor intensive industries
▫ Capital intensive industries ■ Products of mobile Schumpeterian indust.
◪ Products of immobile Schumpeterian ind. ▫ Not classified

Data source: ECLAC/Badecel 2007 and author's classification based on Schrader/ Laaser/Sichelschmidt (2006).

To capture the impact of imports on exports of the classifications based on the factor intensity criteria, Figure 31 was generated. The data reveals that only for Ricardo goods (natural resources-related industries) a surplus was reached. In all other groups, including paradoxically labor intensive industries a deficit contributed to the large deficits previous to the crisis.

Interestingly, some sectors responded rashly to the massive devaluation after the crisis. The production of the Schumpeterian goods (mobile and immobile) displayed an immediate deficit reversal in the years following the devaluation. These sectors led the rash recovery of the economy after the crisis.

Although a large fraction of exports have imports embedded, it seems that there are exporting segments that do react to changes in the exchange rate. This seems to contradict the perception that Mexican exports, given their import bias, might not be real exchange elastic. Therefore, a LS regression is run in 4.3 to evaluate the relationship of exports to the real exchange. The line of reasoning of this effort was that a relative exchange rate inelastic trade structure could be behind the promotion and tolerance of the currency appreciation observed prior to the crisis. However, before this argument is tested, an introduction to the "Maquila Context" and some of its implications follow.

Figure 31 Trade Balance in Industries with Differing Factor Intensity

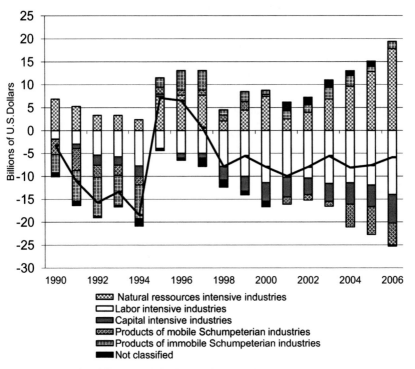

Data source: ECLAC/Badecel 2007 / author's own calculations

4.2.3 Exports and the "Maquila Context"

4.2.3.1 Introduction and the Bazaar Effect

Sinn (2007) coined the term "Bazaar economy" and defined it as the relocation of labor intensive activities within the vertical production chain into foreign countries[100]. The author associates outsourcing and off-shoring to this phenomenon. His thesis of what he calls the "pathological export boom" can be summarized as follows: the interaction of German high wage policy and a welfare state and international low-wage-trend damages labor intensive domestic sectors. The effect is that production factors are excessively directed into capital intensive export sectors and real net output value is inflated. The nominal export data, which shows Germany as the Nr. 1 in goods export, has led according to the author to a recognition and policy problem.

In this sense, Mexican exports have experienced the opposite mechanism with a similar effect. Positive foreign investment trend dating back to the early liberalization period led too, as Sinn (2007) suggests, to an identification and lack of action problem.

The export oriented value added in the Bazaar economies causes a flow of goods that is observed in an over proportional increase of imports and exports. In the case of Mexico the data shows that exports are significantly inflated due to this fact.

Sinn (2007) reports that the reduction in the vertical integration in Germany has been led by the automobile and electronics industries. A condition to profit from the gains of trade is that the exported goods relative to imported goods become more expensive. In other words, the terms of trade must improve. If the terms of trade worsen a country becomes for its exports less imports. This effect is a trade related loss. Sinn (2007) affirms that the profits of globalization are not evident if the plain export statistics are analyzed. Much more relevant are the factors markets, since they support the structural change caused by the international labor division. Some of these aspects encouraged the analysis of the rest of the chapter.

The Mexican export data includes the total value of exports generated within an official assembly program. The scope and effects of this government program, Maquila, will be therefore scrutinized in the next section.

4.2.3.2 The Maquila Program

Up to this point, traditional export data has been used. However, the assessment of the exporting sector requires further reconsideration. The figures portrayed in the last sections do not reflect (with the exception of Figure 31) imports embedded in exports. The inclusion of imports contents of exports, which enlarges the export data, is a standard statistic procedure all over the world. Moreover, the trend of developing countries towards a high share of pre-imported inputs in export is nothing out of the

---

100 The author presents in a non technical book, a critical analysis of the real sector in Germany.

ordinary. However, Mexico, given its "privileged" geographical situation, has developed a distorted export structure based on a governmental program that encouraged this development.

Maquila[101] is an institutional "export" program introduced in the sixties by the Mexican government to foster employment. In the pre-crisis period this endeavor was relevant since there was no free trade within the NAFTA region[102]. The program consisted of the temporary introduction of duty and tariff free imported inputs to perform marginal activities (such as assembly) to then return them as exports to the country of origin, in most cases the U.S. Legally, the domestic content was limited for fiscal reasons. Therefore, "Maquila exports" mainly regard the assembly of pre-imported inputs, which constituted already in 1994 over 80% of the total "export value" (Figure 32).

Figure 32 Composition of "Maquila Exports"

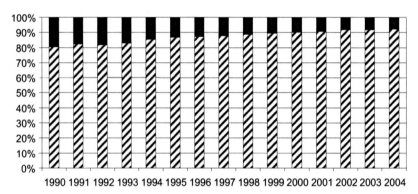

☑ Imported Inputs ■ Aggregate Value

Data source: INEGI / author's own calculations.
Note: Aggregate value includes the labor costs.

Palma (2006) affirms: "It is difficult to imagine any other activity that has such weak direct production linkages (forward and backward) with the rest of the economy".

---

101 However, a few additional facts regarding the Maquila Program would enable to draw significant policy implications. Export statistics are divided into definitive, maquila and temporary. Maquiladora refers to a Mexican company operating under a special customs regime, which enables it to temporarily import into Mexico free of duty machinery, machinery, equipment, materials, parts and components and other items needed for the assembly or manufacture of finished goods for subsequent export (www.maquilaportal.com). Nevertheless, while the Maquila program was the first to be implemented (1966) and has the greatest impact on the statistics, there are similar programs created before the crisis that promote temporary imports for subsequent exports such as PITEX (Programa de Importación Temporal para la Exportación). PITEX exports present a statistical challenge since they should be handled as maquila exports, are however included in the non-maquila export data. Exact PITEX data prior to 1995 is not available. The main inference from this fact is that the while Maquila is not the only program, the existence of PITEX magnifies the impact of the conclusions regarding Mexican exports drawn in these sections.

102 After becoming effective in 1994, in 2010 practically free trade is foreseen within all three North American countries: Canada, U.S. and Mexico.

Dussel (2003) describes how the then existing tax framework generated incentives to keep domestic content low. Maquila production was, conditioned by the domestic tax rules until 2003 to a specific maximum amount of local contents. Maquila production is additionally not subject to tariffs and value added tax. Further, their corporate tax, according to the author is insignificant in real terms (compared with up to 35% that local firms are required to disburse). Schatan (2002) calculated for 2000 an effective taxing rate for maquiladoras of -7.2 %. Consequently, both traditional business start ups and the integration of domestic contents were discouraged by policy. These aspects are fundamental to support Dussel's (2004) assessment of the "relatively primitive processes of the majority of Mexican exports"

De la Garza (2005) describes the Maquila sector as being dominated by large plants, subsidiaries of U.S. based multinational firms, which import most of its inputs and export most of its output. The author affirms that the low domestic content was not only fiscally motivated. In his view, two additional factors are behind this disappointing trend. First, corporate policies of the holdings controlling maquiladoras determine the source of the inputs. Finally, the deficiencies of domestic producers, such as lack of a continuous just-in-time; quality and cost benefits.

Figure 33 Mexican Exports by Type: Maquila & Non-maquila

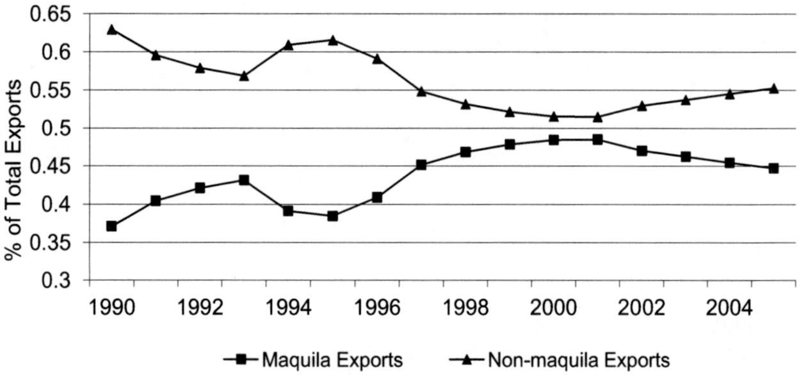

Data source: INEGI online (2007)

4.2.3.3 Revision of Exports in the Maquila Context

The "Maquila context" gains importance once its impact on overall exports is examined (Figure 33). Up to 1994, subsequent trend upwards, of the total reported exports approximately 40% corresponded to "Maquila exports". This figure implies that previous to the crisis roughly one third of the total exports were originally pre-imported inputs within this program. The presumed export boom is relative when the impact of Maquila imports is considered, as seen in Figure 34. The approximation[103] of domestic content reveals the low domestic value. Therefore, the exporting sector must be reconsidered within the "Maquila context", which significantly inflates the export data in diverse sectors.

There are multiple implications to consideration of the "Maquila context". First of all, once reassessed, the importance of Ricardo and Hecksher-Ohlin goods is more evident than if only the nominal data is taken into account.

Figure 34 Total Exports and Maquila-Associated Imports

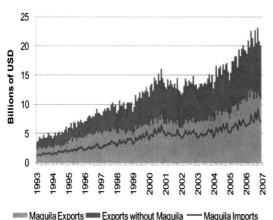

░░░ Maquila Exports ▬▬ Exports without Maquila ▬▬ Maquila Imports

Data source: INEGI online (2007) / author's own calculations

Figure 35 reveals that Ricardo exports in 1994, mainly oil, still constituted 30% of all exports, double as much as indicated by the nominal data[104]. The reevaluation of Heckscher-Ohlin and Schumpeter goods posed a greater statistical challenge. SITC Rev. 2 Maquila-disaggregated data is not available. The only source of this type of data, relevant to disentangle sectorial Maquila effects, is available under a different classification[105].

A further implication is that "Maquila exports" have caused distortions in the external sector. Since their domestic value added is minor, "Maquila exports" tend to be exchange rate insensitive. The interaction of this argument, defined in this thesis as the Maquila effect, and exchange rate overvaluation in a self-reinforcing framework is evaluated along with exchange rate elasticity in section 4.3.

---

103 Recall that due to statistical limitations this is only an approximation of the factual import content. Other import contents, which are not officially labeled as maquila imports, cannot be discerned from the information. Therefore, this approximation can be seen as the minimum. However, given the benefits of this tax regime, probably not far from its real value.

104 Only with Ricardo goods it can be safely assumed that exports are Maquila- and similar-free.

105 Classification of the Sistema Nacional de Cuentas by the Statistics Ministry (INEGI).

Figure 35 Ricardo* Exports

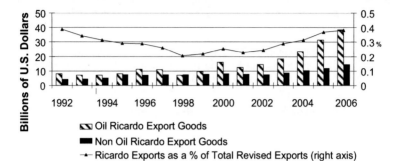

Data source: INEGI/ author's own calculations
*Associated to natural resources.

Trade information received from the Ministry of Trade upon request revealed exports based on a different classification: permanent, Maquila or temporary (Figure 36). This supplementary information backs up the thesis that the main portion structure of Mexican exports is insensitive to real exchange movements.

Figure 36 Exports by Type

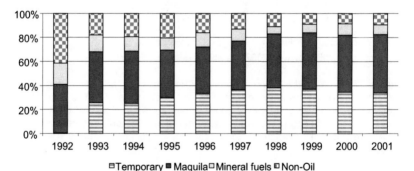

Data source (on inquiry): Secretaria de Economia (2007)/author's own calculations

Figure 36 shows how, as early as 1993, over eighty percent of exports can be classified as temporary-[106], Maquila- or mineral fuel-exports (oil), which are not affected by

---

106 Temporary exports are defined by INEGI as goods that leave the domestic territory to remain in a foreign country for a limited period of time with a transformation and/ or repair purpose. These goods would thereafter return to Mexico.

changes in the behaviour of the real exchange rate.[107] Since roughly 80% of Maquila value is pre-imported, the impact of currency overvaluation only, if at all has long-term facility reallocation effects. The latter due to a lost in competitiveness of the cheap labor argument compared to other regions of the world. Other effects through this channel are discarded.

In 1994 four classifications made up 58% of all final (definitive) exports: mineral fuels, automobile/motor industries and fruits and vegetables. Figure 37 Export Structure displays a revised composition of exports which reflects a contrasting active industrial policy behind the automotive and the Maquila sectors. The former was initiated during the import substitution period to cover domestic demand and had domestic content requirements that were only reduced gradually[108]. The latter, dominated by electronic products[109] is linked to a negligible domestic content (assembly) which inflates the data and was introduced along Mexico's entry to the GATT. Despite the higher domestic contents in automobile sector exports, Arndt/Huemer (2002) found out that there is no correlation between a dollar appreciation and the vehicles and motor sector.

Figure 37 Export Structure

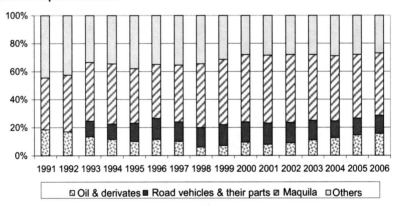

Data source: INEGI (2007) & ECLAC/Badecel (2007), own calculations.

---

107 A more detailed analysis regarding the real domestic value added of exports across industries is given the available statistical data impossible. Oil prices are quoted in U.S. dollars, so any kind of statistical correlation should be mere coincidence.

108 In 1962 the minimum local content was set at 60% and decreased to 36% in 1989 (Ramos 2008) The domestic market for automobiles had one of the longest deregulation periods within NAFTA.

109 Schott (2004) affirms that empirical tests find only "scant evidence in favor of endowment-driven trade at the industry level". The author finds a positive correlation between goods export prices and capital intensity of production. The relevant implication of his work, based on US trade data from 1972-1994, is that factor endowment is relevant in determining trade within (and not across industries) product categories. According to this evidence, "capital- and skill- abundant countries use their endowment advantage to produce vertically superior varieties; i.e. varieties that are relatively capital or skill intensive thereby commanding a relatively higher price". This appears as an adequate explanation of the development of the electronic export industry in Mexico.

4.2.3.4 Terms of Trade

This section briefly displays the long-term development of Mexico's terms of trade. The terms of trade are defined as the relative prices of a country's exports in terms of imports.[110]

The terms of trade of oil exporting countries tend to be more volatile due to statistically significant exogenous price changes. Figure 38 exhibits the behavior of this ratio for Mexican exports and imports. The oil shocks of the early eighties had a severe impact on this indicator. In the nineties and thereafter, the volatility has been lessened. Around the crisis period (1994) there are no signs of significant changes which could indicate impulses from the real side to the crisis, particularly considering the scope of the shock. After a larger rise in 1999, the terms of trade have slightly increased in a continuous matter.

Figure 38 Terms of Trade

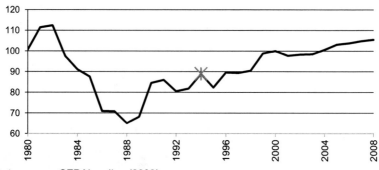

Data source: CEPAL online (2009)

4.2.3.5 Final Remarks on Mexican Exports before the Crisis

The export structure can be described as vulnerable and non-diversified. Most exports reveal Mexico's resource endowment, either natural sources or labor. The market is practically geographically limited to the U.S: Oil, Maquila exports, and to lesser extent road vehicles, dominate the picture. Vulnerability on the above mentioned fronts characterizes the main exporting sectors.

In Dussel's (2001) view, the integration of the electronics, car and their parts sectors was a "relevant success of NAFTA". In his opinion, "integration globally and in the case of NAFTA has resulted in an important growth of intrafirm and intrasectoral trade". The author reports a new North American industrial organization, where Mex-

---

110 An increase in the ratio reveals that a country requires fewer exports to pay for its imports.

ico performs the lowest segment of the value-added chain: assembly, revealing Ricardo's comparative advantage and Krugman's geography and trade[111].

Mexican exports, in the upsurge of trade liberalization exhibit significant growth rates. However, in 1994 external imbalances, measured in terms of a large current account deficit became unsustainable. Behind this deficit was the surge of the import of intermediate inputs, crucial element of the Maquila import-export program.

The "inflationary effects of previously imported inputs" is a phenomenon observed worldwide. However, Mexico's Maquila program reaches atypical levels. The results deflate, only using Maquila data, the official export numbers up to a third in the precrisis period (Figure 34). It seems that the "Maquila context" in the case of Mexico is crucial to analyze exports due to three main factors. First of all, based on its significance as percentage of the total exports (roughly 40% of the total), second of all considering its relative low level of domestic contents (under 20%) and finally, the fact that Maquila export take place within an institutionalized program which explicitly limited national contents.

The classification of exports also suggests a relevant inference, which is studied in section 4.3. As of 1994, at least 55 % of all nominal exports (40% Maquila plus 15% oil) could be considered as not directly affected by fluctuations in the nominal exchange rate. This convenient situation led to the support of an overvalued currency, which was an important pre-condition of the crisis.

The latter conclusion seems straightforward considering the revised trade structure presented in the last sections. However, the sudden reversal of trade deficit classified by factor intensity after the sharp devaluations might be an indication of some exchange rate elasticity. In this sense, in the next section the responsiveness of an export/import index vs. changes in the real exchange rate and the U.S. business cycle is tested.

4.3 Trade Structure, Exchange Rate Appreciation and Exports Performance: Regression Analysis

4.3.1 Introduction and Rationality

The Mexican trade structure moved from being predominantly oil-based up to the late eighties, to be assembly-oriented after the structural reforms in the early nineties. This development, promoted by public policy[112], seems to be crucial to the accrual and tolerance of the real exchange rate appreciation that took place before the crisis.

---

111 Krugman/Obstfeld (2000:138) define "pseudo-intraindustry" trade as the flows between low- and high-wage countries that are classified within the same industry but are rather driven by comparative advantage. The authors affirm that "such "pseudo-intraindustry" trade is particularly common in the trade between the United States and Mexico".

112 Official Maquila and PITEX export "promotion" programs that focused on the assembly of pre-imported inputs.

Exports are influenced by the real exchange rate, so conventional wisdom. In this sense, real exchange rate appreciations negatively affect exports' performance and induce imports. Therefore, a country expecting to use exports as the motor of the economy should avoid appreciation of the currency to keep exports competitive in the world market.

Alternatively, using an exchange rate peg serves to control inflation since the peg functions as the nominal anchor of the economy. However, since inflation differentials to the basis country persist, the peg does not prevent real exchange rate appreciation and a resulting balance of payment problem (Mishkin 2007: 346).

The peg-led stabilization in Mexico and the thereof resulting appreciation in 1994 did end up in a current account problem, also discussed in the macroeconomic sections. Exports only covered roughly four-quarters of imports; excluding oil exports their level of coverage was low as fifty percent (Figure 39).

Figure 39 Exports/Imports Index

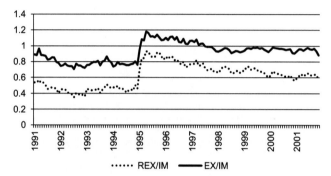

Data source INEGI online (2008) and author's own calculations
*REX includes only non-oil exports, all variables without price adjustments in U.S. dollars.

The Mexican trade structure, as discussed in previous sections, presents some structural weaknesses. Exports might be exchange rate inelastic to some extent since for large fractions they either have high shares of foreign contents or the prices are determined in the world market in foreign currency. Nevertheless, the rash export growth after the exchange rate overshooting in 1995 (Figure 31 and Figure 39) reveal some kind of responsiveness. Imports on the other side, appear to react more intensively than exports to movements in the real exchange rate.

In order to determine the factors which explain the pattern followed by an export/import index, regression analysis was applied. The rationality behind was to evaluate if exports tend to react differently to currency appreciation than expected in theory. In this sense, less exchange rate elastic exports vs. imports create perverse incentive towards appreciation and current account deficits. Such trade related mechanisms increase the country's vulnerability and make it more crisis- prone.

4.3.2 Methodology and Results

In this section, simple[113] regression analysis (LS) was used to determine the relationship between export performance measured as an export/import index and variables with explanatory power, such as the real exchange rate behaviour and the U.S. business cycle between 1991 and 1996.

The goal of this study was to explore the argument that exports before the crisis were relative insensitive to the real exchange rate. Given the particularities of Mexican trade structure, adjustments[114] of the gross data were crucial to analyse its development. To deal with these Mexican specifics, oil exports were excluded since they are currency inelastic, the former priced in U.S. dollars. The effects of the "maquila context" are cancelled since both Maquila exports and imports were included in the index. The here performed adjustments lead to non-traditional conclusions on non-oil and-Maquila exports, which might be influenced by domestic factors.

The dependent variable, an export/import index (REXIM) was constructed using the official INEGI data[115] deducting oil exports from the dividend (exports). Official data on real U.S. GDP (LNUSGDP= Log (real GDP)) was used to determine the relationship between Mexican trade and the business cycle. Natural logs for both figures were used to deal with heteroscedasticity. The log of the real exchange rate data was used to convert the regressions results to an elasticity coefficient. By using the log of the real exchange rate (LOGREEXCLO), the calculated coefficients reflect the elasticity of exports and imports. To deal with serial correlation, a variable to calculate the first order correlation is included. The results are displayed in Table 11.

Table 11 Regression Results

Variable	Coefficient	Std. Error	Probability
REXIMLN (-1) *Previous observation*	0.722851	0.060329	0.00000
LNUSGDP Natural log of U.S. GDP	0.492589	0.244166	0.0478
LOG(REEXCLO) Natural log of the real exchange rate	-0.42484	0.100572	0.0001
Test Parameters:	0.94178		
R-squared of the regression			
S.E. of regression	0.076326		
Durbin-Watson stat.	2.433487		

---

113 Please note the simplicity of this econometric effort.

114 Other possibilities were analyzed and discarded such as using original data and oil price or to consider Chinese imports to the U.S as an explaining variable (using nominal data).

115 In U.S. dollars, therefore, no inflation adjustment was done.

The regression analysis suggests that U.S. business cycle is an important explanatory variable of the elasticity of Mexican exports and imports[116]. The U.S. economic performance, following the intuition and the facts on this market concentration, also shows the right sign. A one percent change in the U.S. GDP implies that exports grow 0.49% faster than imports. A real appreciation of 1% indicates that exports grow 0.42% slower than imports. These results, excluding currency inelastic oil exports, apply to slightly less than half of total exports. Even considering this adjustment, the reaction of exports to currency appreciation changes seems moderate. The coefficients are statistically significant at the 5 percent level.

The equation seems to fit well the data (Figure 40). The plot of the residuals and the Durbin-Watson statistic indicate the absence of a strong serial correlation in the residuals (see Appendix 2 for further results) and the robustness of this regression.

Figure 40 Regression Results

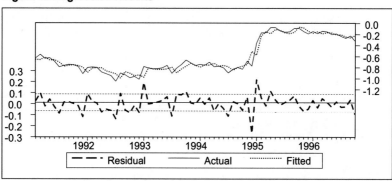

The bottom-line of this simple but robust effort is that the main explanatory factor behind the Mexican export growth is the U.S. economy and that exports in general react much slower to appreciation than imports. The here studied relationship supports the thesis that the interaction of the structural weaknesses of the Mexican trade structure and the real exchange appreciation contributed to the accumulation of imbalances in the external sector, which subsequently led into the 1995 crisis. Further, it indirectly questions the viability of an export-led strategy in a country with high marginal import propensity[117].

---

116 Other variables such as the increase of Chinese imports to the U.S. were statistically discarded.
117 See section 3.3.2 for a compact discussion on the marginal propensity to import or Pacheco-Lopez (2005) for a more detailed evaluation. Also see Razmi/Blecker (2004) for a study on possible limitations to this strategy.

4.4   Final Considerations on the Trade Structure and its Implications on the Mexican Crisis

The evaluation of the trade structure performed in section 4.2 seems to indicate that export concentration (roughly 2/3 of the conventional nominal data) in exchange rate insensitive sectors might have lessened the real effects of the significant and continuous peso appreciations on exports. However, the dynamism of exports after the exchange rate overshooting pointed towards mixed reactions.

The nominal export data does not reveal the structural weakness discussed in this chapter, associated to a low level of domestic aggregate value. However, it served as a basis for policy choice making. Its revision might suggest that the magnitude of the currency appreciation under a fixed regime was allowed at least partly, by the use and public diffusion of this type of data reporting. A presumed export boom occurred simultaneously to currency appreciation, a paradox considering traditional trade theory.

In the search of evidence to support the thesis that the Mexican trade tends to be exchange rate inelastic and that this pattern indirectly supported the real exchange rate appreciation, basic regression analysis was performed. Despite the fact that performed statistical analysis was rather rudimentary, it is safe to affirm that changes in the economic path of the U.S., specifically expressed by GDP, allow exports to move half as much in the same direction vs. imports. However, if a real appreciation occurs, imports react much faster than exports.

The U.S. economy and real currency appreciation are significant factors to explain Mexico's export/import behavior. In 1994, the real appreciation of the peso of roughly 20% implied that exports grew over 80% slower than imports. This trend might explain the large current account deficit observed. A vicious cycle of import-dependent exports, current account deficits, low growth and crisis vulnerability is associated to the Mexican flawed structure.

Pacheco-Lopez (2005) also links the lack of economic growth after trade liberalization to a rise in the long run elasticity of income demand, which has not been offset by an increase in exports. This increase is partially explained by the considerable reliance of the domestic producing system on foreign inputs. "Trade liberalization has exacerbated and reinforced this dependence, promoting and facilitating access to a wide variety of imported goods". Moreover, Dornbusch et al. (1995: 3) associated the exchange rate to the lack of growth: "Mexican neglect of a competitive real exchange rate is an important factor in the poorer performance." Dussel (2001) considers that an overvalued exchange rate "has become a constant of liberalization strategy as a result of controlling the inflation level". Overvaluation should be a faux pas according to elementary "liberalization manuals" as suggested by Edwards (1994).

Frankel/Romer (1999) found that trade had "only moderately statistically significant positive effects on income". Wacziarg/Welch (2008) after analyzing a set of 39 liberalizing countries found that liberalization has, on average, robust positive effects on growth, openness and investment rates within countries. Mexico's case is, whatsoever, an exception with a negative growth effect of liberalization

The appreciation in real terms, which seemed to serve the anti-inflationary goals without explicitly constraining "export growth", was decisive in the building of a current account deficit. The described trade structure built a self-reinforcing mechanism together with real appreciation, large capital inflows, exchange rate elastic imports and low growth. This cycle was a significant cornerstone of the development of a large current account deficit and paved the way to the 1995 crisis.

As Bracho (2003) sharply explained: Mexico "can and must be blamed for allowing time to pass without enhancing its export profile". The persistence tolerance of currency overvaluation and a lack of a sound instrumented trade policy have exacerbated the structural problems analyzed in this section. While many of the observed patterns emerge from the policies followed or omitted in the structural reform process, the elaboration of a more coherent trade and economic policy should be subject of further research.

III. Financial Elements of the Mexican Crisis: The Real Culprits

5 International Capital Markets in the Early Nineties

This chapter is divided into two main parts. The first deals with macro aspects of international flows. This section begins with an introduction on selected trends of the international capital markets both in developing and developed markets. The next segment specifically approaches both the materialization and the grounds behind surge of capital inflows to Mexico. While external conditions determined the availability and willingness to invest abroad, domestic factors were behind the boom of portfolio inflows up to 1994.

Subsequently, an evaluation of micro aspects of the stream of funds that poured into the country is presented. This assessment, conditioned by limited statistical data, sheds light on the disparity between the behaviour of domestic and foreign capital, explicitly that of institutional investors, to respond to market volatility. The main conclusion is that, contrarily to widespread convictions, domestic and not foreign capitals triggered the crisis in 1994. Institutional investors did not foresee the upcoming trend reversal and based their behaviour on traditional fundamentals.

This section is organized as follows: after an introduction to the international capital flow framework and the developments in Mexico, a compact literature review on capital flight and on the origin of the aforementioned thesis are presented. Then, the available data on the origins of capital portfolio inflows, for both public and private securities is displayed. The last section summarizes the findings and discusses some policy challenges.

5.1 Macro-aspects of International Capital Flows

5.1.1 Capital Inflows to Emerging Markets

Private flows, markedly portfolio investment, increased notably in the first half of the nineties. Capital inflows to Mexico followed the international pattern observed in most developing economies. Structural changes in the U.S. pension system positively affected the availability international portfolio funds[118]. Decreasing interest rates in 1993 in the U.S. and other industrialized nations eased the way for the funds to head emerging markets, such as Mexico. (Culpeper 1995: 25).

Table 12 displays the upsurge of capital flows to developing countries in the 1990-1996 period. The most substantial rise took place in 1993. This increase can mainly be attributed to portfolio inflows, which quadrupled in size within one year. FDI showed in the same year a more modest increase (56%). However, by February

---

118 Culpeper (1995) describes how the demographic development of the U.S. population, with the aging of the so called "baby boomers" caused large increase in the availability of pension funds. The number of mutual funds alone in the U.S market doubled between 1987 and 1993. The author also relates the dramatic increase in funds availability to changes in their preferences towards the professional management of their portfolio.

1994, portfolio investment showed a sharp decline following a rise in the short-term interest rates in the U.S.

Table 12 Aggregate Net Capital Inflows to Developing Countries

(in billions of U.S. dollars)

Type of flow	1990	1991	1992	1993	1994	1995	1996
Total private flows:	44.4	56.9	90.6	157.1	161.3	184.2	243.8
a) Portfolio flows	5.5	17.3	20.9	80.9	62.0	60.6	91.8
Bonds	2.3	10.1	9.9	35.9	29.3	28.5	46.1
Equity	3.2	7.2	11.0	45.0	32.7	32.1	45.7
b) Foreign Direct Investment	24.5	33.5	43.6	67.2	83.7	95.5	109.5
c) Commercial Banks	3.0	2.8	12.5	-0.3	11.0	26.5	34.2
Others	11.3	3.3	13.5	9.2	4.6	1.7	8.3
Aggregate Net Resources Flows	100.6	122.5	146.0	212.0	207.0	237.2	284.6
Private flows' share (% of total)	44.1	46.4	62.1	74.1	77.9	77.7	85.7

Data source: World Bank Debtor Reporting System, in: World Bank (1997).

Mexico and China were the top destinations for private foreign capital between 1990 and 1996 (Table 13). Nevertheless, the composition of the inflows started to differ in 1992. FDI to China presented yearly increases between 100 and 300%, (from $4.4 in 1991 to $35.8 billion in 1996). Unlikely, Mexico received relative stable levels of FDI averaging $4 billion yearly in 1991-1993. The sharp increase in total capital inflows in Mexico, which summed $11.2 billion U.S. dollars in 1993, was caused by a sudden and large increase of portfolio inflows (World Bank: 1997). One argument behind this development is summarized by the IMF (1994): "The returns available in the emerging markets were so high and so well publicized that many institutional investors could not afford to ignore these assets".

Table 13 Net Private Capital Inflows to Developing Countries (Top Destinations)

(in billions of U.S. dollars)

Type of flow	1990	1991	1992	1993	1994	1995	1996
Total private flows:	44.4	56.9	90.6	157.1	161.3	184.2	243.8
Top recipient countries							
China	8.1	7.5	21.3	39.6	44.4	44.3	52.0
Mexico	8.2	12.0	9.2	21.2	20.7	13.1	28.1
Brazil	0.5	3.6	9.8	16.1	12.2	19.1	14.7
Malaysia	1.8	4.2	6.0	11.3	8.9	11.9	16.0
Indonesia	3.2	3.4	4.6	1.1	7.7	11.6	17.9
Thailand	4.5	5.0	4.3	6.8	4.8	9.1	13.3
Argentina	-0.2	2.9	4.2	13.8	7.6	7.2	11.3
India	1.9	1.6	1.7	4.6	6.4	3.6	8.0
Russia	5.6	0.2	10.8	3.1	0.3	1.1	3.6
Turkey	1.7	1.1	4.5	7.6	1.6	2.0	4.7
Chile	2.1	1.2	1.6	2.2	4.3	4.2	4.6
Hungary	-0.3	1.0	1.2	4.7	2.8	7.8	2.5
Share (%) of top destinations	83.6	76.8	87.4	84.1	75.4	73.3	72.5

Data source: World Bank Debtor Reporting System, in: World Bank (1997).
Note: Country ranking is based on cumulative 1990-1995 private capital flows received.

5.1.2 Developments in the International Financial Markets in 1994

The sustainability of the upsurge of capital inflows to developing countries was already questioned before their reversal in the first quarter of 1994. As expressed by the IMF (1994):

"...the flows have been huge, but is difficult to know how much of it will be sustained once the recovery gains momentum in the industrial world and interest rates there return to normal levels".

In the first quarter of 1994, interest rates increased sharply in industrialized countries. Between February and March, the yields on ten-year government bonds increased between 50 and up to 167 basis points[119]. Table 14 displays the volatility in the international bond and equity markets of and the more moderate[120] movements in the exchange rate during an eight week period in developed countries (IMF 1994: 3 ff.).

Table 14 Developments in Financial Markets of Selected Industrial Countries

Country	Long-dated bond yields (b.p. change)	Equities (% change)	Exchange rate (% change vs. U.S.d)
United States	96	-8.6	–
Japan	51	-3.0	-4.7
Germany	59	-0.2	-3.3
France	94	-10.3	-2.7
Italy	78	2.9	-3.4
United Kingdom	130	-11.4	1.3
Canada	144	-5.4	3.9
Netherlands	76	-7.5	-3.1
Australia	167	-10.6	-1.7
Switzerland	63	-8.1	-2.2
Belgium	69	-3.8	-3.8
Sweden	147	-11.3	-0.2

Data source: IMF (1994)
Notes: Ten-year Benchmark government bonds, with the exception of Germany (9 years). Share indices used are: FT-SE 100 (U.K.), Dow Jones Industrials (U.S.), DAX (Germany), CAC 40 (France), Nikkei 225 (Japan), MIB General (Italy), Composite (Canada), AffärsvärldnGen (Sweden), SBC General (Switzerland), CBS TtlRtnGen (Netherlands) and ASX All Ordinaries (Australia).

---

119 The ranges are as follows: Japan, Germany, Belgium and Switzerland (50-70 basis points), Netherlands, France, Italy, and U.S. (70-100 basis points), UK, Canada, Sweden and Australia (130-167).
120 Smoothed through intervention in the exchange markets according to this IMF document.

For developing countries, the first quarter of 1994 implied the end of the boom in capital inflows and equity prices that peaked in 1993. Bonds were the preferred instruments, as bond placements in emerging markets were almost five times larger than equity placements. As the IMF (1994) affirms, the political turmoil in Mexico and decreases in interest rates marked the reversal in capital inflows to emerging markets:

> "The market ran into turbulence in the first four months of 1994, as the increase in the U.S. interest rates as well as the political uncertainty in Mexico, helped bring bond and equity flows down sharply from their peaks of the last quarter in 1993."

In the equity markets, inflows sharply decreased in March and in April, for the first time in two years, there was a net capital outflow. The trend was reversed in the summer but resumed again in the fall (IMF 1995: 55).

5.1.3 Capital Inflows to Mexico

5.1.3.1 General Trends

The signature of the Brady Plan marked the return of capital inflows to Mexico.[121] Through this project, Mexican officials negotiated determined with its creditors and reached an advantageous mechanism of external debt reduction[122]. Following the liberalization of the financial sector in 1989 and the closure of debt deal, large-scale voluntary capital inflows picked up on to reach record levels. This "modest" debt renegotiation triggered a transformation in the economic picture:

> "International investors saw the debt deal as a part of the package of reforms that they believed would work. Debt reduction went along with free markets and sound money; free markets and sound money mean prosperity; and so capital flows into the country that follows the right path" (Krugman 1996:142).

FDI increased significantly during the period. Nevertheless, portfolio investment flows grew at a more rapid pace and exceeded FDI since 1991. Particularly large were portfolio inflows in 1992-1993, which reached over seven percent of GDP in 1993 (see Table 13 and Table 15).

Mexico became the benchmark to measure the risk of new sovereign debt issues for those countries with sub-investment grade ratings in Latin America and other regions. The spread paid on Mexican sovereign bonds over T-bills decreased from about 800 in 1989 to roughly 200 basis points at the end of 1993 (IMF 1994: 19).

---

121 The public debt renegotiation, which started in 1982 as the Debt Crisis erupted, ended in 1990. This agreement with foreign commercial banks included large voluntary lending repaid before schedule through the reduction of interest payment and principals (Dornbusch & Werner 1994: 256).

122 See Vazquez (1996) for a description and a critical evaluation of the Brady plan.

Table 15 Mexico's Capital Account

(as percentage of GDP)

Year	Capital Account	Portfolio Investment	FDI
1988	-0,2	0,6	1,6
1989	0,9	0,2	1,4
1990	3,1	1,3	1,0
1991	7,9	4,1	1,5
1992	7,3	5,0	1,2
1993	8,0	7,1	1,1
1994	3,6	2,0	2,6

Data source: Banco de México (2007)

However, following the U.S. interest rate rises in the first quarter of 1994, the upward trend of the capital account was reversed. In 1994, the capital account reached $11.6 billion U.S. dollars, $21 billion less than in 1993.

Quarterly capital account data in Figure 41 provides a valuable insight into the different scenarios in the first half of the nineties. Although the volatility and partially excessive reactions to economic prospects and political instability in the stock market were patent, sudden capital reversals (and capital flight) during 1994 were largely originated by changes in the tenure of government securities. The capital account shows a reduction of the latter in the fourth quarter of 1994 of $5.2 billion, compared to negative foreign investment flows out of the stock market by $0.38 billion.

Figure 41 Mexico's Capital Account by Type of Flow

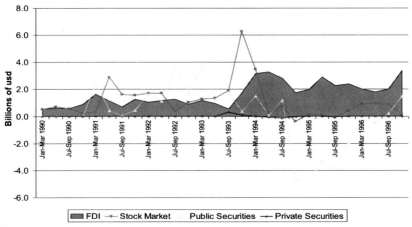

Data source: Banco de México online (2008)

The surplus of the capital account in the crisis year was composed of $16.2 billion foreign capital inflows ($8.2 of portfolio investment), $0.9 net foreign loans and capital flight by residents of $5.5 billion (Banco de México 1994: 35).

5.1.3.2 Factors Behind the Inflows

Capital inflows to Mexico can be explained taking two main strands into consideration. The first are the international "push" trends towards emerging markets, discussed in the previous sections. Others, which are the main focus of this section, are specifically related to Mexico. Fernandez-Arias (1996) suggests that this domestic related (pull) factors are the most important cause of the surge in capital inflows[123]. Probably the confluence of both types can explain the abnormal inflows in 1993 and 1994.

Dornbusch/Werner (1994: 258) attribute the large capital inflows to different factors such as:

- Improved prospects on the private sector
- Increase flows of capital toward emerging markets,
- Crowd-in effect due to more balanced public finances
- Boom in the stock market, both as an effect and cause of the capital flood. The stock market rose 125% in 1991, 25% in 1992 and almost 50% in 1993.

Gurría (1995) also considers a relative worsening of the terms of trade to be associated to the capital inflows.

A significant factor was the improved international opinion of the country up to early 1994, the year when the crisis erupted. Mexico's reform efforts were considered exemplary and were praised internationally[124]. In the spring of 1994 the IMF elicited "a strong and unqualified endorsement of Mexico's economic management" (DeLong 1997).

The upsurge in capital inflows was underpinned by the positive expectations not only of policy makers but also of investment bankers and rating agencies. Edwards (1997) suggest the "invention of a miracle" despite a clear divergence between economic policy and performance. In his view, "a tremendous faith that many analysts had in the reforms themselves" were behind the enthusiastic approach towards Mexico (1997:4).

---

123 The author found out by performing econometric analysis, that Mexico constituted an exception in the study of thirteen developing countries. For the remaining countries, push factors seem to explain the increase in capital inflows.

124 Delong/Eichengreen (2001) summarize:
"When Secretary Bentsen visited Mexico City in mid-February, he gave no public indication of concern, telling reporters that Mexico's economic policies had "become an example for all of Latin America". The IMF reported in the spring of 1994 that Mexico's economic fundamentals -- a balanced federal budget, a successful privatization campaign, and financial liberalization among them -- were strong enough to similarly elicit a strong endorsement of the country's economic management...both Treasury and IMF staff were optimistic about the sustainability of Mexican economic reform and economic growth" (Delong/Eichengreen 2001:9).
The international press coverage in 1994, according to Sachs et al. (1996) was "optimistic about Mexico's future and about its investment opportunities" and did not expect prior to the eruption of the crisis neither the sudden peso devaluations nor a debt default.

Edwards (1997) compiled twenty-one reports of major investment bankers from Nov. and Dec. 1994. The author concluded that the majority remained optimistic and did not expect devaluations. De Luna (2002) also highlights the deficient risk management of institutional foreign investors. He further explains that even in the month prior to the eruption investment bankers were pleading for a better ranking by the international rating agencies.

The evaluations of private rating agencies did support the positive economic outlook and further boosted capital inflows. Sovereign debt rating (Table 16) was initially assigned to Mexican foreign debt in the early nineties. Moody's upgraded Mexico's score shortly after its introduction. The ratings received prior to the crisis were the highest of the speculative grade. Salinas (2000) references positive reports of diverse[125] investment institutions in the weeks before the massive devaluation and abandonment of the peso peg[126]. Some of these reports suggested the possibility of giving Mexican bonds investment grade[127].

Table 16 Long-Term Sovereign Debt Rating

	Standard and Poor's	Moody's
Assign	BB+ / July 1992	Ba3/Dec. 1990
Downgrade	BB+/Feb. 1995	
Upgrade	BB+positive/ March 2000	Ba2/Feb. 1991 Ba1/Ago. 1999

Source: Brankovic, Azra, "Emerging Markets Debt Quarterly", Merrill Lynch, October 2000, in: Bustillo and Velloso (2000).

In retrospective it can be stated that the rating agencies did not foresee the risks of a crisis led by the accumulated currency appreciation in 1994. Further, it seems that investment bankers were eager to invest in Mexico and that rating agencies supported their bullish behavior.

Cline (1995) early identified the inherent risk of the lack of institutional arrangement for policy evaluation. Private credit-rating agencies (primarily Standard and Poor's and Moody's) might "become captives of client countries". Therefore, the author suggested the creation of an international bondholder institution that provides unbiased ratings, coinsurance and coordination in the case of illiquidity[128].

---

125 J.P. Morgan Emerging Markets Outlook 1994 (various issues) , Chemical Bank Newsletter (Nov. 1994), Swiss Bank Corporation Newsletter (Dec. 1994-Jan. 1995) and Bear Sterns Nov. 1994.

126 In Oct. 1994, shortly before the eruption of the crisis, Standard and Poor's (S&P) evaluated different government bonds. The long-term Bondes and Ajustabonos were raised to AA- and the short-term dollar-indexed Tesobonos ratings were enhanced to A-1+. Therefore, Tesobonos were considered as the instrument most capable to punctually meet its obligations and through the positive sign, it further indicated an "extremely safe" investment (Salinas 2000: 1079).

127 A Fidelity Investment analyst explicitly stated: "Mexico may receive an investment-grade rating of BBB before (1994) the year is over." (http://www.secinfo.com/dmnbp.bd.c.htm).

128 The in 2008 originated international financial crisis evidenced the fragility of the analysis based on ratings performed in the currently existing manner. The creation of such an institution or of mechanisms which correct the current perverse incentives is still an important topic in the design of a more functional financial architecture.

Furthermore, not only internationally but also domestic residents shared the positive economic outlook prior to the 1994 crisis (Table 17). The public opinion turned optimistic about the future, both as a result of NAFTA coming into force and the encouraging macroeconomic indicators.

Several factors that contributed to the crisis, such as foreign portfolio investment and consumer and credit booms were influenced by the optimistic economic outlook. The financial mechanisms that predominated in the nineties were an important element of what Edwards (1997) describes as a "self-feeding phenomenon that has historically characterized many bubbles".

Table 17 Public Opinion in National Press and the Pact
(percentage of total articles by sector)

	First Phase (12/97-02/98)	Second Phase (03/98)	Third Phase (04/98-05/98)
Private Sector			
Uncertainty	47.22	28.57	5.88
Government to blame	11.11	7.4	0.00
Optimism	41.67	64.29	94.12
Workers and Peasants			
Uncertainty	71.88	22.22	17.39
Other sectors to blame	18.75	11.11	21.74
Optimism	9.38	66.67	60.87

Data source: Aspe (1993: 54)
Created from a random sample of 131 articles published in national newspapers from Dec. 1987 to May 1988

The pegged exchange rate was at the core of this phenomenon. Investment bankers expected the currency to remain stable for profitability reasons. These foreign institutions were supported by rating agencies and the government. The latter hoped to serve different goals through the peso stability: inflation control, maintain capital inflows by serving the interests of investment bankers and preserve the reputation achieved. This self-reinforcing mechanism contributed to the balance of payment problem originated in the private sector and financed through large foreign capital inflows.

5.2 Origin of International Capitals and their Diverging Behavior

5.2.1 Dynamics of Mexican Capitals

5.2.1.1 Literature Review on Studies of Capital Flight and on the Behavior of Mexican Capital

In the literature, it is generally assumed that the portfolio reversals that caused the December 1994 devaluation and exacerbated the posterior crisis were performed by foreigners. This argument is only partially correct. Despite the fact that data collection and particularly dissemination[129] was scarce and incomplete in the period, the prevalent premise concerning foreign capitals precipitating the Mexican crisis can be refuted. This section attempts to find support for the hypothesis that Mexican investors triggered the 1994 devaluation, which ended up in the currency and financial crisis in 1995. Additionally, while indirectly, it suggests that the observed behaviour of domestic investors in Mexico does not represent an isolated case. For this purpose, selected work on capital flight followed is examined.

Massive capital flight followed the Debt Crisis of 1982. It is estimated that some $18 billion U.S. dollars left the country between 1983 and 1987 (Nunnenkamp 1992: 19). Later on, as a result of the reforms implemented, capital gradually returned the country. Table 18 shows the amounts of capital repatriated to Mexico in the pre-crisis period. Roughly $14 billion of domestic capital returned to the country up to 1993 according to data obtained at the domestic securities regulating agency by Vargas (1994).

Table 18 Capital Repatriation to Mexico by Type of Institution 1990-1993

(millions of U.S. dollars)

Year	Banks	Brokers	Total
1990	1137.1	2839.3	3976.4
1991	1343.2	1965.5	3308.7
1992	882.7	1477.3	2360.0
1993	1350.0	2781.0	4131.0
Total	4713	9063.1	13776.1

Data source: Comisión Nacional de Valores, in: Vargas (1994).

However, the trend was reversed in 1994. According to the Annual Report of Banco de México (1994), recorded foreign assets held by Mexican residents increased by $5.5 billion. Roughly half of this capital flight corresponds to bank deposits by the non-financial sectors. This movement corresponds to almost half of the losses of the international reserves during 1994.

The increase in non-bank sector assets by Mexican residents in banks of BIS reporting countries was in Dec. 1994 $3.7 billion (BIS 1996b). Allen (2000) claims that a large portion of capital flight out of Mexico was mostly not reported in the balance of payments, since it was moved to off-shore dollar markets. However, it can be roughly

---

129 Data regarding resident capital flows is difficult to obtain in developing countries. The BIS bank deposit statistics and the IMF reports face several limitations. Among them are the facts that not all assets are held in banks and that not all assets are accounted for, based on the financial center and the identity of the holder. Further limitations include the coverage between country and institutional reporting. Schneider (2003: 3) references Landell-Mills (1986) to affirm that IMF and BIS statistics are partially estimated from other sources, such as the balance of payments, to complete the data sets and remedy their inconsistency. The US Treasury data, also used to estimate resident capital flows contains data on the liabilities of US banks and brokerage houses to the private non-banking sector of foreign countries (U.S. Treasury Bulletin (Washington D.C).This source includes only the flows of capital into the US in bank and custody liabilities. However, the author considers this data as: "the minimum measure of the external assets of a developing country" (Schneider 2003:3).

estimated from the available data.[130] The BIS additionally indicates that there signs of capital outflows from Latin America towards the end of the year and highlights the substantial share of the private non-bank sector in the new deposits received from Latin America (45% of total deposits from that region after three years of repatriation) (BIS 1995:173).

Table 19 shows the capital movements and reserve changes in Mexico during the early nineties. Foreign capital outflows represent, according to this official data presented by Cabello (1999), roughly one third of the reserve losses. The remaining 2/3 or $12 billion U.S. dollars must therefore correspond to capital flight prior to the crisis. This is another piece of evidence of the role played by domestic residents in the capital stampede of 1994.

Table 19 Capital Flows to Mexico

(in billions of U.S. dollars)

Type of flow	1990	1991	1992	1993	1994	1995
Total private inflows:	1.7	21.0	23.9	30.3	9.7	-15.4
Official Inflows	2.0	2.0	1.7	-0.9	0.3	25.7
Changes in Reserves	0.6	8.2	1.2	6.1	-18.9	9.6
Total foreign capital outflows	4.0	3.3	2.4	4.1	6.9	n.a.
Of which:						
Through banks	1.2	1.3	0.9	1.4	2.4	n.a.
Through securities brokers	2.8	2.0	1.5	2.8	4.5	n.a.

Source: Inflows: BIS (1996), Outflows: Cabello (1999) with the Comisión Nacional de Valores data

Note: Outflows in 1994 refer up to June.

Schneider (2003 b) estimated capital flight in 1994 to be $13.4 billion, similar to the figure calculated from Table 19, and $9.2 billion in the subsequent year. The author finds that despite the data limitations, the Mexican Crisis is discernible from the estimated capital outflows.[131]

Kaminsky (2000) analyzed 102 currency crises in 20 countries to identify composite leading indicators of a crisis. The author refers when discussing sudden capital reversals to: "inverse and offsetting capital flows, with domestic residents often choosing to invest their savings in international capital markets at the same time that they are seeking external finance". The author recognizes the difficulty of integrating the simultaneous foreign borrowing and investing in domestic and external markets within traditional debt models and references the work by Frankel/Schmukler (1996, see next subsection). Further, according to her findings, domestic assets reported in BIS Banks – while not capturing comprehensively capital flight- increased significantly in the eve of currency crises.

---

130 The available information offers indirect support. According to the author is as reported to the IMF: In 1992/1993 LDC fuel exporters (Mexico incl.) had no changes in their dollar reserve but in 1994 there was a $20 billion loss despite $20 billion in "net financing in dollars" in 1993 and $25 in 1994.

131 The author adjusted the values for debt forgiveness and cross currency valuations to be $10.9 and $11 billion usd respectively.

Schneider (2003) analyzed domestic capital flight data in sixteen developing countries to search for common explanatory factors. Differences are observed while trying to identify general capital flight determinants. The author reached the conclusion that the behaviour of Mexican investors has the lowest degree of explicability of the complete data set. In other words, common factors that explain capital outflows in other countries have practically no explanatory power for Mexican capital flight. However, on the other side, Charrette (1993) empirically examined the factors that influenced capital flight in three Latin American countries[132]. The developed model fits the data best for Mexico and concluded that the U.S. interest rate and the absence of capital controls were significant determinants of capital flight between 1978 and 1991.

In August 21st 1995, the IMF published in its International Capital Markets Annual report:

> "The available data show that the pressure on Mexico's foreign exchange reserves during 1994, and in particular just prior to the devaluation, came not from the flight of foreign investors, but from Mexican residents" (ref. in Frankel/Schmukler 1996: 1).

The Fund associated the differing behaviour to asymmetric information. The document contradicted the widespread conviction that Mexicans and not foreigners exerted pressure on the international reserves prior to the eruption of the crisis. In this document, the IMF affirms that $4.7[133] billion (over 2/3) of the $6.7 billion reserve losses during Dec. 1994 were asset liquidations performed by local investors[134]. Estay (1997:62) underscore the fact that "the volatile and speculative character is not exclusive of foreign portfolio investments...and massive capital flight are principles also practiced by many of the major Mexican capitals".

Gil-Diaz/Carstens (1996) affirm that even though the December currency purchases have been predominantly made by Mexican residents, they have not been caused by individuals favored by asymmetric information. Their view appears to be at least partially[135] valid since the Mexican public, confronted with recurrent devaluation crises,

---

132 Mexico, Argentina and Venezuela.
133 Quoting the document:
> "In the run-up to the devaluation, that is, from November 30th to December 19th, foreign investors had net sales of about $326 million in Mexican government debt securities, and there were net purchases of equity, while reserves fell by $2.8 billion. For the entire month of December 1994, foreign investors were net sellers of about $370 million of debt and equity, while Mexican foreign exchange reserves fell by $6.7 billion, only $1.7 billion of which was accounted for by the trade deficit."
134 The BIS (1995) alternatively reported that the "exodus of domestic and foreign capital from Mexico" was one of the main factors behind the abrupt decline in capital inflows to Latin America, which indirectly supports the notions expressed by this section.
135 Salinas (2000) disclosed information about a meeting of the industrial sector with policy makers in the eve of the widening of the fluctuation band. The former president states that they were privileged with asymmetric information and started panic U.S. dollar purchases. However, Serra Puche, Minister of Finance at the beginning of the crisis denied categorically the existence of such an information leakage. The report of this denial was stated on a Conference on Feb. 24th 2010 accounted for in the domestic press, on the last week of February 2010 (see for example El Universal at http://www.emedios.mx/testigospdfs/20100225/267085-5d2b00.pdf). It seems impossible to decipher the truth amid the statements of both policy makers.

hedge through currency purchases in periods of uncertainty. Dabat/Toledo (1999: 95) describe a "final speculative assault led by panic buys and sells of large national capitalists favored by privileged information":

Frankel/Schmukler (1996) explicitly explore the argument presented by the IMF by developing a "divergent expectations"[136] hypothesis. In the view of the IMF, according to this paper "local investors led the stampede out of Mexican assets in December 1994, much as they had done in the earlier crisis of 1982". The authors examine the performance of three Mexican closed-end country funds and their Mexican counterpart NAV's.[137] In their interpretation, Mexican country funds' price –traded in Wall Street- reflect the expectations of U.S. investors while their NAVs , which are determined in the Mexican stock exchange- replicate the information and expectations of resident investors. Under these assumptions, a large discount would signalise that Mexicans have more positive expectations than U.S. investors and a matching premium the opposite case.[138]

Their empirical findings were in line with the conclusions reached by comparing the funds' (MXE) and NAV's (MXENAV) prices and their differentials prior to the crisis. NAV's prices plunged two weeks before Dec. 20th 1994 compared to the funds' values in New York. This piece of evidence supports the argument of divergent expectations by foreigners and Mexican nationals. [139]

The authors conclude that: the short-run elasticity of price to NAV is expected to be less than one, while the long-run elasticity approaches one.[140] They further suggest

---

136 On this regard, Aguilar (1994) refers to the "contrasting vision of the (JP Morgan team) foreigners with the fright, apathy and dependence on governmental action showed by Mexican entrepreneurs" as the firm was about to establish a subsidiary in the country.

137 The funds are instruments to hold Mexican equities. A closed-end country fund consists of a fixed number of shares that are invested in a set of stocks of a specific country. Close-end funds are not allowed to issue new shares whereas existing shares cannot be redeemed. These funds can only be traded in secondary security markets, both in NY at their U.S. dollar price and as Net Asset Values (NAVS) –which are the aggregate to usd translated value of the individual equities in the home market. Theoretically, in perfectly integrated efficient markets both prices should be equal. However, as the authors point out, this is rarely the case, price differentials are large and variable and "it is well known that country funds, as well as domestic closed-end funds, trade at an average discount". The here studied funds are the Mexico Fund (MXF), Mexico Equity (MXE) and Income and Emerging Mexico Fund (MEF). The first was established in 1981, the other two in 1990 (Frankel/ Schmukel 1996)

138 The authors find and describe different barriers to arbitrage which indicate that the price gaps exist and the time lag with which large gaps tend to decrease.

139 Kaufmann et al. (1999) used a comprehensive data survey including managers' expectations of 58 countries to test if they possess an informational advantage regarding exchange rate volatility. Their findings indicate that asymmetric information is present, partially confirmed by country fund discounts and the observation that local residents left the country before international investors did. Additionally, just like it is argued for the Mexican crisis, the authors point out that "market participants-like international mutual funds- and market analysts -like currency forecasters and rating agencies- largely did not expect the Asian crisis". Managers appeared to possess better-quality information than the macroeconomic and financial available data that can help them predict exchange rate fluctuations. One of their main conclusions was that as opposed to local managers, financial markets have only limited possibilities to foresee a crisis. No reference is made to the source of information.

140 In other words: there exists a stationary long-run relationship between each price and its NAV. Given a constant average discount, an innovation in the funds' NAV is expected to be fully trans-

that different expectations might help to unravel the causes for differentials in NAVs and funds prior to the crisis. The authors argue that if a NAV's price fell first or more sharply than the country funds –implicated by a premium- it would be an indication that local investors anticipated the crisis and acted differently to their foreign counterparts based on their negative expectations.

Heath (1996) proposed differentiating the behavior of Mexican and foreign investors reacting to changes in the expected exchange rate. Local residents rashly reacted to the expectation of devaluation by exchanging their capital into U.S. dollars. Historically, sudden devaluations[141], the forced conversion of dollar deposits into pesos and the introduction of exchange rate controls have motivated this collective pattern. Instead, foreign investors use the available information to make rational decisions based on risk evaluations. Foreigners based on their rational expectations, decided in 1994 to keep their capital in Mexico.

The author used available data on tenure of government bonds and concluded that: "Mexican portfolio investment proved to be more speculative and volatile than the corresponding foreign investment" (see Table 20). According to Heath (1996) the best example of this differentiated behaviour took place in March-April 1994.[142] The international reserves decreased from $28.3 billion U.S. dollars within thirty days by almost $11 billion, of which 80% corresponds to Mexican dollar demand. The total holding of government bonds decreased in April by $6.5 billion or 16.4% compared to the previous month. This decrease was caused roughly 75 % by Mexican investors and 25% by foreigners.

---

mitted to the fund's price in the-long run. On the other hand, a change in a NAV is expected to be only partially transmitted to its price, changing the average short-run discount.

141 One of the most prominent cases took place in 1982 where, after the President announced that the peso would not be devaluated and that he personally would "defend it like a dog", it lost almost 500% in that year. Other sudden devaluations took place in 1976, 1985 and 1987 (Heath 1996: 36).

142 After the murder of the presidential candidate of the ruling party for seven decades.

Table 20 Changes in Government Bond Holdings by Mexican Residents and Foreigners in 1994

(in billions)

Period	March-April	May-Aug	Jan-Nov.
Reserves	↓$11 usd		↓$12 usd
Gov. debt holdings	↓21.3 mxp($6.5 usd)	↑13.5 mxp($4.2 usd)	↓14.1 mxp($4.1usd)
of which:			
Residents			
Total Position Changes	↓15.9 mxp(-12.2%)	↑1.3 mxp($0.4 usd)	↓22.4 mxp ($6.5 usd)
Cetes	↓17.6 mxp		
Tesobonos	↑$6.3 mxp($2 usd)		
Foreigners			
Total Position Changes	↓5.5 mxp(-4.2%)	↑12.2 mxp($3.8 usd)	↑$8.3 mxp($2.4 usd)*
Cetes	↓14.9 mxp		
Tesobonos	↑13.6 mxp($4.3 usd)		

Data source: Heath (1996)
* Considering the November exchange rate of 3.45 mxp/usd instead of 3.2 for the rest of the calculations.

The changes in the government bond markets in the above mentioned period can be described as follows: total Cetes holdings decreased significantly; however, most foreigners only exchanged their Cetes against dollar-denominated short-term bonds Tesobonos (Figure 42). Through this strategy, international investors hedged against devaluations. Unlikely, the total outstanding stock of Mexican residents' bonds decreased significantly. In the following four months, mainly foreign capital (90.7% of the total) re-entered the country to purchase government bond markets. Up to the fall 1994, this development did not represent liquidity problems for the country since there were plenty of international reserves.

Shortly after the eruption of the crisis, the Tesobono strategy was widely held responsible for the crisis. This argument has some explanatory power only if additional factors such as the scale of the supply, the background of the demand, (see chapter 7), currency appreciation and international reserves levels are taken into account. "Effectively, this was a double-or-nothing bet."(De Long/Eichengreen 2001:22). However, while the unlimited emission of this type of bond is considered critical, in this section the focus is on the asymmetric behaviour of domestic and international investors.

Between December 1994 and February 1995 Mexican residents got rid of over 28% of their held assets (20% alone between Dec. and January) contrasting with 6% of foreign holders. Local residents withdrew in the period funds from their portfolio amounting $7 billion[143]. The exact destination of the funds cannot be traced back. However, it is plausible to assume, given the volatility observed and the capital outflows that characterized this period, that Mexican residents attacked the currency. The data further indicates that foreign capital probably financed the capital flight that

---

143 Considering the exchange rate at the end of December 1995. Using the exchange rate prior to the Crisis, December 19th 1994, this sums $10.2 billion.

took place during that year. In Heath's (1996) opinion, Mexican residents acted rationally based on their historic devaluation experiences.

Figure 42 Tesobonos, Cetes and International Reserves in 1994

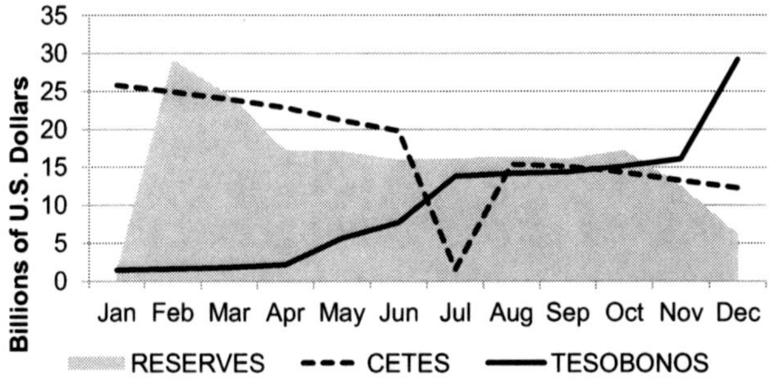

Data source: Banco de México online (2008)

The behaviour of resident investors might be described as:

> "In general, one can also argue that a narrow reliance on local investors limits liquidity. Recent episodes tend to confirm that local investors can bring about destabilizing behavior." (Jeanneau/Tovar 2008 :81)

The studies reviewed provide support to the argument that local residents precipitated the currency crisis. Nevertheless, this phenomenon seems to be not particular of Mexico, but as suggested by Schneider (2003) rather common to other developing countries.

5.2.1.2 Further Evidence on the Behavior of Domestic Capitals

Official data supports the arguments presented in the previous section. Figure 43 compares the Mexican data on changes in international reserves and the assets of non-banking residents. The juxtaposition of the movements in central bank reserves and in foreign asset holding by private, non-traditional banking residents shows a certain correspondence, especially notorious in the eve of the devaluation in Dec. 1994. In November[144], the value of reserve losses corresponds to 85% of the here measured capital flight of domestic investors.

Figure 44 displays the stocks of foreign assets of Mexican financial sector residents.[145] In 1994, these assets roughly tripled between January and November (prior to the crisis) and quadrupled in December, after the currency crisis.

---

144 A report of Nov. 17 1994, see Garcia (1994), calculated that alone on the 16th and 17th of the month, 0.7 billion Central Bank reserves were required to service the market.
145 The modus operandi and motivation that led to a surge, specifically of securities brokers is elaborated upon in 7.2.

Figure 43 Changes in Central Bank Reserves and Foreign Assets of Mexican Non-traditional Banking Residents in 1994

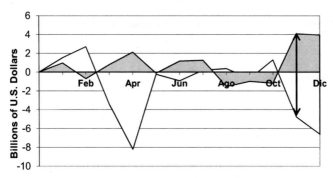

☐ Changes in central bank reserves (excluding gold)
◪ Foreign assets of other bank and non-financial institutions

Data source: IMF International Financial Statistics and author's own calculations

The different estimations, probably not fully accurate, provide a reliable indication of the direction of domestic capital in the years around the crisis. Significant capital flight with a crisis triggering effect from Mexico in 1994 seems to be irrefutable. Foreigners only exacerbated the trend set by domestic investors.

Figure 44 Foreign Assets of Mexican Financial Institutions

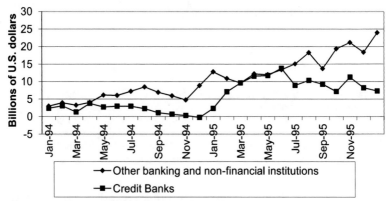

Data source: IMF International Financial Statistics

Salinas[146] (2000), favoured by asymmetric information, affirmed to this regard:

---

146 Mexican president between 1988 and 1994.

"the capitals that were pulled out in Dec. 1994 and that caused the maxi-devaluation and the drying up of the reserves were not those deposited in Tesobonos, they were the resources of Mexican investors."

5.2.2 Dynamics of U.S. Institutional Investment in Mexico

Institutional investors' flows started to pour into the country as early as 1990 and showed significant growth rates up to the eruption of the crisis in Dec. 1994. Government bonds were the most demanded assets by institutional investors with round 70% before the crisis (Figure 45).

In 1993 the bond and equity markets reached their peak and experienced a change in their composition. The investor base broadened to include not only the traditional wealthy individuals and capital flight investors, but also the more moderate institutional investors (IMF 1994: 17).

Figure 45 Portfolio Composition of Institutional Investors in Mexico

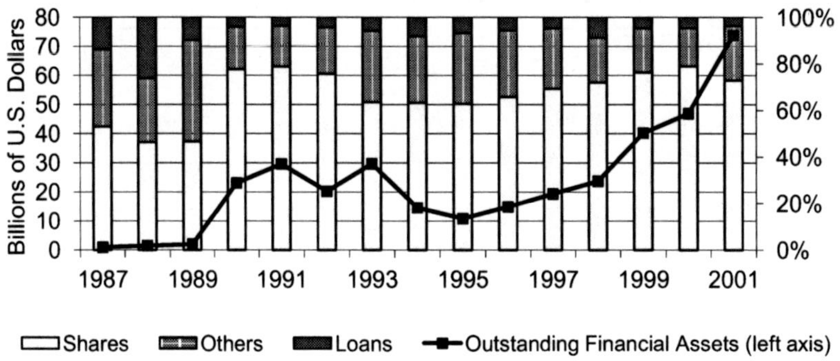

Data source: OECD

Institutional investors can be broadly categorized into mutual funds, pension funds and insurance companies. The organizations of this type of industrial countries manage funds worldwide, which vastly outnumber the market capitalization of emerging markets. Therefore, swings in investment preferences can cause considerable effects on the financial market of the issuing country. The IMF (1994) stated likewise: "major institutional investors are not necessarily long-term buy and hold". While in general, their trading activity levels vary[147] it can be said that all of them would "if a

---

147 Mutual funds face performance standards over a very short-term horizon and actively trade to meet these performance levels, pension funds are evaluated on annual or multi-annual basis " a praxis that is also encouraged by their desire to hold longer maturity assets as to match the maturity structure of their liabilities", and insurance companies that even though tend to share a longer-term view, but at the same time appreciate and safeguard their reputation as safe investments (IMF 1994: 18).

perceived deterioration in the underlying quality of those (risky) assets, were in store, they would move quickly to reduce their holding of emerging market bonds and equities"(IMF 1994: 18).

Information on the position of the U.S. international investors (Table 21) further reveals that loans, as opposed to the 1982 Debt Crisis, did not play a significant role. The data is consistent with the assumption that the government bond markets were at the epicentre of the capital flow volatility.

Table 21 Financial Assets held by U.S. Institutional Investors in Mexico

(millions of U.S. dollars if not otherwise indicated)

Year	Total Financial Assets	% Bonds	% Loans	Shares	Others
1990	23,081.1	80.0	0.8	15.5	3.7
1991	29,612.9	73.5	1.0	20.9	4.7
1992	20,220.7	60.6	1.7	29.8	7.9
1993	29,657.5	76.6	1.3	14.8	7.2
1994	14,544.3	68.7	2.6	19.8	9.0
1995	10,768.7	66.8	2.3	20.9	10.1
1996	14,866.6	74.8	1.4	16.6	7.2

Data source: OECD (2008)

Figure 46 Portfolio Liabilities (flows) vs. Changes in Financial Assets of Institutional Investors

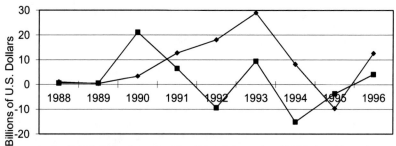

—■—Annual changes in oustanding financial assets of institutional investors
—◆—Mexican Portfolio Liabilities (flows from BoP)

Data source: OECD, IMF and author's own calculations

Note: In 1994, the change in pesos in the outstanding assets of institutional investors corresponds to a reduction of 15%, as compared to a 49% decrease in their dollar value.

Figure 46 exhibits the position changes, both of Mexican portfolio liabilities and of financial assets of institutional investors. They reflect, excluding the exchange rate losses in 1994-5, the instable behaviour of this sort of capital. However, further presumptions on the volatility of the holdings of institutional investors are out of the scope of this thesis.

Yearly data available on U.S. institutional investors shows that they played a role, in exacerbating the crisis (Figure 47). The capital outflows by the U.S. institutional investors (-$12.8 billion) while larger than those of domestic residents, only seem to have followed the stampede by Mexican private sector residents (-$7 billion).

Figure 47 Position Changes in the Bond markets by Mexican Residents and U.S. Institutional Investors in 1994

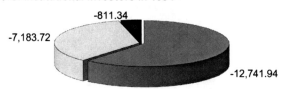

□ U.S. institutional investor's bond position change
□ Mexican private bond holders position change
Data source: OECD (2008), Banco de México (2008) and author's own calculations

5.2.3 Appraisal of the Official Data

5.2.3.1 Available Information on Public Securities

Mexico was in 1993 and 1994 the largest recipient of bond flows worldwide (Table 19). Nevertheless, the availability, comparability and reliability of information on foreign portfolio investment can be considered as limited.[148] For government securities it is moderately better than for the equity markets.

Figure 48 shows the level of outstanding government securities classified by residents and non-residents.[149] The number of bonds issued by the government increased in 1994 by 17.9%. The tenure of Tesobonos increased by twenty-two fold ($29[150] billion worth Tesobonos were held by the public in Dec. 1994 of which $16 billion were held by foreign addresses) in the same period (Banco de México 1994: 210 and online). Tesobonos represented the 83% of the total foreign investment on bonds in January 1995 (Banco de México 2009 online).

---

148 The UNCTAD (1999:5 ff.) offers a representative conclusion on foreign private investment (FPI): "There are different sources of FPI data: the IMF, the World Bank, the Institute of International Finance, source countries (such as United States Treasury) and some commercial companies tracking investment funds (such as Micropal of Standard and Poor's). Needless to say, data shown by different sources widely differ....In short, there is no single source of data on FPI and it is difficult to have a precise indication of cross-border portfolio flows. The IMF seems to have the most reliable figures provided by recipient countries, although the country coverage is far from complete and it is difficult to identify exactly the nationality of the purchaser or seller, or issuer of securities."
149 Data on private securities flows based on the origin of the funds was not available for the period.
150 BIS (1995) reports $21 billion, $17 billion foreign owned, $7 billion of which matured in 1995/ Q1.

Figure 48 Outstanding Securities by Type of Owner

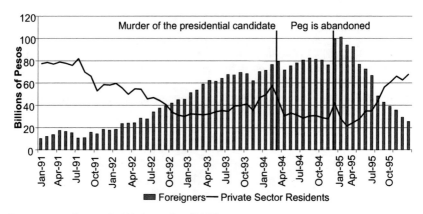

Data source: Banco de México online (2008)

Interestingly, the trend of both groups suggests marked periods where they go in the opposite direction. In 1991 the data reflects large amounts of repatriated capital (see also Table 20). The latter was a result of restored confidence based on favourable expectations and the comprehensive economic reforms. However, already at the end of 1991 the holding of national securities by residents had lost momentum. As opposed to the behaviour of local investors, non residents were increasingly interested in Mexican bonds. Until October 1992, local residents' holdings exceeded those of foreigners. At the end of 1993, a cut in the Fed's rates caused a temporary trend reversal. Both residents and foreigners decreased only shortly their position.

Clearly different reactions took place after the political instability caused by the murder of the presidential candidate in March 23rd, 1994. Foreigners decreased their bond holdings only marginally, starting in April, as compared to local investors which suddenly sold off large amounts of their bonds in March 1994 (see both Figure 48 and Figure 50). In December 1994, the month of the abandonment of the peg[151], the large devaluation was reflected in the increase of the peso value of both foreign and domestic investment. Nevertheless, the withdrawal of foreigners from the public bond market was gradual in the first semester of 1995 as the instruments matured.

Data on domestic tenure of government securities shows the increasing intervention of Banco de México (Figure 49). The private sector, including corporations, individuals and commercial banks decreased their bond holdings in pesos by 46%, or over $7 billion between January and November 1994.[152] The reserves loss in the year summed about $10 billion (Banco de México online 2008). According to SECOFI data, in January 1995 foreign portfolio capital consisting of $17.2 billion U.S. dollars abandoned the country (IIEc-UNAM 1995).

---

151 The currency depreciated roughly 50% within 10 days or 71% accumulated in the year.
152 A former executive of one of the three main commercial banks, currently working as academic, refers that the referred bank took additionally credits during 1994 to secure dollars.

Figure 49 Domestic Holders of Government Securities by Type of Resident

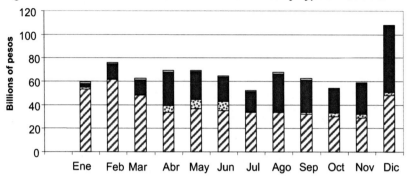

Data source: Banco de México (2008)

The peso value of government securities increased overall in 1994. While foreigners increased their bond tenure by 32.6% (reflecting the December devaluation), residents reduced their holdings by 12.5 % (Banco de México 1994: 210). Figure 50 reveals that Mexican private sector residents abandoned the bond markets already earlier that year, as political and financial turmoil began. Foreign entities had much more stable investment patterns throughout 1994.

Figure 50 Holdings of Government Bonds by Private Enterprises & Individuals

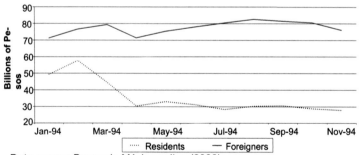

Data source: Banco de México online (2008)

The data seems to support the arguments suggested by Heath (1996) and Frankel/Schmukel (1996) and backed by the author of this thesis. Mexican nationals, based on their experience, triggered through public securities sell off and the resulting capital flight the devaluation of 1994, in a volatile environment followed by U.S. institutional investors.

Although it is unfeasible to fully describe the rationale behind the demand for domestic bonds, Chapter 7 elaborates on the investing behaviour of resident and foreign financial entities. Non-traditional investment was behind these changes in ownership.

5.2.3.2 Available Information on Private Securities

Capital inflows to the private sector also increased rapidly in the early nineties. In addition to the favouring factors mentioned in the past sections, changes in the U.S. SEC Regulation 144-A simplified (reducing both in time and costs) for local firms equity issuance in the U.S. markets (Culpeper 1995:42).

Before 1989, equity flows were practically inexistent. According to the IMF (1995), the increase in equity issuance was partially caused by the privatization of public sector companies. Mexican firms led the new equity placements in the developing world between 1990 and 1994 ($11 billion vs. China's $5.6 billion). However, after the conclusion of major privatizations, their peak was reached in 1991 with $3.8 billion, and decreased thereafter continuously to roughly 40% of this amount in 1994 (IMF 1995: 38 ff.). Figure 51 highlights the preponderance of the telecommunications sector in the primary emissions of equity.

Figure 51 International Equity Issues by Sector, Mexico

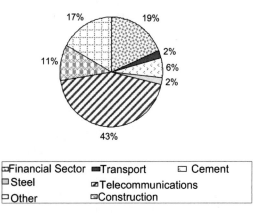

Financial Sector	▬Transport	▢ Cement
Steel	▨Telecommunications	
Other	▨Construction	

Data source: IMF (1995)

The picture in the secondary markets looked somewhat different. In 1993 equity experienced the greatest value increase in the period. However, the inflow upsurge did not match the market value expansion observed up to November 1994 (Table 22). The IMF (1995) reports that the Stock Exchange index rose 436% in dollar terms from 1990-1993. The gap between the actual investment and the market value (which reached 300% of the original inflows in 1992) was the result of a speculative bubble and represented an unforeseen risk to the economy (Cabello 1999: 274).

Table 22 Foreign Investment and Capital Outflows in the Stock Market

(millions of U.S. dollars)

	1990	1991	1992	1993	1994	1995
Market value	4,080	18,543	28,668	54,484	Nov:50,311 Dec:34,395	Feb: 18,946
Accumulated investment	1,670	4,552	7,082	17,898	21,981	n.a.
Yearly flows	1,256	2,882	2,630	10,716	4,084	n.a
Capital gains	2.44	4.07	4.05	3.04	1.56	n.a.
Percentage of ADR's[1]	51.15	74.06	73.79	62.33	57.75	66.57
Capital repatriation (to foreign countries)[2]	2,839	1,965	1,477	2,781	4,537	n.a

Source: Cabello (1999) with data from Secretaria de Comercio y Fomento Industrial and Bolsa Mexicana de Valores (BMV) Anuario Bursátil 1993, 1994 and BMV Indicadores Bursátiles (Nov. 1994 and March 1995).
1 American Depositary Receipts
2 Data source: Comisión Nacional de Valores. For 1994 the information refers up to June.

Culpeper (1995) indicates that between the second and first semester 1992 and 1993, respectively, the stock market corrected the overvaluation and prices decreased by 25% from October to June.

The concentration observed in the primary markets was reflected in the secondary markets as well. Data as of end of Dec. 1993 assigns 40.5% of the total market value to one single company: Teléfonos de México.[153] The market value of ten further companies accumulated roughly 40% of the value market (Gurria 1995: 279).

Further, data from the U.S. Department of the Treasury regarding the value of the acquisitions (in the primary and secondary equity markets) of Mexican securities in the U.S. valued them to be $7 billion in 1991 and $8.4 in 1992. The author attributes the intensified interest of U.S. financial intermediaries to the previous capital flight periods and to the increasing trade links to the region (Culpepper 1995: 38).

According to the World Bank (1997), the stock exchange total market value stood at about US$200 billion at the end of 1993. Mexican share prices fell 35% ($70 billion) in December 1994, mainly in the second half of the month. The Library of the U.S. Congress reports that roughly 75% of equity held at the end of 1993 corresponded to Mexican investors, but only 0.2% of all residents possessed brokerage accounts. New share emissions fell in 1994 by over 25% compared to the previous year (Banco de México 1994).

Based on the March 1994 Survey[154] of U.S holdings of foreign portfolio investment, long-term[155] securities held by U.S. residents in Mexico totaled $51.5 billion. Equity

---

153 Telmex was sold to a group of investors led by Carlos Slim. The Forbes Magazine considered Mr. Slim as the world's richest person in 2010.
154 The survey was a joint undertaking of the U.S. Treasury Department, the Federal Reserve Bank of New York, and the Board of Governors of the Federal Reserve System. The 2006 survey was

holdings summed $34.7 billion and long-term debt securities equaled $16.9 billion (U.S. Department of the Treasury 2007).

The majority of equity titles held by foreigners were held by U.S. residents. However, Griffith-Jones (1995) highlights the involvement of European investment, especially British, in the Latin American equity markets.

The data suggests that foreign investment in the equity market, similarly to the trend observed in the public securities market, weakened only after the large devaluation took place. The stock exchange index reported by the BIS (1995) confirms the pattern expressed by the IMF: "Indeed, foreign investors did not start to sell their Mexican equity holdings in any sizable quantity until February 1995." IMF (1995:7-8).

Finally, despite the rash development of Mexico's financial markets the BIS (1995) argued, that price volatility was considerably higher than in industrialized nations. However, interestingly after calculating a volatility indicator[156] for the 1986-1990 and 1991-1994 period, it found that price volatility was lower in the latter period, characterized by financial liberalization. It concludes that: "there is reason to believe that the widening range of investors may have helped to make markets more stable".

5.3 Conclusions on Capital Inflows

A wave of capital account liberalizations and structural changes in the supply of capital in industrialized countries elicited massive portfolio inflows to emerging markets in the early nineties. Toledo/Dabat (1999) considered the crisis was caused due to overexposition of the economy (or disproportionate absorption of foreign flows). Mexico, as a result of push and pull factors, was the major recipient of bond capital inflows in the world in 1993 and 1994. This fact should have been a mattern of concern. As Harberger (1985: 166) affirms: "countries should begin to worry when capital inflows reach unsustainable rates". Oppositely, Mexican Policy makers were eager to offer unlimitedly Tesobonos and absorbing the exchange rate risk.

Endogenously and exogenously originated volatility began in the first quarter of 1994. Subsequently, domestic and foreign investors, mainly of U.S. origin, reacted divergently. In this sense, their contribution to the precipitation of the crisis is dissimilar.

This section provided some evidence to the argument that Mexican investors, based on a specific devaluation expectations pattern, were the forerunners of the Mexican crisis of 1994. This effort was confronted with the fact that data availability is limited, due to the lack of digitalization of statistics and the deficient transparency policy

---

the seventh survey of U.S. ownership of foreign securities conducted by the United States, with prior surveys conducted as of March 31, 1994, December 31, 1997, December 31, 2001, December 31, 2003, December 31, 2004, and December 31, 2005 and December 31, 2006.

155 Long-term securities are defined as those without a stated maturity date (such as equities) or with an original term-to-maturity in excess of one year. Short-term securities' data is not available for 1994.

156 The standard deviation of month-on- month changes in equity prices in usd. The index decreased in Mexico from 15.9 to 10.4 as it did for all but two of the studied countries.

reigning in the period previous to the crisis. However, a mainly qualitative review of the existing information evidences the implication, generally disregarded in the prevailing literature, of local residents in the currency run that lead to the Dec. 1994 devaluation.

International equity flows, previous to liberalization quasi inexistent, increased rapidly due to major privatizations and changes in SEC regulations. The market was previous to the crisis very concentrated in few sectors with the telecom sector outstanding. Important to point out is that there were not any indicators of volatility in 1994 stemming from the equity markets leading to capital flight and major losses of the central bank reserves. This type of investment rather was affected after the large devaluations in December 1994 and first quarter of 1995 and the market weakened importantly only a posterior, in early 1995.

The volatility of domestic capital in Mexico and other emerging countries poses a grim policy challenge. Policy makers face painful options which vary from maintaining high levels of reserves, which imply opportunity costs, to the introduction of capital curfews, which might be punished by the markets. While the policy choice is out of the scope of this document, this section introduced an implication relevant to both financial analysis and policy making. Local nationals tend to react to currency volatility with capital flight and elicit in this manner a self-reinforcing mechanism that can contribute to a currency crisis. Foreigners, on the other hand-side appear to have a more rational behaviour based on the available information. However, once capital flight starts, regardless of its origin, the risk of herding and its perilous effects are always latent. The next chapter continues to explore the financial markets from a domestic perspective with banking practices at its core.

6 Inefficient Credit Allocation and the Banking Sector

Mexican banks in the early nineties were overwhelmed with financial resources, as a result of the increased availability of capital and the crowding in by the government. The in 1992 privatized financial institutions were under significant pressure, since the domestic industrial groups which purchased them, had to leverage heavily in a flawed privatization process. Further, efficient credit allocation skills were not developed neither in the phase of state ownership nor in the diverse branches of origin of the new owners. Therefore, at the beginning of the decade, the financial institutions followed aggressive credit allocation patterns, which supported the credit and consumption booms previous to the crisis.

Some pernicious aspects were behind the credit portfolio growth. Moral hazard, through the circumvention of the existing regulation in the form of an exchange of lending to related parties was an issue that amplified the credit boom. Nevertheless, the most important effect of the deficient and rash credit expansion was the worsening of the portfolio to dangerous levels, which were actually understated by local accounting standards. Other collateral effects of the credit surge for the economy were the strengthening of the import and consumption booms.

In this document, the thesis suggested by De Luna (2002) that the Mexican banking crisis would have been possible without the eruption of the currency crisis is supported. In his view, the causes of the crisis are of structural nature. The inefficiency and insufficiency of the institutional conditions for credit allocation are at the heart of this affirmation (De Luna 2002: 144).

This chapter is organized as follows. The first part introduces some historical aspects of the banking sector in the period prior to the re-privatization. These include market concentration and profitability based on inefficient but non-perilous practices. The following section describes the divestiture process, characterized by regulatory shortcomings and excessive leverage to acquire the banks. Subsequently, the credit boom is analyzed. The financial burden caused by the leveraged buy-out and the lack of financial skills were behind the disorderly credit allocation practices. Finally, conclusions on the poor banking performance are drawn and the related engagement of financial groups into derivatives introduces the following chapter.

6.1 Antecedents of the Private Banking Sector and the State Banks (1982-1992)

In 1981, a year before the nationalization, the banking sector was characterized by a strong concentration originated due to regulatory changes in 1970 (Vega 1999:120). The author references Gonzalez (1989) and presents information regarding the financial sector. Accordingly, the two largest banks had a share of 20% each of the total resources in the banking system. Six institutions controlled 75% of the resources. There were basically three types of institutions: those linked to industrial groups (ex. Serfin), those concentrated in financial services but acquiring financial groups (Bancomer and Banamex) and hybrid (without a holding and links to industrial units such as Cremi).

The banks operated with a financial margin[157] of roughly 13% in 1981. The profitability of the sector was according to Vega (1999) attributed to the market concentration and the gains in the exchange markets. Table 23 presents some financial indicators and the involvement of the major bank in exchange rate-related businesses:

Table 23 Profitability of Mexican Banks 1981

(billions of pesos)

Institution	ROE	Exchange market profits	Gross Profits	Net profits	% of total exchange rate profits
All banking	38.9%*	8.9	18.4	10.1	100%
Banamex	42.7%	1.3	4.3	2.8	14%
Bancomer	42.6%	2.5	7.0	2.9	28%
Serfin	53.9%	.96	1.4	1.0	11%

Data source: Comisión Nacional Bancaria y de Valores referenced in Vega (1999: 132 and 136) and authors' own calculations
* Refers to commercial banking only, based on August 1981 data.

Due to the financial repression, the price signal function in the economy was distorted. Real interest rates had wide fluctuations in the 80's. Financial controls had other effects on resource allocation. Banks were subject to increased intermediation costs and channeled funds to non-profitable activities. Limited and restricted private funds available through the banks and low (and negative) interest rates supported the development of a large informal credit market. As a result, the performance of monetary policy was also limited (APEC and Banco de México 2003: 205)[158].

The three largest banks with 50% of the market share contributed with a similar percentage to the speculative gains of the branch, which played a role in the 1982 devaluation and crisis. Other sixty institutions of different size and scope accounted for the remaining 43% of the gains in the forex markets. In most of the cases, exchange rate induced profits constituted roughly one third of gross profits (Vega 1999).

The deficit in the financial services account represented four fifths of the total current account deficit in 1981, which increased 85% within one year (Vega 1999: 139). The increasing imbalances of the fiscal sector reached 15% of the GDP in 1981 and resulted in a crisis in 1982. Domestic credit was soon insufficient and private investment was crowded out. The financing sources of public spending were international

---

157 The difference between active and passive rates.
158 In the period after 1982, the nationalized banks had a more limited performance. Aspe (1993: 67) states that the financial system was too rigid and did not allow proper adjustment in periods of moderate to high inflation. The monetary control was hindered by the fact that the minimum reserve requirement in an inflationary environment was established by the borrowing requirements of the public sector and its deficit. In this case, the ability to influence the money mass was limited. However, since interest rates were fixed and were not able to respond to inflation, the currency depreciated and credit had to be rationed, since people took their funds to place them abroad.

public debt, inflation and negative interest rates. Banks were not financing private investment, rather mainly public expenditure (Rubio 1999: 4-6).[159]

The currency and debt crisis in 1982 was associated to capital flight, hyperinflation and subsequent devaluations, a quasi-national insolvency and the nationalization of the banks. Vega (1999) reports the rupture[160] of the banking associations and the government, where the former considered that the latter, due to inflation and public external mismatches, was to blame for the crisis. According to the author, bankers did not recognize their contribution to the 1982 crisis through the dollarization of the financial sector and capital flight.

The bank nationalization introduced after the stabilization measures in 1982, intensified capital flight.[161] However, Vega (1999) states that the expropriation[162], as opposed to conventional belief, represented an advantageous business for the main banks (Table 24). These institutions had faced large losses in their speculative transactions after large and continuous devaluations.

Table 24 Bank Indemnization per Share

Bank	Share price Aug. 1982 (pesos)	Actual indemnization per share (pesos)	Increase (%)
Banamex	70	298	326%
Bancomer	31	257	729%
Serfin	125	588	370%

Data source: Diario Oficial de la Federación 22 Agosto 1983 in: Vega (1999: 159).

6.2 The Privatization Process 1991-1992

After almost a decade under governmental rule, in 1991 a process of bank privatization was started[163]. The divestiture caused great expectations among nationals and foreigners; however, foreign participation was virtually banned. The financial liberalization and the re-privatization of the banks supported the expectations of a more efficient channeling of resources. Foreign capital was expected to fuel economic devel-

---

159 Prior to 1988 three regulatory instruments of the banking system were being used. First the legal reserve requirement that forced credit institutions to grant credit to the public sector at no cost or low rates. Second, quantitative credit controls that forced intermediaries to assign a specific quota of their lending portfolio to certain sectors of the economy. Third borrowing and lending rates were set by the authorities and remained generally fixed for long periods (Aspe 1993: 67).

160 Vega (1999: 133) describes a dynamic process of mistrust and speculation towards the end of the presidential term since the "economic elites" perceive (and abuse) the fact that the authorities are to leave office. The author defines this notion as the "psychological foundation" of the typical crisis of the end of the six-year term.

161 In Vega's (1999) opinion, it was the result of a complicated process and not only of an interventionist spirit of the authorities.

162 The author refers to a change in the total valuation of the banks introduced after the presidential term which more than doubled from the 1982 original valuation. What the author does not reference is inflation, however, the increases in their adjusted capital valuations are by large higher than this rate.

163 This process was concluded in 1992.

opment and the banks should serve as an engine to a sound economic growth (Kessler 1999: 92).

As expressed by Aspe (1993), the financial outcomes for the government of the bank privatization surpassed the expectations of the external advisors to this matter (Table 25). Moreover, the prices obtained by the sale of Mexican banks were high compared to other international experiences in the eighties.

Table 25 Price obtained for commercial banks

	Times book value
Mexico	3.08
U.S. and Europe	2.2

Data source: Aspe (1993:214)

Willson et al. (1998) exemplify the widespread critics on the bank privatization, referencing the Wall Street Journal (1/25/96):

"the mainstreams of critics arise from the high prices paid which might have contributed to under-capitalization and that an adequate prudential regulatory framework was only implemented in 1996".

Nevertheless, even though it is widely discussed in the literature that banks were overpriced, a less evident fact is not as publicized (Vega 1999:237). An independent examination of the assets and bidden prices for banks was performed a posteriori. As a result, bankers were compensated for the value of bad quality loans. The authorities returned a percentage of the total price paid for the financial institutions. As established by the independent auditors, there was only one case where the quality of portfolio was not in line with the paid price for the bank. A summary of the adjustments is displayed in Table 26.

Table 26 Posterior Price Corrections on Banks

Adjustment/ Total bidder price	Number of institutions
Under 3.5%	11
Between 5-9%	4
24%	1
Not-adjusted	2

Data source: Vega (1999: 237)

An industry source[164] regarded the poorly capitalized banking sector "where buyers of these banks had stretched themselves" as an underlying cause of the banking crisis. However, the excessive leveraging required by domestic investors reflects both the profitability[165] of the branch, and therefore its high price and also the determination to ban foreign investors from the process. Therefore, the conventional argument

---

164 Former N.Y. based investment banker.
165 Mexican banks have a tradition of large spreads in the active and passive rates. This subject is elaborated upon in the following sections.

that banks aggressive risk-taking practices prior to the 1995 crisis were caused by an overpriced divestiture policy in the re-privatization process is only partially correct.

6.3 Early Performance of the Re-privatized Banks: the Disproportionate Credit Expansion

The dynamic growth of credit allocation started in the period of governmental control[166] and grew at an accelerated pace after the privatization. However, the valuation of the state owned banks performed by First Boston, intermediator of the privatization process, considered in 1991 the assets of the banks to comply with high standards. In their view, as quoted in Vega (1999: 230): "the situation of the quality of credit portfolio is significantly superior to that of the U.S., France and Spain". Table 27 presents their findings:

Table 27 Financial Situation of Mexican Banks

Concept	End of 1988	End of 1989	End of 1990
Assets	108	162	268
Of which: Repos & futures*	9.8%	11.6%	18%
Passives	100	152	252
Capital	8	10	16

Data source: First Boston (1992) excerpted from Vega 1999: 207, 210
*similar percentage of passives

Torre (1999: 29) affirms that the privatized banks further supported the credit expansion with risk valuation methods, organizational and information systems that were inherited from the nationalized bank. After 1988, the amount of granted credit increased dramatically. From 1988-1994, it moved from 14 % of the BIP to 45% (Figure 52).

Banco de México (1994) reports an overall increase in credit of 32% alone in 1994 following a previous annual rise of 16.5%. Credit to the business sector (which accounted for roughly ¾ of total credit) rose by 39% in 1994.

---

166 Harberger (1985) reports a similar development of the Chilean banking system prior to the 1982 Crisis, where regarding what he describes to be "excessive capital inflows" and credit bank expansion explains:

"Some share of the blame also rests with the international bankers, whose zeal seems to have exceeded their prudence in Chile, where there was a special element of riskiness in the portfolios of most banks, probably as early as 1975.. The "false demand" for credit stimulated by the continual rollovers of essentially bad (or at least dubious) loans was surely a main cause of high real interest rates.... Chilean bankers, obviously, must take a share of the blame. They were hopeful that economic prosperity would carry weak and failing firms out of their troubles... the biggest mistake of the policymakers ultimately lay in overlooking the need to keep the banking system under a stricter discipline." (Harberger 1985:248)

Figure 52 Credit granted by Private Banks
as a percentage of GDP

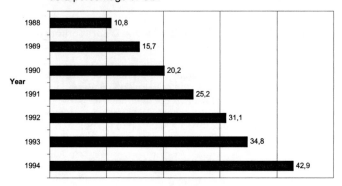

Data source: Banco de México (1994)

The operative results of the financial sector in the first three quarters of 1994 showed mixed outcomes (Table 28). These results are based on Mexican accounting principles which, as unveiled after the crisis, undervalued the embedded risks (Vega 1999).

Table 28 Summary of the Operative Results of the Financial Sector in 1994

In millions of pesos/ %

Area/Firm	Amount / %
Banking sector profits	6700
Banacci, Bancomer, Serfin	62.4% of the sector
Losses: Arka (29), Sureste (83.8), Interacciones (37), Fina-Value (9.2)	159
Most significant changes: Banco Mexicano Probursa Confia	8.3 / -98.2% 33.7/ -85.4%, 88.3/-43.4%
Brokerage firms profits	505
Inbursa, Accival and OBSA	97% of the sector

Source: Aviles (1994)
Note: Revaluation of assets is not considered

The main effect associated to the credit expansion was the worsening of the credit portfolio (Figure 53). Regulations in this regard were enough for the more conservative credit assignation during the governmental period but proved insufficient afterwards. The amount of non-performing loans almost doubled in the semester after the first large devaluation in December 1994.

Figure 53 Nonperforming Loans Dec. 1994-1995

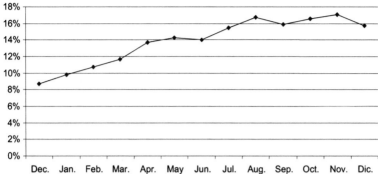

Data source: Banco de México Informe Anual 1995

Other collateral effects of the credit boom were the underpinning of the import boom of consumer goods and the credit expansion to non-banking financial entities (Vega 1999: 239). The support of the import propensity in the productive sectors probably profited from this trend as well. However, lack of disaggregated data in this regard makes the elaboration on this argument unfeasible.

The Mexican Accounting principles enabled the undervaluation of non-performing loans. Credit provisions were not sufficient given the risks caused by the credit multiplication. Credit was given to firms in the non-tradable sector and the incursion in derivatives gave the impression that market risks were non-existent (Vega 1999: 233). Salomon Brothers estimated that the ratio of past due to total loans under US GAAP was approximately 170% of the figure under Mexican GAAP (Federal Reserve Bank of Chicago 1996: 25).

The vulnerability of the commercial bank balance-sheets reached their peak in 1994. The total assets of the commercial banks, including repo operations, amounted almost 70% of the GDP (Sidaoui: 2005). This quasi-unregulated rash expansion of the sector after the privatization implied a large systemic risk in case of difficulties in the financial sector. This proved to be the case after December 1994.

6.4 Factors Related to the Credit Boom

The factors that led to the credit expansion during this period according to Torre (1999: 18) were:

- financial liberalization,
- strengthening of the public finances,
- stabilization of the economy,
- increased expected income and positive economic outlook,
- wealth effect caused by a boom in the sock and real estate markets and

137

- the appreciation of the peso in real terms.

According to Ortiz (1998: x) bank credit increased at a time when supervision was inadequate, despite the efforts made, and that privatized banks had not established internal controls to assign credits prudently. Additionally, the state-owned banks had mainly experience with granting credit to the public sector. Therefore, had not been able to develop effective credit evaluation, market risk or loan performance skills. Furthermore, not only employees were inexperienced in market operations, but management teams in the new privatized banks were as well lacking experience in the branch. In addition, moral hazard increased as a consequence of the increase of unlimited backing of banking liabilities (APEC 2003: 209).

Figure 54 compares risk management performed by state owned and private owned banks. Vega's (1999) conclusions have their fundaments, for the state-controlled period on the First Boston report: "the income earnings of Mexican banks are totally insensitive to changes in interest rates. Average due dates of loans and deposits are less than a month". In the period following privatizations, as expressed by the author, bankers followed a policy dominated by a "negative gap" where their income became very sensitive to interest rate hikes, as it was the case in Dec. 1994.

Figure 54 Risk Management State Owned vs. Private Owned Banks

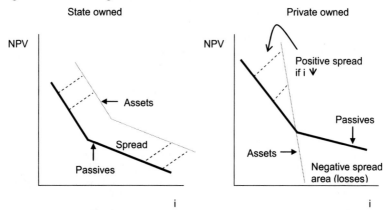

Adapted from: Vega (1999: 233)

The regulations regarding prudential supervision in Mexico are summarized by Lopez (2005). Prior to the crisis (adopted in 1991) they mainly comprised a minimum requirement of 8% of risk capital and a limit to foreign currency liabilities. Related[167] credits had to be capitalized by 100%.

---

167 Credits to shareholders or executives of the bank were limited (see Circular 1186 Comisión Nacional Bancaria y de Valores). According to Barranco (1994) bank leaders exchanged favors regarding related credits to circumvent this rule.

Two additional factors supported the swift credit growth: Credit extended by the development banks, whose operations were not included in the calculation of the public financial deficit and a "strange combinations of operations with derivatives[168] which were not limited and without control of the regulations established by Banxico" (Vega 1999:238).

The "use of synthetic dollars" allowed circumventing the regulations established by Banco de México, since they pertained to passives in foreign currencies (dollars) and a liquidity coefficient for dollar acquisitions. The operations based on Vega (1999: 280) would consist of:

1. The bank would issue obligations in pesos (passive)
2. This amount would be exchanged to U.S. dollars in the spot market (asset)
3. To compensate the long position, the bank sells a U.S. dollar forward (passive) herewith the dollar position is cero.
4. The bank issues a credit to a firm in U.S. dollars (asset).

The outstanding positions would be passives in pesos and assets in U.S. dollars. The profits depend on the forex gains (spot vs. forward), since those must be larger than the difference of interest rates requested (in U.S. dollars) and offered (in pesos).Forward contracts were until the end of 1993 only allowed to banking shareholders that would hold at least 1% of the financial group (Vega 1999: 279). This regulation implied that only "big players" were allowed to speculate in these markets.

In Vega's (1999) view, these types of operations are not pernicious per se, but given the weaknesses of bank supervision, their risk potential was disregarded. The fact that credit was given to firms with mismatches in their balance-sheets was ignored. These types of transactions, complying with the existing regulation[169], started to get into difficulties already in early 1994 as the interest rates hiked (and increased their funding costs). In his opinion, the engagement in this sort of operations magnified the crisis that erupted in 1994. This argument is further analyzed and expanded upon with the scant evidence available in the next chapter.

Poor banking skills, the heritage of the period in public hands, and conflicts of interest played an important role in the bad performance of banks credit in the years preceding the crisis (Sidaoui 2005: 278). The author references the conclusions reached by La Porta et al. (2003). As a result of their research they affirm that:: (1) related-

---

168 Defined by the IMF (Balance of Payments Manual, fifth edition)§:
"A financial derivative contract is a financial instrument that is linked to another specific financial instrument or indicator or commodity and through which specific risks (such as interest rate risk, foreign exchange risk, equity and commodity price risks, credit risk, etc) can be traded in their own right in financial markets. Transactions and positions in financial derivatives are treated separately from the values of any underlying items to which they are linked. Transactions involving financial derivatives may arise at inception, on secondary markets, with ongoing servicing (such as for margin payments), and at settlement."
169 The author presents the example of Banpais, bank intervened in 1995, which used $500 million from a development bank to engage in synthetic operations such as those here described.

lending[170] was a large fraction of banking business; (2) After the crisis, banks in financial distress increased their holdings in related lending loans; (3) related loans were privileged with better terms than unrelated ones; (4) related loans had much higher default rates than unrelated and (5) the worst loans both to individuals and firms were had the closest links to the individuals who controlled the banks.

The domestic financial market was plagued with distortions. Four financial institutions were intervened[171] by the government in 1994 and 1995. Further, Umlauf (1993) reports collusion and asymmetric information by the largest players in T-bill auctions. According to Salomon Brothers, the intermediation margins[172] of Mexican banks were in 1994 the highest of a group of 13 countries[173] and reached up to 8.32% (Gonzalez 1994). The crisis reflects that, as expressed by Mancera (1997: 240), "the Mexican financial system was overwhelmed with the volume of resources –foreign and domestic-that became available as a result of the structural reforms".

After the crisis, the increases in the rates increased defaults and the banks were still engaged in delivering U.S. dollars. According to Sidaoui (2005), the situation was so critic that the first action determined in the bank rescue of 1995 was to provide "emergency loans to the commercial banks". Commercial banks used $3.9 billion of the emergency credit line established by the Central bank, whose peak was reached in April 1995 (Banco de México 1995: 103). In February 1995, as published in Mancera (1997), half of Mexico's banks were not complaining the Basle capital adequacy standards.

A widely critiqued bank rescue package was arranged in 1995. The former president estimated its net value to be 20% of GDP in 1995 and therefore proportionally higher than the U.S. bank intervention (Universal: 2009). Not the nationalization of loses but some kind of punitive action against the private sector would have been appropriate:

> "Deregulation is only effective in increasing efficiency if the reduction in government discipline is replaced by a compensating increase in market discipline. The strongest form of market discipline is potential losses to shareholders, managers and creditors when an institution becomes economical insolvent." (Kaufman 1992: 93)

---

170 Defined by the authors following the definition of article 73 of the Mexican Code of Mercantile Institutions, a related loan is a loan for which the borrower is either: (1) a person or company holding 1% or more of the shares of the bank; (2) family member(s) of the previous group of individuals, related by marriage or blood, up to the second degree; (3) a director, officer, or employee of the borrowing company or of the bank itself with the power to engage into contracts or transactions in the name of the borrowing company or the bank; or (4) a person holding 10% or more of the borrowing company.

171 Their top level directors were imprisoned. A total of eight major financial groups undergo this process until 1998 and charges were filed on 68 directors. Some of the imputations are self-lending and engaging in derivatives and speculation.

172 Defined as the difference between the active (charged on lending) and passive (granted on deposits) interest rates.

173 Including the U.S., Spain, U.K, Chile, Germany, France, Switzerland, Japan, Argentina, Australia, Panama and Canada.

International credit lines were authorized by the IMF and the U.S. government of $40 billion two months after the eruption of the crisis helped to deal with the liquidity bottleneck.

> "Its success can also be seen on how rapidly Mexico recovered its access to the international capital markets and to the fact that the Mexican government fully repaid its loans to the U.S. with several years ahead of schedule" (Lustig 1998: 217)

6.5 Conclusions on the Performance the Banking Sector

The in the early nineties privatized financial sector participants duplicated vicious behaviors and magnified the inherited structural flaws of the previous governmental era. The historical trend towards branch concentration, investments in speculative businesses and inefficient credit allocation practices was accelerated by the private sector in a very scarce regulatory effort to contravene it. This trend seems to be associated, more to the substantial leverage required by domestic groups to finance the buy-out than to a too high price paid as suggested by most literature. Evidence seems to point out that the high-price was to some extent justified by relative healthy balance sheets before the take-over.

A regulatory flaw[174] in the process was to only include domestic investor groups, which neither had a sufficient purchasing power to finance their acquisition without heavily incurring in leveraging nor the required skills. The leveraged purchase forced the newly privatized banks to rashly expand to cover their financial costs. Credit as a percentage of GDP tripled within a six-year presidential term to reach 45% barely in the absence of an adequate regulatory framework.

The credit boom was self-reinforcing as a result of diverse factors: the increased availability of funds, the improved economic perspective, the leveraged buyout of the banks consequentially the need to cover their financial costs, corruption practices and the lack of a solid regulation. After the eruption of the crisis, the banking sector in Mexico was confronted with a doubled amount of non-performing loans within a few months understated by Mexican accounting principles, significant currency mismatches and large passives.

Two unusual factors behind the abrupt credit growth can be highlighted. Related lending was forbidden by regulation, but was relevant in practical terms. Banks exchanged significant fractions of their total credits to their shareholders or executives, which later contributed importantly to the stock of non-performing loans. The second factor refers to the engagement of banks in derivatives and currency mismatches in a lax regulatory framework, which increased the vulnerability of the sector.

The latter has been rarely subject of research, due to the lack of data availability and to a lesser extent, to the continuous emergence of financial crises. Therefore, and

---

174 Probably of politic nature.

because of the significant role they played in the development of the crisis, the use of derivatives by Mexican banks will be elaborated upon in the next chapter.

7 Derivatives and the Role of Synthetic Capital Flows in the Mexican Crisis

Derivatives are financial instruments whose value is derived from the value of some underlying financial instrument or variable. These instruments can serve for hedging purposes by enabling risk-averse parties to transfer risks against a fee. However, derivatives are also associated to perilous outcomes. A major problem of selected derivatives is leveraging, which as evidenced by the Mexican crisis of 1994, can pose systemic risks and have significant effects on the real side of the economy.

The explosive growth of the international derivatives market after 1987 was not matched by a parallel development of an adequate regulatory framework. A specific occurrence evidenced this flaw in Mexico, partially induced by a bank re-privatization process restricted to domestic investors. Considerable amounts of derivative-related, here termed "synthetic capital inflows"[175], poured into the country. In this sense, large amounts of capital flowed into the country and shifted a manageable current account deficit to unsustainable levels. As a result of the confluence of massive capital availability and the weaknesses of domestic banks, credit allocation expanded rash and inefficiently. A financial crisis was triggered in late 1994 by capital flight, an outcome of a sudden devaluation of a moderately overvalued peso.

The interrelation of OTC derivatives and financial crises was a scarcely explored field of study before 2008. This fact is probably linked to the quality and lack of data availability[176], especially regarding the Mexican crisis of 1994. This chapter re-examines the role played by the private and public financial institutions based on their derivatives operations and regulation in the light of the new evidence created by the global financial crisis of 2008-2009.

Many regulatory gaps were closed after the eruption of the global crisis. Nevertheless, structural reforms of the financial system were avoided. It seems that the incentives, market structures, international networking and regulatory framework that predominated until 2008 have not allowed the private gains to offset the public losses. Rather, massive OTC derivative use drove the world economy to a critical global crisis. A challenge in the design of a new financial architecture is to implement a far-reaching reform and take account of the international experiences in this regard.

The misuse of derivatives by domestic financial groups and their contribution to the Mexican crisis is explored in this last chapter. This section is organized as follows. First, a compact literature review on early contributions regarding the awareness of potential risks of derivatives and the unavailability of data introduce the topic. Afterwards, different aspects related to the derivative trading by Mexican financial groups,

---

175 In this thesis, international capital flows that are a mere effect of derivative trading are labelled as: "synthetic capital flows". This specific term seems to have been previously used in the literature only by Yam (1999) for Hong Kong, former Chief Executive of the Hong Kong Monetary Authority.

176 Probably associated to the lack of a competitive market (supply-side) in economic terms. Rudek (2009) points out that the lack of comprehensive statistics is still a current matter of concern: "the demand for them (central banks and the BIS) to produce additional data has increased, motivated by a variety of expectations. However, there is no single type of derivatives statistics that can serve all purposes."

such as regulatory issues, a description of the most relevant types used before the crisis and their magnitude are presented. Subsequently some of the scarce evidence indicating the existence and accuracy of the existing estimations is presented. This section precedes a critical analysis of the role played by derivatives in the unwinding of the crisis and the policy reforms. The last section draws conclusions.

7.1 Literature Review on Potential Effects of Derivatives: Stand of Awareness in the Early Nineties

In December 1994, the Bank of International Settlements BIS (1994b) released its first conceptional publication related exclusively to derivatives and their potential risks. This fact reflects the deficiencies regarding prudential regulation[177] and transparency that prevailed in the early nineties. Considering the growth of derivative trading in the markets since 1987[178] it can be safely stated that international and domestic institutions were far behind the developments of the markets.

The first available statistics on open derivatives positions in the global over the counter (OTC) derivatives markets were published by the BIS in 1996. Sarialoglu-Hayali (2007:4) confirms the lack of over the counter (OTC) derivatives data for emerging markets during the decade. The IMF (2002) reports that analysis was "seriously hampered by data availability". The fund explicitly affirms that anecdotal evidence and ex-post reports on losses by the main financial institutions of developed countries are the key elements to obtain related information.

Despite the fact that data availability was very restricted in the early nineties, reiterated concerns regarding the destabilizing potential of financial derivatives were expressed both in Europe and the U.S. This section, far from being exhaustive, exemplifies some of those publications and shows that the subject was discussed by both academics and international institutions:

> "Even though the gains and losses of the counterparties in a financial derivative transaction constitute a zero sum pecuniary redistribution, the unbundling and trading of elemental risks components and the heterogeneity of derivatives' users imply that real aggregate effects may follow from their introduction." (BIS 1994 b)

Up to 1993 derivatives and their embedded risks were seldom a subject of research. Regulators were, as expressed by Steinherr (1998), "a large step behind the evolution of derivative markets". The rather conservative German Saving and Loans Organisation (Sparkassenorganisation e.V) and the Association of Public Banks also expressed their concern that the aggregate effects of derivatives were still, as of the early nineties, seldom a subject of research (Schober/Störmann 1995: 81).

---

177 Which remained until 2008. Currently (2010) discussions on a "New Financial Architecture" is being discussed in multiple fora.

178 Arnoldi (2004) presents information regarding OTC derivative trading. In mid-1994 the notional value of the open transaction was around $1 trillion.

Yam (1999) expressed to this regard: "The inadequate data on OTC[179] markets make it difficult to understand the nature of capital flows, their movements or their impact on financial markets and the real economy" (1999: 166).

Harberger (1987) reports that the bankruptcy of the largest sugar company in Chile, CRAV, a result of over-borrowing in the domestic market and futures on sugar, detonated the Chilean twin crisis of 1982. It seems that this transaction is the first derivative-leverage-systemic-risk-crisis connection. However, capital inflows in this case, were according to Harberger (1987) rather related to "complacency" foreign lending to domestic banks.

Großmann (1990) analyzed the effects and types of securitization available by the late eighties. He described different types of risk transfer, including interest rate risks. This type of risks, exemplified by the financing of fixed-rate loans with variable rate investments can be traded away through active or passive interest rate swaps. Even exposure to losses can be avoided in the own accounts by banks if the loans are transferred to third parties or if the securities are sold by the first signs of deterioration. According to the author, the risks transfer gives "a sense of safety". This might lead to an increase the readiness to assume risks of banks. Additionally, the strict requirements adopted to allocate credit are not applied by the securitization because the credit risks can be transferred in the secondary market[180]. Securitization leads in general to banks being exposed mainly to market-risk instead of to credit risks (Großmann 1990: 269 ff).

The increase of the systemic risk in the financial system is another aspect foreseen in Großmann (1990). The expansion of risk taking of single market operators augments systemic risk (Blohm 1985). "Innovative techniques namely cannot eliminate risks, but rather distribute them and therefore (cannot) safeguard the system" (Großmann 1990:271 ref. Delamaide 1985 & Fidler 1987a). He concludes that the risks derived of the intensive use of the innovative financial techniques were still difficult to estimate.

Up to the Mexican Crisis of 1994-1995, there were only isolated reports of "spectacular losses" associated to the rash growth of derivatives. At most, these reports caused turbulence in the international capital and forex markets. Systemic risks had not arisen, but "this was no reason not to worry" (Schober/Störmann 1995: 81). The main problems were not speculation or misjudgement, which in their view have been always existent in the branch. Rather, the problematic lies on the possibility of leveraging to hedge and reallocating risks, out of the proportion of the own capital needs, which create a dangerous volume of traded securities.

Schober/Störmann (1995) describe the market structure prevailing in the derivative markets at the end of 1993. The authors and Angell (1992) report a high concentration at international level in the financial centres and a relatively low number of investment bankers. Edwards and Patricks (1992:8) consider the U.S. financial prod-

---

179 Over the Counter (OTC) derivative are privately traded and negotiated contracts between the counterparties. Given their flexibility and their operation mechanics, problems with disclosure and regulation compliance are more likely to arise than in a standardized market.
180 Großmann (1990) references Fidler (1987).

ucts market to lack competition. These market structures[181] translate in a low level of transparency.

According to Schober/Störmann (1995) systemic risks[182] were clearly in sight given the lack of information on the type, scope and associated risks of derivative deals. The authors[183] pleaded for the enlargement and standardization of OTC derivatives markets to both increase transparency and to maintain the stability of the aggregate financial system. Likewise, other authors, such as Folkerts-Landau and Steinherr (1994) made early suggestions in this direction.

Other dangers associated to derivatives are that they are so varied and some even so "esoteric" and complex that even the most sophisticated investors are not fully aware of their embedded risks. "Some of these instruments appear to be specifically designed to enable institutional investors to take gambles which they would otherwise not permitted to take" (Soros 1995 referenced in Steinherr 1998:75).

Angell (1992) suggested the possibility of a systemic crisis based on the interdependence among national financial markets. The origin of an initial price collapse of such an episode would be exogenous; however, these conditions might spill to the cash market. A liquidity crunch would mean that central banks must intervene to improve liquidity into the system, act as a lender of last resort and eventually rescue the banking sector. In his view, authorities should look for fragilities of this type, such as leveraged buy-outs, as a "ready-made current example".

As for public policy, Kaufmann (1992) stated that the challenge for the 90`s and beyond were straightforward. In his view, the challenge was to redesign the U.S. banking system to make it more competitive and safe to avoid from penalties on tax payers in terms of transfers or economic disturbances.

The Basle Committee on Banking Supervision and IOSCO (1995) further advised that trading activities, involving derivatives and on-balance-sheet instruments, had increased rashly in a short period of time. For many large dealer banks, these transactions have been major sources of earnings. "For many of these institutions, notional amounts of off-balance-sheet derivatives transactions now often exceed on-balance-sheet positions by a multiple". In their view, these activities implied risks analogous to traditional banking operations but their expansion and complexity involved new challenges for banks and securities firms.

---

181 Herz'(1987) opinion is that securities are „experience goods" in which banks with an ample reputation and trust have an advantage in their development. Additionally, the author eludes legal barriers to "financial imitators" and start ups in the financial sectors which support market concentration.

182 To control systemic risks stemming from the U.S. banking system, Kane (1992) considered some untypical factors:
"it is necessary to recognize that relative to periods longer than congressional and presidential electoral cycles, crisis pressures are being made worse by short sighted efforts of officials in individual countries to preserve undercapitalized and technologically outmoded competitors and regulatory systems." (Kane 1992: 263-264).

183 In line with the publication: Bilanzunwirksame Geschäfte deutscher Banken in: Deutsche Bundesbank, Monatsbericht 10, 1993.

Research on the effects of derivatives on monetary policy was published in the early nineties[184] (Schober/Störmann 1995: 89). The authors reference the Deutsche Bundesbank (1994) to affirm that the direction and scope of the effects of derivatives to the real sector and the development of inflation is difficult to determine. If the aggregate demand shifts more than the aggregate supply, inflationary pressure arises, which in their view is no reason to be alarmed since it a single (not a process) adjustment. However, already in that period as their essay confirms, there was concern about the changes in interest rates in the presence of a large volume of securities. In their view, the consequences of monetary impulses were difficult to estimate a priori.

Less consensus prevailed on the effectiveness of the interventions by the central banks and the influence of derivatives, as expressed by Schober/Störmann (1995). However as the authors point out, their potential was not completely ignored: "certain derivatives will primarily influence the pace at which pressure on a currency can be observed." Glaessner/Oks (1994) warned about the potential risks and suggested the development of a domestic derivative trading agency.

As a conclusion it can be safely stated that although the potential risks of derivatives were only partially foreseeable before the crisis, there were diverse voices raised all over the world to advice caution. However, Mexican banks were able to engage undisturbed massively in derivatives, overlooking some of the here reviewed dangers, as it will be elaborated upon in the next sections.

7.2 Derivative Handling between Mexican and U.S. Investment Banks in the Mexican Crisis of 1994

7.2.1 Early use of Derivatives in Mexico

Already in the late eighties and early nineties, "state bankers" jointly with foreign investment bankers performed non-traditional financial operations. Futures, forwards and options on the peso and metals were traded previous to the bank privatization. Until 1991, as described by Vega (1999:229), banks took credit in U.S. dollars at LIBOR and invested in CETES, with a spread of 400 basis points. These proceedings continued until Banco de México extended a regulation in 1991 that established that bank's foreign liabilities could not exceed 10% of total passives.

Coberturas cambiarias or foreign exchange forwards[185] and futures[186], introduced in Mexico in 1987, were the most traditional derivatives. These operations became especially interesting for financial institutions after the introduction of the peg. In the

---

184 The author references the monthly report (Monatsbericht) of the Deutsche Bundesbank of November 1994 and the BIS Hanoun-Report of 1994, which both deal with this topic.

185 Up to 1993 peso forward transactions were only allowed to shareholders of the financial groups holding at least 1% of the holding (Vega 1999: 279). In August 1995, Banco de México introduced regulations that imposed risk-management and responsibility of the board of directors to act according an "ethical code" in the forex future and options markets (http://www.iiec.unam.mx/ Boletin_electronico/1995/num08/finanzas.html).

186 Futures and Forwards are derivatives which establish the purchase or sale of an asset at a previously specified price. Futures are standardized contracts which can be traded and forward is a non-standardized contract.

absence of large volatility in the exchange market, cobertura suppliers were likely to retain the paid fees. Foreign exchange forwards[187], based on the expectation that the exchange rate would stay fixed, became an important source of revenue for the banks and financial intermediaries. Capital market brokerage operators, which have been private ever since, were also involved in these transactions[188] (Vega 1999:299). Garcia (1993) rated the market as "lacking experience and expertise" and overfilled with brokers and individuals which used credit lines to operate. The underlying risks were associated to the potential pro-cyclical activities in case of exchange rate volatility, which might worsen the conditions in an already unstable market.

In 1992, policy makers raised the 10% foreign currency-peso liability ratio of banks to 20%. Of the additional 10 %, four percent had to be channelled to importers or exporters of goods. Glaesner/Oks (1994) consider the impact on this increase very limited in view of the fact that most of the large banks were holding foreign currency-peso liability ratios of more than 20%. However, this did support smaller banks to expand their foreign borrowing. Additionally, this policy might have increased their availability to extend foreign-denominated credits not only to exporters, but also to importers.

Vega (1999) describes different off-balance transactions performed by financial intermediaries and reports that this type of practices was common already in the eighties (prior to the bank privatization). Other types of derivatives such as future gold loans and flexible forwards (options) were operated[189] by major banks Banamex and Cremi already before they were privatized (Vega 1999: 231).

Garcia (1993) reports that in November 1993 derivatives concerning Cetes, Bondes and Ajustabonos[190] were due and subject to renewal. The operations, made by the three largest banks and a brokerage house, represented a significant currency mismatch. This development caused nervousness in the foreign exchange market, as suggested by the author. Conservative calculations valued them in $4 billion.

Vega (1999) refers to a "mini" crisis related to Ajustabonos[191] in 1991-1992. Reference to Ajustabono repurchase (repo[192]) operations, which supports the author's in-

---

187 Vega (1999) affirms that alone one operator, called the "forward king", had short dollar forward positions of over $1 billion. Garcia (1993) refers to a similar number in 1994 and reveals his identity: Hector Gómez. These transactions were leveraged according to the latter by a Bank Group Cremi-Union that was already intervened a few months before the eruption of the crisis. Mr. Gómez was imprisoned with fraud charges as of 1996.

188 According to Vega (1999), operating a stock exchange/financial broker was a way to compensate former bankers for the nationalization of the banks. They were until the crisis the only financial operators allowed to bid on Cetes (main government bond type).

189 The author describes an informal "back office" in charge of off-record transactions, which was ignored by the monetary authorities.

190 Cetes, Bondes and Ajustabonos are Mexican government securities.

191 Ajustabonos were inflation-indexed three year government bonds. During the high inflation period, their yield was very high and leveraged buys were profitable. However, as inflation and active interest rates decreased and passive rates remained the same, several banks ran into trouble.

192 Repo operations are defined as the operation through which a "repurchaser" acquires securities, receives a credit from the "reporter" and commits to transfer the property of the securities to a "reporter". Finally, the securities are repurchased after a specific period against the original price

formation, is found in the regulation of financial institutions effective in 1994 (art. M42.62[193] and M83.22.[194]). The problematic started in 1991, as the leveraged positions in Ajustabonos emanated losses. Feliz/Welch (1993) consider this situation as an additional factor to exchange rate volatility. The authors estimated the losses related to the Ajustabono operations of 1992 to be $1 billion U.S. dollars. The Mexican Central Bank swaped Ajustabonos with a 3.5% yearly rate against 17% rate and absorbed the losses. Some conflicting effects of this financial distress were summarized by the authors:

> "the maneuver created turmoil because the other banks demanded equal treatment. The problems ultimately led to the relaxation of the restrictions on foreign borrowing by Mexican banks and the problems seem to have abated for now." (Feliz/Welch 1993: 6)

The central bank increasingly sent the signal that it was willing to witness significant financial losses as seen in the Ajustabonos episode (Glaessner/Oks 1994). Banco Mercantil Probursa determined in the third quarter of 1994 a 7% worker layoff and losses[195] on Ajustabonos junior notes (Rivera 1994). Other Ajustabono-holders recurred to other OTC derivatives, such as the structured notes described by Partnoy (1997) and those described by the history of Weston Group.[196]

As suggested by this section, Mexican banks had engaged in risky derivative operations already in their governmental period. However, until 1993 they did not pose systemic challenges. Further, the monetary authorities might have encouraged derivative trading by indicating their willingness to absorb losses and act as a lender of last resort.

7.2.2 Selected Regulatory Issues

This section concentrates on a revision of the regulation ruling banks and financial institutions in 1994. Selected extracts are presented and reviewed. The here performed assessment of the effective regulatory framework indicates that this regulation[197] introduced important concepts[198]; however, it was still vague and had significant loopholes that paved the way for massive engagement in derivatives in 1994.

---

plus a premium. Based on art. 259 of the General Law of Securities and Credit Operations. Available at: (http://www.banxico.org.mx/tipo/disposiciones/OtrasDisposiciones/Reglas-reporto.html).

193 Available at: http://www.banxico.org.mx/sistemafinanciero/disposiciones/circularesAbrogadas/200894/Circular%202008-94.-%20M-4.pdf

194 Available at: http://www.banxico.org.mx/sistemafinanciero/disposiciones/circularesAbrogadas/2008-94/Circular%202008-94.-%20M-8.pdf

195 These losses represent 90% of net profits of the financial group in ¾ of a year. This change represents a decrease of over 85% in their profits compared to the prior year. It is important to note that actually only the marginal widening of the band caused these exchange rate based losses.

196 Banco Nacional de Mexico (Banamex) S.A US$ 185 million underwrote and placed the first fixed rate Mexican peso denominated notes with a maturity greater than one year (1993) (http://www.westonfinancial.com/history_underwriting.html).

197 Published in February 1994 and effective in March 1st, is available at: http://www.banxico.org.mx/sistemafinanciero/disposiciones/circularesAbrogadas/2008-94/Circular%202008-94.-%20M-6.pdf

The prudential regulations were very limited until 1994[199]. Vega (1999:231) reports that the regulating agencies ignored forward and future operations and what he calls "synthetic dollars". The (20)2008-1994 circular, which included subordinated obligations, repo operations, futures and forwards, limited foreign liabilities of banks. However, it specifically excluded the passives held by securities brokers and other financial institutions (art. M.13.2). In general, financial groups owned securities brokers and meant de facto a possibility to circumvent this directive.

Probably historically based, coberturas or currency forward operations were relatively strictly regulated in section M.53. A less astringent regime evidences the involvement of financial institutions in Ajustabonos repos. According to this regulation, these organizations were allowed to progressively decrease their obligations to comply with the foreign liability limits.

Repo operations were also regulated through this decree. According to this guideline: Institutions should reframe from: "performing these operations (repos) in conditions and terms contrary to the general policy of the institutions and healthy practices and uses of the market" (art. M41.12.3.). A further vaguely formulated article forbids repo operations that foresee the anticipated payment of passives by credit institutions (M 41.8).

Section M.6 regulated foreign currency positions based on the difference of assets and passives. Banxico established that either short or long[200] positions were accepted. However, they should not exceed 15% of the capital and should include the transactions covered by firms both foreign and domestic that exceed a 50% stock holding. Further, it established which passives and assets should be included to compute the foreign exchange exposure. Among them were:

- Tesobonos
- Tesobono repos[201]
- Forex forwards and futures
- Operations with precious metals
- Other similar passives and assets

However, securities brokers and other financial institutions were again excluded from this regulation (M.64) leaving plenty of room for handling.

---

198 Based on a public statement of the central bank director, Miguel Mancera, Quintana (1994) reports that the head of the central bank repudiated derivatives and perceived a trend towards mishandling and imprudent use in the absence of a regulation. Mancera announced therefore, that their development path in Mexico should follow slow and based on deep reflected decisions. Garcia (1994) reports the discontentment by U.S. financial firms regarding his vigilant and prudent approach towards derivatives stated in March 1994.

199 Banco de México (1994) introduced, for example, regulations regarding repo operations performed by brokerage houses in 1994 and leverage transactions involving a foreign financial firm were regulated in Nov. 1994. The limit for the repo operations should not exceed 25 times their capital if they engage in repurchase (repo) operations.

200 A long position is related to the purchase or ownership of a currency or asset and a short position to sale of a borrowed currency or asset with a repurchase intention (extracted from http://www.investopedia.com).

201 Swaps would not fall into this category.

The prudential regulation scheme that started to get implemented in the previous months of the crisis was enhanced only ex-post. Several financial reforms, compiled by (Sidaoui 2005), were implemented only after 1995 to promote market discipline:

i) Establishment of a limit to deposit protection insurance;
ii) Disclosure requirements were increased to enhance market discipline;
iii) Establishment of credit bureaus;
iv) Introduction of capital adequacy rules;
v) Elimination of limits to foreign ownership (recapitalization);
v) Adoption of international accounting standards;
vi) Prudential regulation regarding derivatives[202];
vii) Corporate governance; and,
viii) Creation of risk management units

As seen in this section, decisive but insufficient steps towards a tighter regulation were undertaken in 1994. However, these efforts focused on the creation of a strict regulation to deal with the evident foreign exchange problematic. Regulatory loopholes and the complex ownership and risk schemes of derivatives enabled domestic banks to massively engage in derivatives markets. However, the attempt to regulate proves both the information stand and the resulting concern of the authorities. Their efforts were not sufficient to contain the large and hazardous level of derivative operations that led to the 1994 crisis. The next section deals with this subject and with operative details on this engagement.

7.2.3 Financial Institutions and Derivative Operations in 1994

As previously discussed, most Mexican financial groups followed an aggressive expansion pattern[203] based on credit assignment and an increase of foreign liabilities in 1993 and 1994. As of the beginning of 1994: "the dollar exposures of Mexican banks will have to be watched" (Glaesner/Oks 1994: 36).

Foreign liabilities of non-bank financial institutions almost doubled from 1992 to 1994 (Figure 55). Those of banks also increased, however their growth was limited, as discussed in 7.2.2, by the available regulation that capped their ability to acquire passives in foreign currency. After liberalization, the creation of financial groups comprising diverse types of financial institutions under a corporate unit was the rule in the branch. Therefore, while the regulation for banks limited their foreign liabilities, this could be circumvented by diverting operations to other non-regulated areas of the financial conglomerate, such as securities brokers.

---

202 See for example, the Anexo 9, Circular 2019/85 Banco de México.
203 Some of the causes behind this behavior were various, according to Torre (1993). Lack of experience of bureaucrats in project valuation, the new owners were mainly non-bankers, deficits in legal and judicial systems, moral hazard induced by self-selection (perverse incentives to assign credits to risky projects in the presence of a bad loan fund) are among them. Specifically related to supervision and regulation deficits the author elaborates on the following: legal reforms from 1989/90, which were not able to stop growth of NPL's, the lack of resources of the Regulating Agency (CNBV), the absence of credit bureaus and standardized credit requirements and the use of local accounting standards (which underestimated the amount of NPLs).

Figure 55 Assets and Liabilities of Banks and Other Financial Institutions

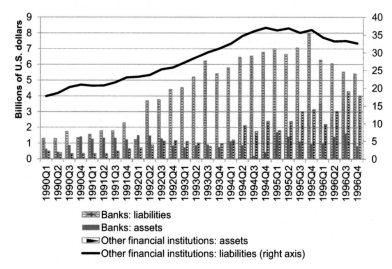

Banks: liabilities
Banks: assets
Other financial institutions: assets
Other financial institutions: liabilities (right axis)

Data source: IMF Financial Statistics

In fact, banks were mainly repurchased by securities brokers[204], which were not affected by the 1982 nationalization of the banks (Vega 1999). The disincorporation process is behind the rash development of the external liabilities of non-bank financial institutions. The leveraged purchase of the banks forced financial groups to pursue a hard business line. [205]

Garber (1998) affirms that even in the absence of currency forward speculation, "Other derivative products may be present in sufficient quantities to affect the dynamics of a crisis. The Mexican peso crisis is such a case." In his view, the derivative positions related to the crisis were taken by a weak banking system "hungry for current income". The bank privatizations had been financed the aggregate $12 billion price through leverage and the purchasers were forced to repay their interest.[206].

---

204 Twelve out of eighteen privatized banks ended up owned by brokerage houses. Their market participation, calculated based on their 1991 assets, was according to Vega (1999) 62%. This indicates the preponderance of financial groups owned by an existing brokerage house.

205 Interestingly, the on-sheet increase of the aggregate liabilities of the non-bank financial institutions between the conclusion of the legal bank privatization process and the eruption of the crisis (ten quarters of a year) is based on IMF data $16.3 billion, matching the amount calculated by Garber (1998, $16.1 billion U.S. dollars) of Tesobono swap liabilities.

206 The authors' rationale behind the increasing credit and market risk taking was confirmed by an industry source, a former executive for Latin America of a major N.Y. based investment bank.

In the literature there is only one source that specifically estimates and describes the use of derivatives[207] by Mexican banks in the previous months of the 1994 crisis. Garber (1998, 2000), referencing information of the IMF and the financial industry[208] in diverse publications describes different types of OTC derivative products which were used by Mexican banks before the crisis.

Garber (1998) describes operations with derivatives[209] such as Tesobono swaps and repos, equity swaps and structured notes, which played an important role in the Mexican Crisis. These instruments, according to the author, share some common characteristics:

- Only a small fraction, if at all, is reflected in the capital account of the balance of payments.
- Can be constructed in a way that they evade prudential regulations.
- Can drive the dynamics of currency volatility due to the leveraged offered.
- Apparent risk positions can be misleading and can enhance market risks.

7.2.4 Selected Types Derivative Operations

In this section only[210] single currency swaps, Tesobono swaps and the nearly equivalent repos, will be described based on the information gathered by Garber (1998). The decision is based on two grounds: first, because they all share common features and second, since the operations of this type display the most straightforward effect to the crisis. Recall that Tesobono dollar liabilities (Figure 42) were behind Mexico's illiquidity problems in early 1995.

Tesobono swaps were a variety of single-currency interest rate swaps. The latter involve the exchange of fixed-rate securities against floating rate ones, without incurring in exchange rate risk. Based on Garber's (1998) information, Tesobono swaps, off-shore transactions between foreign investment bankers and domestic banks, were the most substantial type before the Mexican crisis of 1994. The typical transaction involved the domestic bank financing their fixed-yield Tesobono purchases through a credit based on a variable rate LIBOR plus a margin.

The mechanisms of the Tesobono swaps can be analyzed by first scrutinizing the virtually comparable, simpler operation called Tesobono repo. A Tesobono repo implied the following transaction: After the deposit of a margin by the Mexican institution, a large U.S. investment firm would lend dollars for a year against a Tesobono

---

207 To circumvent the regulation established in 1992 regarding a ceiling to foreign currency denominated liabilities of commercial banks.
208 The sources of the information were interviews held with banking executives.
209 Single currency interest rate swaps. For a full description on these types of instruments, also massively used in other developing countries, see Garber (1998), (2000), Garber/Lall (1996).
210 Other derivatives, such as equity swaps functioned in a similar way as Tesobono swaps, but they used the total return on the recently privatized Teléfonos de México (Telmex) as the object to swap. The equity risk would be held by Mexican banks and investment bankers would function as lenders of foreign currency at LIBOR + 3%, as exemplified by Garber (1998).

collateral and the promise to repurchase (repo) at the original price plus an interest rate.

Figure 56 shows diagrammatically an example of the Tesobono repo deal. In this example, the Mexican bank financed Tesobonos worth $1 bn. U.S. dollars by borrowing $800 million from U.S. investment bankers, which themselves borrowed at LIBOR. Mexican banks had to disburse 20% of the total. As an exchange, the domestic banks borrowed 80% at LIBOR plus 100 points. The economic incentive for the Mexican banks was, in the first months of 1994, that they received fixed Tesobono yields equivalent to LIBOR plus ca. 300 points on 100% of the notional amount. Investment bankers obtained LIBOR plus 100 points while borrowing themselves at LIBOR. The official data on Tesobonos holdings would only show foreign investment on this type of bonds, since these were acquired through off-shore offices of Mexican banks in order to circumvent the existing regulation.

A Tesobono swap has a similar risk structure for both participants as the repo transaction (Figure 57). In this example, the U.S. investment banking firms swaps Tesobono yields (notional value = 100%) against LIBOR plus 100 points. The Mexican bank must deposit 20% as collateral to guarantee the fulfillment of the contract. To hedge, the U.S. firm acquires itself Tesobonos, on the notional, total value, borrowing 80% at LIBOR and using the collateral. The balance of payments registers a capital outflows performed by the Mexican bank of 20% (collateral) and a foreign capital inflow on the remaining 80%. However, this capital inflow is only a result of the derivative transaction. The differential on interest rates is held by the Mexican financial institution and Mexico as a country borrows to finance its capital inflow.

Figure 56 Derivative Transaction: Tesobono Repo

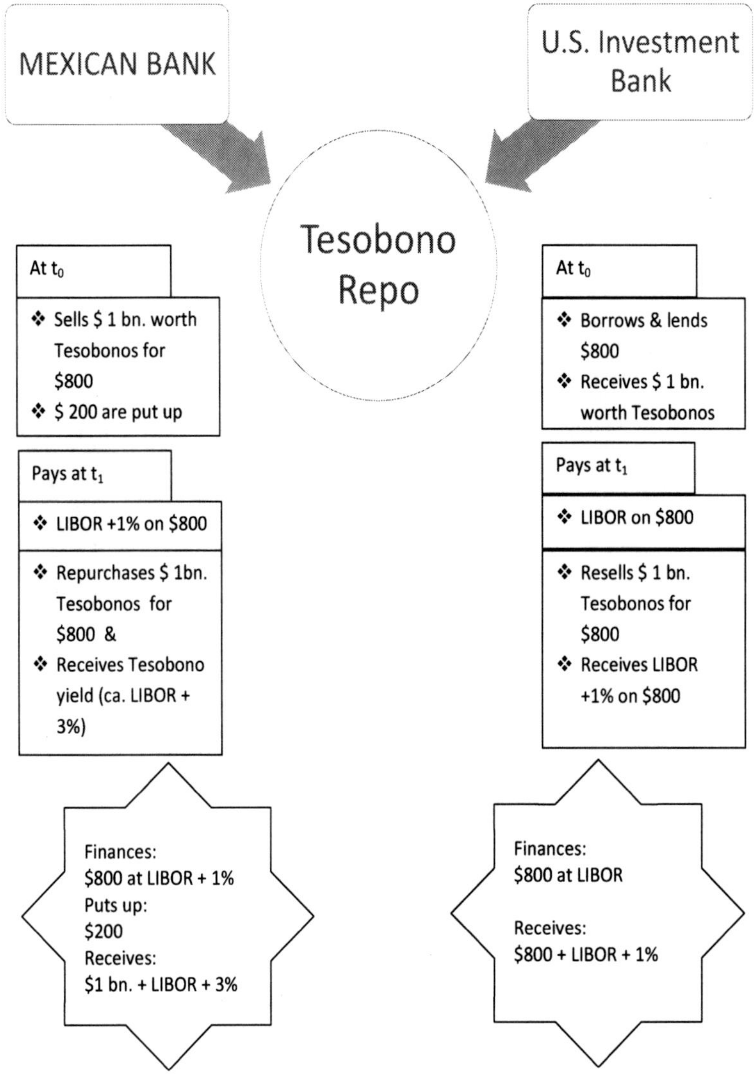

MEXICAN BANK

U.S. Investment Bank

Tesobono Repo

At t_0
- Sells $ 1 bn. worth Tesobonos for $800
- $ 200 are put up

Pays at t_1
- LIBOR +1% on $800

- Repurchases $ 1bn. Tesobonos for $800 &
- Receives Tesobono yield (ca. LIBOR + 3%)

At t_0
- Borrows & lends $800
- Receives $ 1 bn. worth Tesobonos

Pays at t_1
- LIBOR on $800

- Resells $ 1 bn. Tesobonos for $800
- Receives LIBOR +1% on $800

Finances:
$800 at LIBOR + 1%
Puts up:
$200
Receives:
$1 bn. + LIBOR + 3%

Finances:
$800 at LIBOR

Receives:
$800 + LIBOR + 1%

Data source: Garber (1998)/ author's own illustration

Figure 57 Derivative Transaction: Tesobono Swap

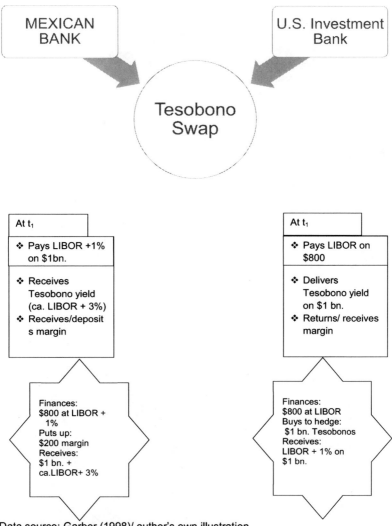

Data source: Garber (1998)/ author's own illustration

These types of operations were performed within the regulatory framework. They offered both financial parties advantageous conditions given the willingness of the authorities to retain capitals in 1994 at the cost of currency mismatch. The seriousness of the derivative problematic was linked to the extent to which these operations were performed and their interrelation to the real side of the economy. Per definition a capital account surplus finances a deficit in the current account, mainly associated to negative net exports. Therefore, if derivatives magnify capital inflows, a larger current account deficit can be financed through very liquid, often leveraged funds. This dynamics represent the main menace for the economy.

7.2.5 Magnitude of Derivatives Use and Conditions in 1994

Official statistics on derivative operations of Mexican banks did not exist in 1994. Garber (1998) was the first academic to quantify, based on industry sources, the engagement of Mexican banks in derivatives. According to his estimations, Tesobono swaps amounting $16 billion were open previous to the December 20th devaluation. Garber's work is extended in this section by placing his estimation in the Mexican context in 1994 and by searching for more evidence in the following.

Official statistics Tesobonos reflect their drastic increase in demand, as a result of political turmoil in the first trimester of 1994 (Figure 42). The chart also depicts the continuous losses of central bank reserves. Tesobonos, as opposed to regular Federal Treasury Bonds (Cetes) eliminated currency risk. In January 1994, only 3% of the total government debt instruments were dollar-linked Tesobonos. However, ten months later, this figure jumped to 40% (Table 29)[211].

Before the eruption of the crisis, $29 billion Tesobonos were outstanding (see Table 29). Foreign residents owned Tesobonos worth $16.3 billion according to Banco de México (Informe Anual 1995). The central bank reserves in 1994 fluctuated from $29 to $5 billion before the freeing of the peso in December 1994.

Alone the by Garber (1998) estimated Tesobono swap-related capital inflows, $16 billion, financed over half of the unsustainable imbalances in the real sector. These "synthetic capital inflows" represented 57% of the high current account deficit (7.7% of GDP) of 1994. The existence of Tesobono-linked "synthetic capital inflows" worsened Mexico's financial position at the end of 1994. The country was confronted with an alleged short-term illiquidity, which fostered capital flight. In their absence, the current account deficit would have been less than 4% of GDP, an evidently more manageable deficit.

The rationale behind policy makers to supply such a large quantity of short-term dollar denominated Tesobonos is questionable. This strategy appears as a capital policy error and was taken advantage of by domestic and foreign bankers. This constellation proved costly for the central bank and for country. As Table 29 evidences, Banxico had to heavily intervene and repurchase foreign passives of domestic banks in 1995.

---

211 Recall that Mexico was the second largest recipient (developing countries) of private capital inflows worldwide in 1994 (Table 13). Most of the capital flowed into government bonds (see section 5.1.3.)

Table 29 Selected Financial Indicators and the Current Account

in U.S. billions if not otherwise stated

Concept :	1993	1994	1995
Current Account Deficit / + Surplus			
In U.S. billions	-23.4	-28.8	+.6
As a percentage of GDP´	-6.5%	-7.7%	+.1%
Foreign portfolio investment	28.9	20.2/8.2"	-10.4
Open Tesobono positions		29.2	.3
Banxico Tesobono repurchase (from domestic banks*)			-5
Banxico's amortization of foreign passives by (commercial banks) of which:			-4.2
Interbank payments			-1.9
Other passives			-2.3

Data source: Informe Anual 1995 Banco de México and IMF Financial Statistics
´ As a percentage of GDP excluding devaluatory effects
* Through credit swaps with the Banco de México
"After capital flight

7.2.6 Evidence Supporting the Magnitude and Existence of Derivative Trading

Selected sources, scarce but existent, found by the author of this thesis suggest that Garber's (1998) arguments are correct. This section attempts to gather information to corroborate the author's primary information. Most of the available literature assumes its correctness based on the lack of identified official information sources. The here performed search suggests three assertions: first, the short-supply and the dispersion of the information, second, the large extent of the derivative trading in 1994. Finally, Garber's (1998) estimations are corroborated with official information.

In its first Annual Report after the crisis (published in 1995), the Central bank refers to several factors complicating the possibility of sustaining the peg. One of those is:

"the ease to leverage in positions in different currencies through derivatives operations and the leveraging opportunities offered by external financial intermediaries" (Informe Anual 1994: 62).

Additionally, the central bank refers to a small group of banks that were operating with intense problems not revealed in their financial information; actually, in some cases with operations out of the existent regulation and prudential bank practices (Banco de México 1995: 97). Mancera (1997) refers to "some[212] commercial banks operating with serious problems that were not noticeable from the information disclosed to financial authorities".

---

212 Vega (1999: 601) describes the treasury of Banpaís bank as being leader of innovative products such as derivatives, inverse derivatives, forwards, junk bonds, financial and exchange swaps.

158

Moreover, a detailed analysis of various issues of the Annual Reports of Banco de México yielded a significant and specific piece of evidence to support Garber's (1998) work. In the Statistical Annex[213] of the Annual Report 1999, Banco de México used a revised methodology of resources and obligations of the financial system and the tenure of government bonds by different sectors. The in year 2000 released data is probably the only source of official information in this regard.

Table 30 Government Bonds and Financial Sector Repos

in millions of pesos

	Total Gov. Bonds (outstanding)	Repos	% of Repos of total bonds*	Repos as % of GDP*
1991	171,654	4,193	2.4%	0.44 %
1992	134,755	5,225	3.8%	0.46%
1993	138,318	8,286	6.0%	0.66%
1994	228,885⁺	69,910	30.5 %	4.90 %
1995	136,000	0	0%	0%
1996	161,572	0	0%	0%

Data source: Banco de México (Informe Anual 1999: 208 and 163, 164) and
*author's own calculations
⁺ 55.2% were Tesobonos

Table 30 shows how the repos of the private financial sector had a sudden increase in 1994 to reach 30% of the total public government debt. Consider Tesobonos alone, which for the end of 1994 represented 55.2% of the total public bonds. Total repos by the financial system correspond to 55% of the $29 billion outstanding Tesobonos. This estimation represents almost one third of all outstanding government bonds. Recall that Mexico was in the world in that period the main recipient of portfolio inflows, mainly government bonds. As a result and calculated based on the official data, repos amounting $16 billion were held by the financial sector. The here performed assessment of the official data indicates that Garber's estimations based on industry sources were both accurate and correct. In 1994 repo operations amounted a remarkable 4.9% of GDP.

7.3 Effects of Derivatives and their Contribution to the Crisis Dynamics

Both Garber's (1998) primary information and the last sections seem to provide enough evidence to suggest the existence of large amounts of derivative operations. In this subdivision, exogenous elements and the dynamics triggered by these instruments are displayed. Recall, however, that according to Steinherr (1998) two further kinds of financial instruments were heavily used by Mexican banks to evade prudential regulation: structured notes and equity swaps[214].

---

213 No reference to this data was found in the remaining of the extensive document. Further, there is no data disaggregation or any details on this information.
214 Equity swaps function in a similar way as Tesobono swaps, but they used the total return on the recently privatized Teléfonos de México (Telmex) as the object to swap. The equity risk would

In 1994 the economy was confronted with different challenges: increasing external interest rates, political uncertainty and the peso overvaluation. Figure 58 shows the spread between Tesobonos and LIBOR. The differential of both rates at the beginning of the Tesobono growth period (April 1994) was high enough to appeal to attract domestic and foreign banks into the transaction. However, unexpected rises in LIBOR started to put pressure on the operations already in September 1994. The excessive leveraged positions undertaken by the Mexican banks were not profitable already in the fall of 1994.

Figure 58 Spread Tesobono vs. LIBOR and the Commissions on Investment Banks (1-2%)

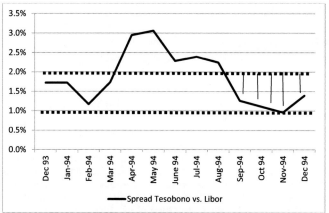

——Spread Tesobono vs. Libor

Data source: Indicadores Económicos de Banco de México (1995),
http://www.wsjprimerate.us/libor/libor_rates_history.htm
and authors' own calculations

After the volatility started in December 1994, the Tesobono market value in U.S. dollars plummeted, as some of the auctions were dismissed. This decrease in market value lessened the value of the collateral and triggered immediate margin calls to transfer dollars or close out the positions. Garber (1998) exemplifies that if the Tesobono value fell by 15%, the collateral would have to be adjusted by the same percentage. The author estimated overnight margin calls amounting $2.4 billion in the period. Additional margin calls on Equity swaps were estimated by the author to be $1.6 billion. The actual reserves losses accounted for almost $4 billion the week before the peso was floated.

The existence, magnitude and dynamics of derivative trading in Mexico contributed significantly to Mexico's unsustainable external imbalances and to trigger capital flight. The crisis, traditionally associated to rational investment capital inflows, can be

---

held by Mexican banks and investment bankers would function as lenders of foreign currency at, as exemplified by Garber (1998) LIBOR + 3%. See also Garber (1998) for the description of structured notes and other types of derivative trading in Mexico.

directly related to synthetic capital inflows. The next section reviews some of contributions regarding the link between derivatives and crisis in the real sector.

7.3.1 Effects of Derivatives on Crisis: Literature Review

Dodd (2000) links directly the financial crisis in Asia[215] to the derivative markets. The author analyses the impact of this type of instruments on different fronts focusing on the East Asian crisis, however, references the Mexican crisis indirectly. His studies constitute together with Garber (1998) the early cornerstones of research in the area, as referenced by the IMF (2002).

As highlighted by Garber (1999), the analysis of the sources and dynamics of sudden capital outflows and balance-of-payments crises is based on balance-sheet information. However, if large volumes of derivatives exist, the available information leads to incorrect conclusions and policy prescriptions. The author cites, exemplarily, claims such as the short maturity of public debt as the origin of crises. In his view:

"Subaccount data, such as portfolio investment, equity investment, foreign direct investment, or long- or short-maturity fixed interest rate lending, are illusory in the presence of substantial volumes of derivative products" (Garber 1999: 388).

According to Dodd (2000) there are two main aspects linked to derivatives and a reduction in transparency. On the one hand side, derivatives distort the balance-sheets of banks, central bank accounts and national accounts and limit their explanatory power. On the other hand side, OTC derivatives are hard to regulate.

Derivatives allow banks to conceal liabilities, eliminating them from their balance sheets. These mismatches do not allow prudential supervision and might lead to financial vulnerability. The IMF (2002) has a clear position:

"In particular, the use (or rather misuse) of derivatives can potentially allow financial institutions to move certain exposures off balance sheets, thereby magnifying their balance sheet mismatches in ways that may not be easily detected by prudential supervisors and, as a result, may lead to a gradual buildup of financial system fragilities."

As reported by Garber (1999) and the IMF (2002: 67), in the Tesobono swap case only an outflow of bank deposits linked to collateral payment by the Mexican bank and a U.S. dollar inflow resulting from the purchase of Tesobonos by foreign investors were recorded in the balance of payments. Under this perspective, the traditional balance of payments offers an enhanced and inaccurate picture of flows and risks. From this data, foreign investors appear holding government securities. In fact, the external financial institution provided a short-term dollar term with high yields and the local bank assumed the Tesobono swap risks.

---

215 Menkhoff (1999) refers to the implication of banks of industrialized countries in the inefficient risk structures in Asia previous to the crisis.

Padoa-Schioppa (1998: xi) acknowledged the increasing concern of regulators about off-balance sheet exposure[216] to credit and market risk of large international banks. The author refers to several cases where problems of this type were highlighted and points out: "the lack of accounting transparency in the Mexico crisis on the dollar exposure of Mexican banks."

There are diverse critical aspects related to the massive engagement in derivative operations. Dodd (2000) sketches them as:

- Derivatives reduce transparency.
- Derivatives can serve to circumvent prudential regulations.
- Derivatives might endanger the stability of fixed exchange systems.
- Derivatives accelerate and deepen crises.
- Derivatives increased systemic risks and contagion.
- Derivatives complicate post-crisis policy making.

Steinherr (1998) discusses different[217] well publicized debacles related to derivatives. He concluded that:

1) OTC derivatives pose specific and enormous challenges that are not observed in exchange traded instruments.
2) Not all large losses associated to the use of derivatives led to financial crises.
3) Failures are usual in any large growing industry.
4) Substantial economic benefits fulfilling private and social purposes are linked to the massive derivative trading.
5) Regulators control lay far behind the development of the derivatives.

Capital inflows in 1993 and 1994 were induced in Mexico significantly by the availability of derivatives. The IMF (2002: 63) expresses to this regard:

> "There is a broad consensus that the rapid expansion of derivatives products during the past 10 to 15 years was an important factor that facilitated the growth of global cross-border capital flows. "

Yam (1999) highlights not only the speculative nature but also the magnitude of the transactions resulting from derivative trading. This type of "synthetic" capital inflows, typically arising from OTC operations: "are subject to very little if any supervision" (Yam 1999: 166). In the view of the author, the use of derivatives for goals other than genuine trade or hedging might generate large capital outflows leading to contagion to "traditional" portfolio investors and endanger the financial sector stability.

Most derivatives are issued by commercial and investment banks and authorities might be forced to act as a lender of last resort and eventually rescue the financial

---

216 Großmann (1990:27) reports a significant increase of this type of activities as early as 1984 by the investment bankers in the USA.
217 The stock market crash (1987), the Metallgesellschaft losses (1993), The EMS crisis (1992), Barings Failure (1995), Banker's Trust (1994), Orange County (1994), the Mexican Crisis (1994).

system. Therefore, "authorities have both a right and an obligation to supervise and regulate derivative instruments" (Soros 1995 referenced in Steinherr 1998:75).

A further collateral effect is the amplification of volatility[218]:

> "Also, due to their very nature (i.e., the fact that they allow market participants to establish leveraged positions), derivative instruments tend to amplify volatility in asset markets. Thus, a negative shock to a country with already weak economic fundamentals, which typically triggers a sell-off in local asset markets, can also lead to an unpredictable and rapid unwinding of derivatives positions that can in turn accelerate capital outflows and deepen the crisis." (IMF 2002: 67).

Garber (1998) associates the presence of large capital inflows to systemic failures in the financial sector via the rash incursion of banks into "unfamiliar businesses". While the privatized bank engaged largely in "synthetic dollars", few suspected that the Mexican financial system was being exposed to an immense systemic risk, credit risk and potentially a high market risk. All these risks erupted immediately after the crisis (Vega 1999: 229).

The IMF (2002: 67) affirms that structured notes and swaps magnified the balance-sheet mismatches and contributed to increase the exogenous volatility of the financial markets in the Asian and Mexican crises. However, in their view, "deteriorating fundamentals...were the main causes of the recent emerging crises, but derivatives amplified the(ir) impact". Dodd (2002) also states that the use of derivatives exacerbated the Mexican (and the Asian) Crises.

7.3.2 Possible and Factual Policy Reforms after the Crisis

After the crisis different policy measures were undertaken. This section presents and briefly discusses a selection of alternatives of possible (based on Dodd 2000) and actual policy responses to the 1994 crisis. In general, it can be stated that the regulating agencies improved the financial regulation and closed most of the regulatory loopholes after the crisis. However, although some room for improvement was left, most of the reforms would require international coordination to restrict the excessive ability to contract risks.

A) Improving direct regulation

As reviewed in section 7.2.2, regulatory ambiguity was behind the massive and inadequately capitalized derivative trading in 1994. The most straightforward aspect

---

218 Soros (1995) disagrees with the "conventional wisdom" considering that financial markets tend to equilibirium and discount the future correctly. In his view, a boom-bust cycle develops when the market presents a trend-following pattern. The main reasons behind this trend are the performance measurement by mutual funds and dynamic hedging involved in derivatives. According to Soros (1995) the difficulty arises from the fact that derivative issuers usually protect themselves by delta or dynamic hedging. That means, that if the market shifts against the issuer, he is obliged to move with the market. This dynamic amplifies market disturbances and if changes are constant would only lead to increased volatility, which increase derivatives demand as a result.

was the exclusion of the bank-related securities brokers of the regulation introduced in the year of the eruption of the crisis.

Mexican policy makers modified[219] a posteriori the regulatory framework on different fronts. The IMF Technical note on Derivatives Markets (2007) assessed the market and concluded that "the supervision of derivatives activities follows international standards[220] and good practices". This appraisal is motivated by aspects such as the effective regulation and the enforcement procedures. Specifically the document highlights a capitalization rule of at least 90% of the market and credit risk, which are evaluated (both risks and compliance) periodically by different governmental institutions.

B) Enhancing transparency

Some authors such as Yam (1998) and Dodd (2000) pleaded for increasing transparency of the open operations. The regulations introduced after the crisis compel financial institutions to file in periodical reports on mark-to-market value, value at risk and the composition of their trading and investment portfolios (the latter on a daily basis) (IMF 2007: 15). In this regard the Mexican authorities successfully amended their supervision to make up for their omissions of the early nineties.

C) Indirect regulation

Yam (1999) suggested encouraging indirect regulations to reduce leverage and improve risk management. These could take the form, for example of increasing margin and collateral requirements (Yam 1999: 171). Guidelines for a longer-term oriented performance evaluation of traders would be a possible indirect regulation to modify the incentive scheme of short-term gains. Actions in this direction, as indirectly suggested by the IMF (2007) were not undertaken after the crisis. International practices, linked to dangerous leverage levels were continued.

D) Creation of structured markets

OTC markets are related to more flexibility but also to lack of transparency and ineffective risk management. Structured markets with standard financial products are less complex and easier to regulate. MexDer, the Mexican derivatives exchange was formally created in 1998 after a constituting process of four years. The IMF (2007) considers MexDer's challenges to broaden, deepen the market and reduce transactions costs. Yet, the overall evaluation reflects a development path towards robustness in a better regulated market.

---

219 Yam (1999) considers direct regulation to be linked to difficult and complex issues, such as: the choice of an appropriate supervisory authority, the sheer volume of the OTC markets, the large number and different types of players and migration to 'regulatory safe havens'.

220 As evidenced by the Global Financial Crisis of 2008 international standards did not prevent that the dynamics and operations of derivatives to pose challenges to financial institutions. However, regulations based on those of the Bank of International Settlements, for example, define safer conditions than those effective (and ineffective) during the 1994 crisis.

E) Redefinition of Markets and Products

An alternative which is banned out of serious policy discussions is the redesign of markets and products. Derivatives associated to high systemic risks could be ruled out of the market or redefined to minimize risks. A more radical possibility would be limiting derivatives supply only to hedging purposes, taxing this type of operations or reducing leverage significantly[221]. These alternatives, probably to avoid interest conflicts and sending wrong signals to the markets, have not been formally reviewed in the Mexican financial markets.

Nevertheless, the Global Financial Crisis opened up a chance to reevaluate the benefits and intended scope of derivative markets and to use this information to restructure the market to avoid socializing[222] losses caused by "synthetic capital inflows".

In the Mexican case, the opportunity posed by the financial turmoil in 1994 to improve the regulatory framework was seized by policy makers. The domestic derivative market emerged strengthened out of the crisis and financial institutions, as suggested by the IMF (2007), and operates with internal risk management systems which appear to be up to international standards. A further piece of evidence is indicated by the fact that after the 2008 Global Financial Crisis, as it discussed in the postscript of this thesis, hazardous derivative trading in Mexico was limited to a few industrial firms and exchange rate volatility. However, given the improved regulations in the financial sector, no systemic risk was posed by these isolated developments.

7.4 The Public and Private Financial Sector Institutions and their Implication on the Mexican Crisis

The Mexican private banking sector prior to the crisis reflected the lack of competition and incentives inherited from the governmental period and the fact that the authorities, in the modernization haste, defined rules on-the go. Conventional wisdom holds Mexican banks responsible for a rash and deficient domestic credit expansion. However, the domestic financial sector with the support of foreign investment banks should also be blamed for engaging massively and overstretching with derivative trading. An essential factor behind these excessive risk taking procedures was the eagerness of foreign investment bankers[223] to support the demands of the already heavy indebted domestic financial groups.

The magnitude of the engagement of the Mexican financial groups in this type of securities made the financing of Mexico's large external imbalances possible. In their absence, the correction of fundamentals, such as the realignment of the peso and

---

221 Actually, Calvo (2000), referenced by Dymski (2002), suggests that the establishment of derivatives markets in developing countries might reduce economic welfare.

222 Most of the crises' rescue packages are associated to government support of some kind. At the end, all tax-payers end up contributing to remedy problems caused by derivative-related effects. Profits seem to end up in private hands and large losses are absorbed by the State.

223 In Oliver Wayman/Morgan Stanley (2008) the Securities Industry and Financial Markets Association top 25 U.S. security houses pre-tax income losses were in 1994, as a result of the Mexico Peso Crisis, the most severe in absolute terms since 1985.

the closing of the external gap, might have been through a smoother landing. The aggressive risk taking behaviour of the domestic financial sector enabled the bubble-bust-cycle which led to the Mexican Crisis in 1995.

In the liberalization frenzy which characterized the Mexican economic picture of the early nineties, regulators are also to blame for central omissions and policy errors. The bank privatization process, organized transparently, but limited by political tradition, only allowed Mexican nationals to bid. Distortions based on this fact are a result of the lack expertise in the branch and of the required leverage in foreign currency to participate in the divestiture process.

The main line of criticism in the traditional literature against the central bank is the unlimited absorption of currency risks through the emission of Tesobonos. This strategy paved the way for exchange-risk free Tesobono derivative trading. Further, despite the fact that the authorities were partially aware of this type of transactions and their potential risk in the banking sector, regulations introduced in early 1994 did not apply for securities brokers and other financial institutions. This regulatory gap was taken advantage of.

Regulators were overburdened with the growing derivative operations that Mexican financial institutions underwrote in the international financial markets. Further, they did not design an adequate regulatory framework that would limit the potential risks of off-balance operations of the private financial sector. Also for the unlimited emission of Tesobonos and the absorption of most of the bank rescue costs they sould be held responsible. All these failures can be attributed to the regulating authorities. However, as the experience proved in all the crises after 1994, policy makers all over the world were behind the developments of the complex derivatives markets and underestimated their destabilizing potential.

Weak fundamentals are a precondition to crisis proneness. However, considerable amounts of derivative trading related to the size of the current account deficit raise the possibility of a crisis. Therefore, derivative trading should take place in a solid regulatory framework to avoid systemic risks. Under this scheme, the possible effects derived from the willingness to adopt risks should remain by the risk-taker. The redefinition of a new financial architecture might imply breaking with old paradigms to reach this goal. The challenge is to implement transnational reforms with determination to avoid spill-overs from the financial sector into the real sector. Encouragingly, given the Global Financial Crisis of 2008, this subject has gained relevance and became therefore a matter of current research.

7.5 Conclusions: Derivatives' Role in the Mexican Crisis

In the relative scarce literature dealing with derivatives and the Mexican crisis of 1994, consensus prevailed[224] regarding the destabilizing and magnifying role of derivatives to financial and currency crises. In general, the view which predominates is

---

224 See for example Zhang/Lien (2008), IMF (2002), Dodd (2000), Garber (1998).

that even though derivatives did not cause financial distress, they amplified the effects of the crisis caused by weak fundamentals.

For the Mexican case, the author of this thesis confers derivatives more accountability than the conventional view. The leverage involved in some derivative transactions can generate multiple non-intended hazardous effects (Figure 59). A relevant outcome is that these, typically OTC, artificially boost the demand for bonds and equity. These operations also enlarge the availability of funds in the economy. Automatically, these resources, at least in the short-term, are at hand to finance a consumption boom and the excess value of imports over exports (current account deficits) and to extend credit allocation ineffectively. Simultaneously, these might be subject to large and immediate capital reversals, as it was the case in Mexico in Dec. 1994.

Figure 59 Misbalancing Effects of Synthetic Capital Inflows

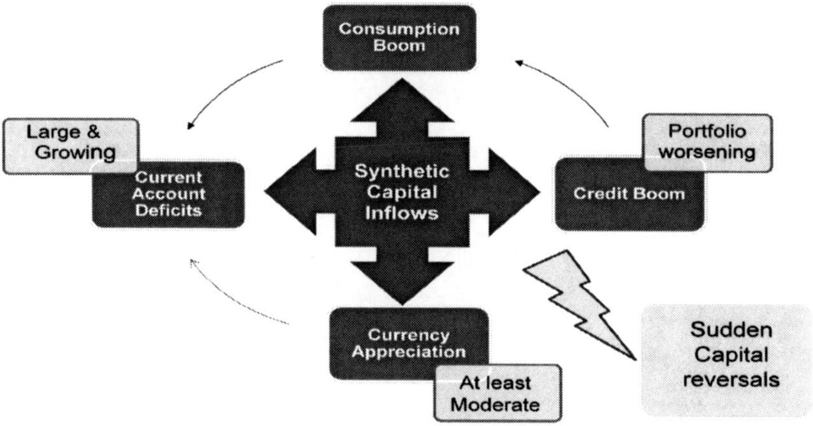

Source: author's own conception

In the absence of derivatives, the unsustainable current account financing that took place in the Mexican case would have not been possible. Garber's (1998) estimations, in this thesis corroborated through official data, indicate that derivative-related capital inflows financed in 1994 over 60% of the large current account deficit. In this sense, not traditional short-term portfolio investment but immoderate "synthetic capital inflows" additionally acted as the push factor which supported currency appreciation and enabled the consumption and credit booms. Exogenous factors, in Mexico such as a sudden devaluation and changes in the Fed's monetary policy, can activate the dynamics of leveraged synthetic capital inflows, instigate a sudden capital reversal and trigger off a systemic crisis.

The financing of the current account deficit in 1994 was much more perilous than in 1982. The liquidity bottle-neck after the oil shock in the eighties was easier to negotiate with the lending banks. In 1994, derivative handling was not only leveraged lending to finance capital inflows with speculative purposes, but also implied immediate capital reversals in strict terms. Margin calls previous to the freeing of the peso contributed importantly to reserve depletion and elicited capital flight.

Derivative trading by domestic banks in 1994 accounted for capital inflows estimated at 4.9% of GDP. In the absence of such flows, the boom-bust cycle would have been much more moderate. The international reserves in a scenario with at least half of the foreign liabilities would have left more room for manoeuvre. More liquidity would have faced the market turbulences that forced the necessary devaluation and might have increased the possibility of a softer landing.

This thesis might suggest an improved understanding of the Mexican crisis. Synthetic and liquid inflows financed most of the current account deficit. By shifting this external gap from a manageable to a hazardous level, derivative trading in this magnitude did not magnify but enabled the Mexican crisis and its operation dynamics elicited the process of capital flight.

8 Conclusions and Contributions to Crisis Prevention

8.1 Research Conclusions

Mexico conducted after the 1982 debt crisis a profound market-oriented structural reform. Stabilization, liberalization of trade and the capital account and diverse privatizations, with the banks outstanding, were achieved before 1994. The optimistic outlook before the eruption of the crisis presented yet some discernible areas of concern. Low growth, moderate currency overvaluation, a large current account deficit financed by short-term portfolio inflows and a consumption and credit boom can describe the evident situation in 1994. At the end of a turbulent year, the abandonment of the currency peg caused capital reversals that triggered the Mexican crisis.

The present work explored three main approaches to explain the Mexican crisis. The first, the most traditional, is of macroeconomic nature. The second, exclusive to this work, are related to microeconomics of trade. The third reviewed both conventional aspects, such as (mis)behavior of the banking sector, and less evident such as the composition of capital inflows and OTC derivative trading.

The first part of the thesis explores and summarizes diverse literature contributions on macro fundamentals and theory. The main conclusions for Mexico are:

1) *No single approach of the abundant literature contributions seems to offer an integral answer to explain the origins of the Mexican crisis.* Most propose valuable elements that partially explain this shock. This thesis attempts to complement the literature by linking macro and microeconomic aspects to specific misbalancing effects stemming from the financial markets.

2) *While weak fundamentals are a precondition for the crisis, they cannot account for its magnitude.* In the Mexican case, the peg and its chronological extension have been often related to the crisis. This argument is partially correct. The peg allowed inflation control, yet it was linked to currency appreciation, acute import surge, economic slowdown and the loss of autonomy of monetary policy. However, while realignment of the appreciated currency was imminent and the international reserves low, the overshooting observed in early 1995 cannot be explained by the fundamentals. Fiscal policy was disciplined and did not follow the path of the crisis of the eighties. A relaxation in the presidential election year did not cause major policy effects. Monetary policy, restricted by the peg, struggled to contain inflation in a framework of continuous capital inflows. Sterilization caused higher interest rates, which further attracted capital.

3) *Mexico's large current account deficits, which peaked in 1994, seem to have more explanatory power for the crisis than other fundamentals.* This argument is related to two issues. The first is the implication of the prolonged currency overvaluation behind this trend. The second is the fact that per definition these deficits are financed by capital imports, which might be liquid or short-termed.

Hence, sudden capital reversals associated to this type of portfolio inflows do not enable a soft-landing to close a large external gap.

4) *The major policy errors were procrastination to realign the currency and to limit the emission of Tesobonos.* In Mexico, these dollar-denominated short-term government securities contributed to maintain large capital inflows after political turmoil intensified in 1994. As in the standard literature is correctly highlighted, the unlimited supply of this type of bonds during 1994 magnified currency risks, fostered further capital inflows, further appreciated the currency and underpinned the deterioration of the current account deficit.

5) *The country's difficulties with the current account deficit in 1994 were mainly driven by the import-bias of Mexican exports and to a lesser extent by a consumption boom.* Challenging expected results, an estimation of the import contents of aggregate demand components in 1994 revealed that roughly 60% of the total imports were associated to exports. Therefore, the following section concentrated on micro aspects of Mexico's import-dependent exports. High-import propensity supports the trends towards current account deficits and conditions growth. The here performed research suggests policy omissions to gradually correct this self-reinforcing mechanism given the national export-growth strategy.

The focus of the second major part of this thesis is on the microeconomics of Mexico's trade. This section explored both the trade structure and the link between by policy supported import-biased Mexican exports and their responsiveness to an appreciated currency. The main conclusions are:

6) *Mexican exports are concentrated in exchange rate insensitive sectors and imports react much faster than exports to real currency changes.* The exploration of this unorthodox crisis literature strand shed some light on its real appreciation and trade interaction. The observed "export boom" was artificially boosted by an over-proportionate growth in imports. Basic regression analysis suggests that changes in the economic path of the U.S allow exports to move half as much in the same direction compared to imports. However, if real appreciation occurs, imports react much faster than exports. Mexico's highly import-dependent exports, fostered but not limited to the Maquila program, contrary to theory only moderately react to real currency movements. The study of Mexico's trade balance by export type suggests the predominant primitive nature of its trade structure, despite modernization efforts. The large majority of positive net exports are of crude oil.

7) *The interaction of trade structural weaknesses and exchange rate appreciation contributed to enlarge Mexico's external imbalances in 1994.* The described trade structure built a self-reinforcing mechanism of real appreciation, large capital inflows, exchange rate elastic imports, large current account deficits and low growth. The second is their significant contribution to current account deficits within an export-growth strategy, which constantly increases the vulnerability of Mexico's external position.

The third section mainly focuses on financial issues of the Mexican crisis. After introducing the dynamism of international portfolio markets in the early nineties, particularities in Mexico are explored. The main conclusions are:

8) *Contrary to conventional wisdom, domestic and not foreign investors triggered the financial stampede that elicited the crisis.* Different information sources gathered in this document evidence this behavior, traditionally associated to foreign investors.

9) *The domestic credit boom was self-reinforcing as a result of: the increased availability of funds, the consumption boom, the large leverage required to purchase the banks, corruption and inefficient practices and the lack of a solid regulation.* This issue is relative widespread, especially considering domestic literature. Credit allocation tripled within a six-year term to reach 45% of GDP. Non-performing loans doubled within a few months, understated by Mexican accounting principles. Related lending, (credit to bank shareholders holding >1% of the shares or their relatives) was forbidden by regulation, but relevant in practical terms. After the eruption of the crisis, the banking sector in Mexico was confronted with a poor credit portfolio, significant currency mismatches and large passives.

10) *In 1994, capital inflows equivalent to 4.9% of GDP were "synthetic capital flows", the mere result of derivative trading.* To circumvent the existing regulation, domestic banks leveraged through their off-shore subsidiaries large purchase of Tesobonos through derivatives. By shifting the available financing of current account deficit from a manageable to a hazardous level, derivative trading in this magnitude did not magnify but enabled the Mexican crisis. Their operation dynamics through destabilizing margin calls supported the process of reserve depletion and the unwinding of the Mexican crisis. The domestic financial sector with the support of Wall-Street-based investment bankers is to blame for their aggressive behaviour portrayed by the magnitude of derivative trading and the credit boom. The monetary authorities acted complacently and did not regulate adequately. The confluence of these factors caused a self-reinforcing spiral of synthetic capital inflows, peso overvaluation, current account deficits and credit increase behind the 1994 crisis.

The bottom-line is that while the Mexican crisis of 1994 can be partially explained by the fundamentals, its magnitude can only be attributed to the misbalancing effects of "synthetic capital inflows", suggested by Garber's field research (1998) and corroborated by this document.

8.2 The Mexican Experience: Contributions to Crisis Prevention

This section attempts to contribute to an improved understanding of crisis dynamics by presenting the key issues behind the Mexican shock in 1994-1995. These are classified into two main sets, depending on if they can be generalized for future reference. While the former reflects aspects which were exclusive to Mexico in the early nineties or might be similar to other developing countries at most, the latter might serve as reference to assess possible crisis vulnerability.

1) The first group is domestic-related, therefore difficult[225] to transfer to other countries when searching for signs of crisis vulnerability:

    a) A far-reaching and prompt market-oriented reform, which was intended to amend the flaws originated during the import-substitution phase. These reforms were a major experiment towards liberalization and the enthusiasm based on them reflected more what Krugman (1995) calls "a leap of faith than a conclusion based on hard evidence" (referenced in Edwards 1997).

    b) The Mexican politically-based "obsessive preoccupation with inflation and hence with nominal-exchange stability" (Dornbusch 1997), also related to an extended period of significant currency overvaluation.

    c) The unlimited supply of short-term, dollar-denominated government securities (Tesobonos) in a pegged-currency framework which pushed Mexico to sudden illiquidity after the devaluation (Sachs/Radelet 1998).

    d) The banking system was vulnerable due to its reprivatization process, which was marked with two major flaws. One was the inexperience of its management. Second the strain put in the system with the massive credit allocation in the face of large capital inflows (Calvo/Mendoza 1996).

    e) The structure of the Mexican real sector, concentrated in a few branches and highly dependent on pre-imported inputs, is a factor behind the high import propensity. This fact is also related to the trend described in h).

    f) Not foreign, but Mexican investors, based on their understanding of the exchange rate dynamics after a presidential change, started the stampede that preceded the peso-collapse. The asymmetric behavior of domestic investors had its origin in divergent experiences and expectations, rather than on asymmetric information. It seemed however, practical from the policy makers' view to blame foreign short-term capitals ("hot money").

    g) The political economy of recurrent crises after presidential successions in the eighties is linked to the lack of credibility of policy makers and capital fight by domestic investors.

2) A second group of underlying factors is of generic nature. This set of occurrences, derived from the Mexican experience, while not exclusive and exhaustive, *might indicate systemic country vulnerability* (Figure 59):

---

225 Even though some of the structural weaknesses and deficiencies might be similar to other developing countries, there is no direct connection to other financial crises, with the exception of domestic capital flight. See Schneider (2003) for a thorough study of the topic.

h) Non-gradual capital surges largely related to financial derivatives, "synthetic capital inflows", are at the core of the process. These flows are not discernible from standard balance of payments information.

i) As a result of the large capital inflows, the currency appreciates regardless of the regime and *considerable*[226] current account deficits are financed[227].

j) A further effect of suddenly available funds in the domestic financial market is swift growth in credit to the private sector. Since the financial absorption takes place abruptly, it is linked to inefficient credit allocation.

k) The operation dynamics of derivatives are fundamental in the development of the sudden capital surges. The leverage-effect associated to derivatives is a factor behind their destabilizing magnitude. Accordingly, they are able to abruptly flood financial markets and compromise domestic liquidity through sudden outflows.[228]

l) The triggering of a crisis can be diverse, but is linked to capital reversals. Unexpected devaluations elicited in the case of Mexico 1994 the crisis.

m) Once the crisis is set off, the capital turn-around requires a sudden closing of the large external gap, which causes a drastic spillover to the real sector.

This thesis, as opposed to most of the literature which proliferated in the crisis aftermath, was developed in a different framework. Several crises with similar patterns have occurred in the last 15 years, with the global financial crisis of 2008 outstanding. These occurrences have a two-fold implication for this study. First, they enabled a different perspective based on the history of financial crises but, they also reflect what Naím/ Edwards (1998) calls a "politically induced learning disability". The Asian, Russian, and the Global Financial Crises suggest that investing patterns and regulatory gaps of the financial sector were not exclusive to the Mexican case.

The challenge remains to design and implement transnational[229] reforms to avoid spill-overs from the financial sector into the real sector. Encouragingly, given the Global Financial Crisis of 2008/2009, this topic has gained relevance and is as of the completion of this thesis subject of intensive research. The last section is a very modest step in this direction.

---

226 If a current account deficit is sustainable or excessive is a widely discussed topic. Reisen (1998) suggests that there is no specific range and rejects the inter-temporal approach (Obstfeld/Rogoff 1994). In his view, large capital inflows and the resulting current account deficits finance productive, preferably in the exportable sector to face the future foreign liabilities. Otherwise, they can be considered as excessive.

227 See Naím/Edwards (1997) for a historical perspective on large and sustained current account deficits and Obstfeld and Rogoff (2007) for a more contemporary view of the topic.

228 In the absence of derivatives, capital flows are reduced to those following the traditional investing pattern. In this case, capital surges are smoother and the economy can absorb them gradually.

229 Fortunately, after the crisis, reforms have been introduced in Mexico and as described by the IMF (2006:14): "The supervision of derivatives activities follows international standards and good practices".

8.3   Subjects for Further Research

It seems pertinent to propose some broad recommendations, in the spirit of suggesting possible matters for further research. These can be classified in two broad aspects: domestic economic policy and dealing with the international financial markets.

As for Mexico, the complement of the growth policy with the following features is suggested:

1) Elaborate a *targeted industrial policy to increase the domestic contents of its strongly biased export structure*. The introduction of tax and unorthodox incentives in this regard should be pursued as a long term strategy. This type of measures would have a double effect, first on growth and second on reducing the vulnerability caused by the perennial current account deficits.

2) Banco de México should, as it counterpart in the U.S., *pursue a dual mandate in the conduction of monetary policy*. Inflation control would in this case not be the ultimate goal of the central bank. The inflation-control fixation[230] of the central bank, based on Mexico's hyperinflation history and given the stability of the last decades, could be complement with a more targeted growth policy based on *moderate active monetary, fiscal and exchange rate policies.* [231]

More generic aspects include:

A) A more aggressive handling with the international financial institutions and markets is suggested. The use and scope of leverage should be questioned and limited to a position where own capital requirements are the main component of all financial products. Through these measures the destructive effects of capital surges would be dampened.

B) The adoption of more strict regulations for credit allocation. Basel III is already an important step in this direction. However, at national level the revision of the prevailing regulatory framework should precede their introduction.

C) To compensate a more strict credit allocation, alternative financing options for SME should be designed and implemented.

As it is discussed in the postscript of this thesis, Mexico has taken decisive measures after the eruption Global Crisis of 2008/2009. The authorities used, if admittedly still with potential, active monetary and fiscal policy to deal with this shock. This is an encouraging step in this direction. Also concerning the regulation of the domestic financial markets, the resilience of the sector was due to the improved regulation in the financial markets, especially regarding investments in derivatives. The way is actually paved for Mexico to continue reforms and grow.

---

230 Suggested, for example, by Dornbusch, R.; Goldfajn, I. and Valdes, R. (1995) and Dornbusch (1997).

231 Bouzas/ Ffrench-Davis (2005) call for research on a "responsible but active countercyclical monetary, fiscal, exchange-rate and capital-account policies" for Latin American countries.

Postscript: Impact of the 2008/9 Global Financial Crisis on the Mexican Economy

The global financial crisis caused the most severe recession in the post war era and affected practically all countries and financial systems. The Mexican economy was hardly hit by these developments and had the one of the largest output losses in its history. However, as it will be highlighted in this final chapter, even though the severe growth decline was comparable to that of 1995, its dynamics and prospects differ considerably.

This chapter is organized as follows. The first section presents the impact of the global financial crisis on macroeconomic indicators and contrasts their behaviour pattern vs. that observed in 1995. The second section reveals the sounder stand of the domestic financial institutions. The third section introduces selected factors that have intensified the current crisis. The last section evaluates and concludes.

Macro-indicators and Trends

The output losses caused by the global financial crisis are similar to those suffered after the 1995 crisis (Figure 60). This section presents key facts that indicate that, while in the former crisis several fundamentals such as a current account deficit and currency overvaluation called for correction, the recovery was prompt through an impressive export growth. In 2008 Mexican fundamentals varied from sound to manageable; however, the global economic recession complicated the replication of such a recuperating pattern.

Figure 60 Mexico's GDP in the 1995 vs. the 2008 Global Financial Crisis

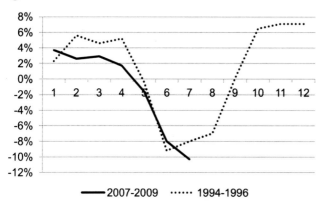

———— 2007-2009   ⋯⋯ 1994-1996

Data source: Banco de México online (2009)

Note: Quarters after initial shocks 1= 1994/1 or 2007/3

The initial propagation mechanism of the 2008 crisis was of financial origin. Financial flows to emerging countries decreased dramatically as the crisis erupted. The leading interest rates had to incorporate a higher risk premium to compensate the increased uncertainty and capital outflows (Figure 61). As a result of the disturbances in the financial sector the industrial and residential sectors in the country faced, as observed worldwide, a credit crunch and decreased liquidity (Banco de México 2009: 36).

The origin of the 1995 crisis was financial as well, but not exogenous, rather self-inflicted. After a capital inflow boom, capital outflows were the response to currency volatility and the sudden abandonment of the currency peg. As it is argued in this thesis, the capital inflow boom was mainly a result of derivative operations by Mexican banks.

Figure 61 Foreign Portfolio Inflows

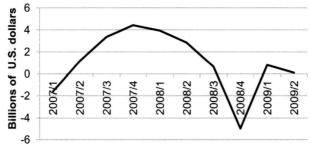

Data source: Banco de México online (2009)

A major factor that affected emerging economies in 2008 and 2009, including Mexico, was the decrease in flows of funds from developed countries. Sharp falls in exports and tourism revenues, remittances[232] and investment were the main causes of output decline and depreciation pressure in the country (Banco de México 2009). The economic contraction in the U.S., Mexico's major trading partner, had a significant effect on these falls.

Output started to contract already in the late 2008 (Figure 62). Investment, exports and domestic demand plummeted in 2009. The first major GDP loss was in the first quarter of 2009 with a -8.2% drop vs. same period in the prior year. The largest contraction was in the manufacturing sector with a -13.8% decrease. (INEGI 2009a). In the second quarter, GDP experienced its sharpest fall ever -10.3%. Main losses were in the services sector (-11.4%) and in the manufacturing sector (-16.4%) (INEGI 2009b).

---

232 Transfer of funds made by a migrant worker to his home country.

Figure 62 Aggregate Demand Components

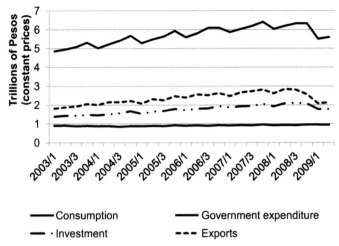

——Consumption ——Government expenditure
— · Investment --- Exports

Data source: INEGI, Sistema de Cuentas Nacionales (2009 online)

Likewise, employment was severely affected by the current crisis. Unemployment[233] rose 48% in the second 2009 quarter to reach 5.2%. Additionally, 11% of the total "employed population" are considered as underemployed and 28% work in the informal sector (INEGI 2009c). These indicators show their worst levels ever and similar levels to those of 1995.

Inflation, however, has been contained for the first time in a post-crisis period (Figure 63). After being lower than in the U.S. in 2007, inflation rose slightly in 2008 (http://www.amcham.com.mx/servicios/analisiseco/Documents/2Chartingenglish09.pdf). In 2009 the inflation rate reached a four year low, it was estimated at 3.57% (Banco de México online: 2010).

Interest rates have followed mixed patterns due to two main counteracting forces. Volatility in the international financial markets has increased the country risk on the one hand side. The interest rates of the Fed have led on the other hand to a dominating effect of the decrease of the leading rates. However, real interest rates are still positive and remain under one digit.

---

233 Defined by INEGI as the percentage of all persons over 14 that were willing and searching for a job and did not earn at least one hour of income of any kind in the previous four weeks.

Figure 63 Inflation

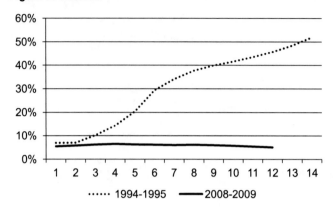

Data source: Banco de México (2009: 145)

1= previous month to intensified volatility = 1994/11 or 2007/9

As a result of the reduction of flows of funds and large OTC derivative losses[234], the Mexican peso faced increased pressure in the last 2008 and first 2009 quarter (Banco de México 2009: 37). Despite intensified intervention, the peso suffered a major loss of value (Figure 64) to only recover after two quarters of volatility.

Figure 64 Exchange Rate Growth Index

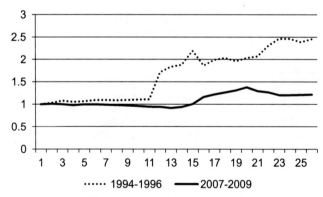

Data source: Banco de México online (2009) and authors' own calculations

Note: X axis: Months after initials shocks 1=1994/1 or 2007/7

Y axis: 1=Exchange rate in period 1994/1 or 2007/7

234 See section on other impacting forces.

The main contagion channel in the 2008 crisis was through the real sector. Exports as opposed to 1995, experience in 2009 the sharpest contraction of history (Figure 65). The exports decline rate in the second quarter of 2009 was -20.2%. The severity of the downturn is associated to Mexico's export pattern. Roughly four fifths of all exports head the U.S. This development matches the reduction reported[235] in the U.S: in non-oil imports (consumer and automotive products mainly) for the same period. Mexican exports should recover in the medium term to the extent that the U.S. economy stabilizes.

Figure 65 Exports and Imports Change Index

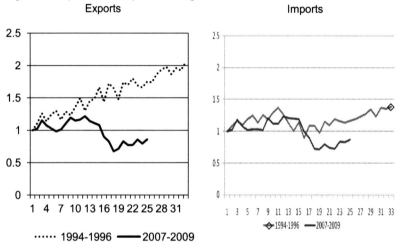

Data source: Banco de México online (2009) and authors' own calculations

Note: X axis: Months after initials shocks 1=1994/1 or 2007/7

Y axis: 1=Exchange rate in period 1994/1 or 2007/7

Imports also shrunk both as a result of the depreciation and of the economic contraction (Figure 65). According to official data, imports contracted in 2009 at a quicker pace than exports (-22.1%) with a reduction in the first semester of -25.1%. This contraction also reflects the in this thesis discussed correlation, which present a large fraction of pre-imported inputs. The perennial but manageable current account deficit gap was lessened in 2009.

---

235 Taken from: http://www.bea.gov/newsreleases/international/transactions/transnewsrelease.htm

Figure 66 Current Account Deficit

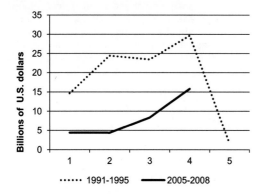

Data source: Anexo Estadístico 3. Informe de Gobierno
(www.informe.gob.mx/anexo_estadistico)

In 2008, the current account deficit reached its highest level in eight years (see Figure 66) estimated at 1.4% of GDP. This deficit was expected by Banco de México (2009) to increase in 2009 by 15%. However, these deficits remain moderate and contrast with the 7% of GDP level reached prior to the 1995 crisis. The peso loss of value was a significant factor which contributed to slowdown the expansion of imports.

Fiscal policy in the global crisis differs significantly to that carried out in 1995. A countercyclical fiscal policy on multiple fronts has been designed and implemented after 2008. The most important instruments are summarized in Table 31.

Table 31 Main Elements of the Countercyclical Fiscal Package 2009

1. Economic Support Program
• Fiscal stimuli for the private sector
• 5% reduction to public insurance contributions
• Reduction of electricity rates in peak times
• Increase in the budget of the national unemployment net
• Increase in the budget of the national oil monopoly
2. Increase of international public debt
• Up to $5 bn. U.S. dollars
3. Growth and Employment Program
• Increase in public investment in infrastructure, mainly on roads (0.7% GDP)

180

- More direct and indirect financing
- Construction of a refining plant
- Tariff reduction for imports from countries without trade agreement
- Gasoline price will remain fixed for a year and gas prices were cut by 10%
- 20% of all government purchases are to be bought from small or mid-sized domestic company.
- Extension of the Temporary Work Program/ unemployment coverage

Source: Banco de México (2009) and Congreso de la Unión, Centro de Estudios de las Finanzas Públicas (http://www.cefp.gob.mx/intr/edocumentos/pdf/cefp/2009/cefp0072009.pdf)

Government spending increased appreciably in constant terms after 2005. Sarabia/Orozco (2009) relate the loosening of the fiscal policy to the oil bonanza previous to the global financial crisis of 2008. However, public indebtedness can be considered as moderate, as of 2008 total Mexican public debt was 32.3 % of GDP (Presidencia online: 2009[236]). The broad public deficit was 1.8%[237] of GDP. The expected public deficit[238] for 2010 equals 2.5% of GDP (SHCP Ministry of Finance online[239] 2009). Even if some elements are subject to discussion, in general the countercyclical measures seem modest but appropriate.

Financial Sector

The changes in the legal framework and financial regulation undertaken as a result of the 1995 crisis underpinned, according to Banco de México (2009), the solidness of the Mexican institutions and financial systems during the global financial crisis. Some indicators in this regard will be presented in this subsection.

Financial contagion within financial corporate groups was not possible because of the existence of regulation limits to operations of domestic banks and their foreign subsidiaries. According to this organization, "Mexican banks did not have in their balance sheets assets linked to the U.S. housing market (the so called "toxic assets")" (Banco de México 2009: 40).

Non-performing loans (Figure 67), particularly consumption credit in 2008, have increased in the aftermath of the global financial crisis. However, their level of coverage is still manageable and far from the level observed in the 1995 crisis (Banco de México 2009:117).

---

236 http://www.presidencia.gob.mx/prensa/shcp/?contenido=42004&imprimir=true
237 Compared to 1.1% in 2007. (http://www.shcp.gob.mx/FINANZASPUBLICAS/finanzas_publicas_criterios/CGPE%202009_060908_VF%20Sin%20Cambios.pdf).
238 The traditional deficit is expected to be 0.5% of GDP. However, debt related to the state oil concern is excluded, which implies an additional 1.8% of GDP. The full deficit, including financial costs totals 3.1% of GDP
239 http://www.shcp.gob.mx/Documentos_recientes/acc_%20091509_comparecencia_cded.pdf

181

Moreover, the reserves required to face credit defaults despite the credit card increase in 2008 (Figure 68), remain higher and satisfactory compared to those in 1995 (Banco de México 2009:117).

Figure 67 Non-performing Loans by Type

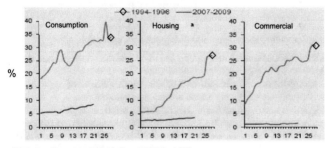

Source: Banco de México (2009: 145)
Percentage of total loans
X axis: months after Jan. 1994 and August 2007

Figure 68 Percentage of Due Loans Kept as Provisions

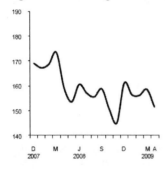

Source: Banco de México (2009: 117) with Comision Nacional Bancaria data

Mexican banks also report significantly lower asset to capital ratios than the U.S. financial institutions (Figure 69). Their performance is close to the minimum Basel II[240] capital adequacy ratio, which is 12.5 times (or 8% capital-to-asset ratio). The data presented by Banco de México supports their argument of the relative soundness of the sector based on adjustments made to regulation after 1995 in this regard.

---

240 http://www.bis.org/publ/bcbs107b.pdf

Figure 69 Assets/ Capital Ratio U.S. vs. Mexican Banks

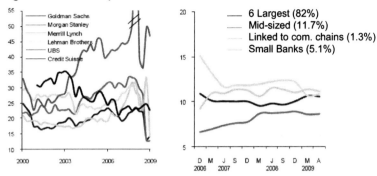

Source: U.S. Banks: Banco de México (2009: 11) with data from Bloomberg
Mexican Banks: Banco de México (2009: 113)
Note: y-axis=Times
*until April 2009 Percentage data in () refers to the share of the total domestic market share

Figure 70 shows an adjusted measurement[241] of the resources available of an operating bank to meet losses and obligations (risk adjusted capital-to-asset ratio). According to Banco de México (2009), a similar index has been used in the U.S and by the IMF. The latter recommends as a reference that the index should be in the 6-9% range. The largest Mexican banks serving roughly four fifths of the financial markets show that indicators are better than the recommended levels by the IMF.

Figure 70 Adjusted Capital-to-assets Ratio of Six Major Mexican Banks

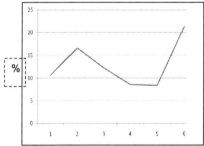

Data source: Banco de México (2009: 116)
Banks ranked by size, up to April 2009
Adjusted capital-to capital ratio = Index of tangible capital= "Tier 1 Common Capital[242]"- subordinated bonds classified as capital-deferred assets classified as capital/assets subject to total risk.

---

241 Which excludes from capital subordinated bonds and other hybrids that only absorb losses in the case of bankruptcy.
242 Calculation based on the Supervisory Capital Assessment Program, Board of Governors of the Federal Reserve.

Other Impacting Forces

Additionally, the economic activity in the country was affected by several non-related factors during 2009. Concerns based on increased criminality have affected the business environment. Further, the emergence of the H1N1 virus and the extreme measures[243] undertaken to stop its spread in the second quarter of 2009 harmed the aggregate economic activity (Banco de México 2009: 9). Tourism revenues plunged as a result of the outbreak of the crisis. Banco de México[244] calculated its impact to be approximately 0.5% of the previously projected yearly GDP.

Prior to the global financial crisis, several industrial Mexican firms (Table 32) had massively engaged in leveraged positions (OTC derivatives) to profit from the continued strength of the peso[245]. Currency derivatives, such as target forwards, were a significant source of profits (and risks) as the exchange rate remained stable. However, as in October 2008 currencies in various emerging markets, including Mexico started to depreciate, the margin calls of open currency derivatives positions further boosted the domestic U.S. dollar demand[246]. As a result of both confluent forces, the peso depreciated 25% alone in one month (Banco de México 2009: 79,81).

Table 32 Major Losses of Mexican Companies on Currency Derivatives 2009

Name of the holding	Sector	Losses* in millions of U.S. dollars
Controladora Comercial Mexicana	Commercial	2200
Cemex	Cement	711
Gruma	Corn products	684
Alfa	Diversified	273
Vitro	Glass	227

Source: Farhi and Sanchetta Borghi (2009)
*Estimated losses considering that some positions were still open by the time of calculation.[247]

Total losses of Mexican corporations in derivative markets in the above mentioned period were estimated to be $8.8 billion U.S. dollars (Reyes 2009). This amount represents roughly one third of all interventions in the forex market done by the central bank in the last quarter of 2008 and the first semester 2009. Nevertheless, these were isolated cases in the industrial sector. Hence, unlike in 1995, no systemic risk or a banking system was at stake. Banco de México followed its managed float strategy. The peso depreciated to some extent and the bank had enough international

---

243 Which included the suspension of nearly all economic activities for 5 consecutive days in May and the cancellation of all educational activities in the country at all levels for two weeks.

244 Through his Governor, Ortiz in Davos.

245 The intermediation role of local subsidiaries of foreign banks is not out of scrutiny, just out of the scope of this thesis.

246 In some cases the firms were not able to meet their obligations and their counterparts had to acquire U.S. dollars themselves.

247 Reyes (2009) reports that up to September 16th 2009, Gruma and Comercial Mexicana (third largest supermarket chain) are still negotiating their derivative related obligations with their counterparts.

reserves to counteract the increased demand for foreign currency. Therefore, the derivatives episode in 2009 translated merely into temporary exchange rate volatility.

A collateral effect was that the cost of funds of non-related large Mexican firms increased as a result of uncertainty caused by the significant and well publicized losses on derivatives of other major companies (Banco de México 2009:9). Both developments had a negative but moderate impact on employment and investment.

Finally, the oil price drops after the global financial crisis have negatively affected a significant source of governmental income (Figure 71). However, Mexico contracted derivatives in the form of oil hedges, which covered all 2009 oil revenues and might reach 1% of GDP[248]. The proceeds derived from these instruments were central in the decision to implement a countercyclical policy.

Figure 71 Government Revenues as a % of GDP

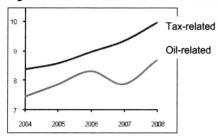

Source: Banco de México 2009: 70

Concluding remarks

The effects of the global financial crisis have been as severe in terms of output growth as the self-inflicted one in 1995. Sound macroeconomic fundamentals did not allow the country to remain resilient to the external shocks and atypical developments that occurred in 2008 and 2009.

Inflation is still after the crisis at levels comparable to the U.S. rate. This represents a major progress, since it is the first time in recent history that it can be contained after a major shock.

Exports had the sharpest decline in history. The fact that roughly 80% of Mexico exports head the U.S. determined its extent. After 1995, the exports rebound allowed a quick recovery, however, the global financial crisis poses a larger challenge. Economic growth will depend on the expansion of Mexican imports in the U.S., investment recovery and on domestic demand.

---

248 http://www.bloomberg.com/apps/news?pid=20601086&sid=aCaPOf8Qtquis&refer=latin_ america

The export structure played a key role in the dramatic drop experienced in 2009. Different factors supported this trend. The concentration on the U.S. market[249] and on the oil, automotive and electronic sectors caused a sharp contraction. Further, exports in the predominating non-oil sectors are highly dependent on imports, which make them vulnerable to nominal currency value variations. The exporting sector is dominated by U.S. foreign firms and by large, often oligopolistic Mexican corporations. Several of these domestic firms, as reviewed in the previous section, engaged in derivative positions and incurred in large losses. Many of the remaining faced more volatility and higher financial costs despite their lack of participation in speculation with derivatives. These structural weaknesses and financial conditions enlarged the impact of the global financial crisis in the real sector.

The contractionary effects of interest rate hikes were complemented by some particularities of the Mexican[250] economy. The high import propensity and a related high import content of most exports and domestic production, discussed in section 4.2.3, are a factor behind the depreciation-inflation spiral and the devaluatory aversion of the monetary authorities suggested by Ibarra (1999: 55) and Ffrench-Davis (2005: 58). Therefore, there is a strong counteracting force of depreciations not only on imports, but also on aggregate economic activity (as opposed to the textbook expansionary effects of devaluations through the export channel).

The conditions in the domestic financial markets seem to be more favourable than in the real sector, as suggested by Banco de México (2009). Important reforms introduced as a result of the 1995 crisis such as a more astringent financial regulation and the introduction of credit bureaus have enhanced the credit portfolios and contributed to a better regulated branch. Further steps to consolidate a branch with more competitive active vs. passive rate differentials should be undertaken. However, the branch has proved resilient to the financial turbulences after 1995.

The pursued countercyclical fiscal policy has been complemented with the available oil revenues and additional credit lines by the IMF. Significant in financial and symbolic terms are the oil income compensations which resulted from derivatives. The government traded away the oil price fluctuations through derivatives hedge transactions. In general, whatsoever, the resources seem to be insufficient to contain the plummet of the economy, which in the second quarter 2009 peaked at -10.3%. Others such as investment in a refining plant seem inopportune since they are of long-term nature. Moreover, much of the technology investment would presumably have to be imported. Others comprise market distortions such as subventions on fossil fuels that only directly increase the disposable income of agents owning vehicles. For the specific case of gasoline, which is paradoxically[251] mainly imported, the impact on the economy is limited[252]. However, the implementation of a moderate countercyclical policy is in Mexico a new way to fight a crisis. Given that public sector balances neared 0% from 2001-2008 and the large impact of the crisis, this effort appears

---

249 For other Latin American countries such as Chile and Brazil, export diversification is the case.
250 Probably to many other emerging economies as well.
251 In spite of the large oil production.
252 Apart from the environmental effects of such measures.

manageable but scarce. The challenge is to assign the funds efficiently to increase the domestic demand in the short term given the observed high import propensity.

The prospects in the real sector are rather grim in the short-term and output will probably only recover progressively as the situation in the world markets improve. The global financial crisis opened up a chance to design and implement structural reforms which foster investment and economic growth. Mexico would benefit from a more flexible labor market and a more active industrial policy based on incentives to generate more domestic contents in the domestic industrial sector and employment. The IMF (2009) after analyzing 88 financial crises concludes: "There is also some evidence that structural reform efforts are associated with better medium-term (output) outcomes". Lack of action and uncoordinated policies are a certain way to worsen output prospects in a country that has expected (and not seen) significant growth rates for the last three decades.

APPENDICES

Appendix 1 Debt Crisis of 1982

Background on the Debt Crisis 1970-1982

The 1982 Crisis is probably the most dramatic in the Mexican history. It was caused by large fiscal imbalances as advocated by the first generation models (Krugman (1979)/ Flood/Garber 1984). The crisis stemmed from the bursting of a bubble after money and foreign loans financed a loose fiscal policy in a fixed exchange rate framework. The run-out of reserves and speculative attacks were important aspects that led to the crisis. Its causes and developments differ from the 1994 crisis mainly in fiscal and monetary terms. However, various others such as a significant current account deficit and the abandonment of a fixed exchange rate as a result capital flight, are some of the main aspect that both crises show in common.

Relevant for this thesis is the ideological legacy of the period to the policy conception and implementation of the structural reform in the early nineties. The most influential issues were related to fiscal indiscipline, inflationary and devaluatory aversion, which are the grounds several macroeconomic measures taken a posteriori. This section reviews some of the most relevant aspects after the 1982 crisis including fiscal policy, debt and financial aspects and the real sector.

The 1982 Debt Crisis

After a decade of economic growth and stability in the sixties, a power switch changed the economic panorama. Starting in 1970 and until the outbreak of the 1982 crisis, the participation of the government in the economy enlarged drastically. The fiscal indiscipline in the late seventies was financed by oil-revenue backed foreign debt[253] until 1982, as the oil prices[254] experienced a significant drop and interest rates in the international markets soared.[255]

The External Sector and the Exchange Rate

In the real sector, Cronin (2003) reports that the significant increases observed in the first half of the seventies indicates a "strengthening and maturation process" that appeared to be countercyclical. According to the author:

> "Suffering from an acute case of "Dutch disease," the country's exports soon were dominated by petroleum, from which the dollar revenues (and loans based on them) soon pushed up the real value of the peso."

---

253 34% of the Planned Annual Budget was to be originally financed through foreign debt.
254 Oil was Mexico's the most important export product until the late 1990´s.
255 The strategies to remedy the 1982 Crisis will only be indirectly dealt with in the section regarding the reform period until 1994. Cline's seminal work concluded: "the quality of domestic economic policy turned out to be the most important determinant of success in dealing with the debt problem" (1995: 352).

The oil bonanza in the late seventies and the peso appreciation[256] in the period inter-
rupted the dynamism observed at the beginning of the decade. The author describes
the exporting-sector as concentrated in a few large firms, which were mainly oriented
to the domestic sector.[257]

Figure 72 Increases in Public Foreign Debt and the Trade Balance 1980-1988

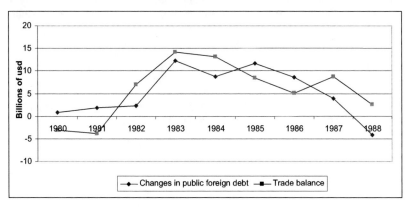

Data source: IMF Financial Statistics

Figure 72 presents the significant increases in public foreign debt and the trade balance movements.[258] Foreign debt partially financed until 1982 the widening current
account deficit. Subsequently, constant devaluations of the fixed currency and the
resulting overvaluation artificially induced a trade surplus after crisis.

Foreign Debt

Mexico and Brazil were according to the World Bank the most indebted developing
countries in the eighties. In the most critical phase, from 1982 to 1987, gross external
debt increased in U.S. dollars by 27%. The cumulative average LIBOR plus a spread
of one percent for the five year period was calculated to be 57.8% (Cline 1995: 42).
Table 33 shows the significance of Mexico's debt to western industrialized countries.
The impact on international banks of the Mexico's suspension on payments was considerable. The main creditors were private U.S. banks[259]. British banks had a less

---

256 The fixed exchange rate and higher inflation rate during the 70's resulted in the appreciation of the
currency as a consequence of the pressure on the balance of payments.
257 The author mentions that only 13% of the 200 largest firms' total sales in 1980 were generated
abroad. He is aware of the appreciation effect on exports and states that after diverse devaluations took place, in 1984, this figure increased only to 17.4%. However, if considering only the top
50 companies the figures are raised to 30.8% and 37.9% respectively. This trend might evidence
the interest of large industrial groups towards trade (import) liberalization.
258 Strict import controls the balance of payments were introduced after 1982.
259 This fact might be a hint of the wide political support offered by the U.S. government and institutions of the following public administrators in Mexico which pursued liberalization in all fronts. This

significant share, whereas German banks portion was relatively low and French banks joined only after the crisis.

Table 33 Selected Debt Indicators Mexico 1982-1988

in U.S. dollars billions (if not otherwise indicated)

	1982	1983	1984	1985	1986	1987	1988
Net External Debt, as % of GNP	52.0	63.8	52.9	52.4	78.2	73.0	57.2
Exposure of nine largest U.S. banks vs. capital (%)	44.4	44.8	40.0	33.3	28.6	25.9	21.1
Total commercial debt, Owed to:	34.8	36.9	42.8	41.8	41.2	34.6	31.8
U.S. Banks	24.4	26.3	26.5	24.9	23.7	22.7	17.9
U.K. Banks	8.5	8.4	8.7	8.7	8.7	8.7	8.3
German Banks	1.9	2.2	3.5	3.8	3.9	4.1	3.7
French Banks	-	-	5.1	5.3	5.5	5.5	4.5

Data source: Cline (1995) with World Bank, Federal Institutions Examination Council, Bank of England, Deutsche Bundesbank and Banque de France data.

Subsequent to the 1982 crisis, the main goal of the exchange rate policy was to use it as a protectionist tool, since the undervalued currency subsidized exporters and served as a non-tariff barrier agains imports. Therefore, starting in 1983 the peso moved along through mini-slids that would allow overvaluation. As a result, substantial surpluses in the balance of payments were achieved. (Cortez 2004: 39).

Table 34 shows some macroeconomic indicators which evidence severity of the Debt Crisis of 1982. The data indicates the difficulties to overcome it, given the 1986 oil shock and the persistence of inflation despite fiscal tightening. Exports, supported by an undervalued currency counteracted the adverse economic situation and contributed to economic growth. Inflationary pressure was related to constant exchange revaluations and other inertial sources (Aspe 1993: 9) and remained two and three-digit in the period.

Table 34 Economic Indicators for Mexico, 1982-1988

	1982	1983	1984	1985	1986	1987	1988
Real GDP growth (%)	-0.6	-5.3	3.7	2.7	-3.7	1.8	1.4
Primary Fiscal Balance (% of GDP)	-7.3	4.2	4.8	3.4	1.6	4.7	8.0
Net Interest Payments (% of exports of goods & services)	37.8	32.1	30.7	30.6	31.6	23.3	21.4
Current account Deficit (billions of U.S. dollars)	-6.3	5.4	4.2	1.1	-1.7	4.0	-2.4
Inflation (%)	58.9	101.8	65.5	57.7	86.2	131.8	114.2
Real Exchange Rate /G6* (1985=100)	117.6	121.4	100.7	100.0	133.1	134.2	109.5

Data source: Cline (1995) with IFS and IMF data.
* Real exchange rate vs. six large industrial countries, deflated by wholesale prices.

engagement would be at least partially related to the generation of a bubble of positive expectations which busted in Dec. 1994.

Up to 1982, public external debt reached a level of 49% of GDP. Furthermore, the growing currency overvaluation and political instability, mainly related to exchange controls and bank nationalization, caused capital flight[260]. These factors and the "extremely high" interest rates in the U.S. caused the insolvency of the country, as the alternative borrow-to-service-debt was after oil prices fell was not longer available (Dornbusch/Werner 1994: 256-257). In August 1982 the government announced its inability to service its international debt. This point marked the start of Mexico's most dramatic economic incident.

---

260 The shifting of domestic assets abroad after the crisis (1984-1987) was estimated to be $ 23 billion U.S. dollars (Cline 1995:112).

Appendix 2 Regressions Results and Residual Tests

Dependent Variable: REXIMLN
Method: Least Squares
Date: 03/11/08   Time: 11:14
Sample(adjusted): 1991:02 1996:10
Included observations: 69 after adjusting endpoints

Variable	Coefficient	Std. Error	t-Statistic	Prob.
C	-4,508253	2,203542	-2,045912	0,0448
REXIMLN(-1)	0,722851	0,060329	11,98181	0,00000
LNUSGDP	0,492589	0,244166	2,017438	0,0478
LOG(REEXCLO)	-0,42484	0,100572	-4,224252	0,0001

R-squared	0,94178	Mean dependent var	-0,603051
Adjusted R-squared	0,939092	S.D. dependent var	0,30927
S.E. of regression	0,076326	Akaike info criterion	-2,251378
Sum squared resid	0,37867	Schwarz criterion	-2,121864
Log likelihood	81,67253	F-statistic	350,482
Durbin-Watson stat	2,433487	Prob(F-statistic)	0

obs	Actual	Fitted	Residual	Residual Plot
1991:02:00	-0.62938	-0.65544	0.02606	. |* .
1991:03:00	-0.5651	-0.66176	0.09666	. | .*
1991:04:00	-0.63813	-0.6157	-0.02243	. *| .
1991:05:00	-0.62795	-0.66915	0.0412	. |*.
1991:06:00	-0.68946	-0.66235	-0.0271	. *| .
1991:07:00	-0.79237	-0.70604	-0.08633	* | .
1991:08:00	-0.76576	-0.7803	0.01454	. |* .
1991:09:00	-0.74627	-0.76293	0.01665	. |* .
1991:10:00	-0.75364	-0.75526	0.00161	. * .
1991:11:00	-0.78694	-0.76847	-0.01847	. *| .
1991:12:00	-0.916	-0.7981	-0.1179	*. | .
1992:01:00	-0.80419	-0.89394	0.08975	. | .*
1992:02:00	-0.79404	-0.81334	0.0193	. |* .
1992:03:00	-0.80168	-0.80737	0.00568	. * .
1992:04:00	-0.88484	-0.80932	-0.07552	* | .
1992:05:00	-0.91656	-0.86637	-0.05019	.* | .
1992:06:00	-0.95096	-0.88976	-0.06121	.* | .
1992:07:00	-1.05481	-0.91764	-0.13717	*. | .
1992:08:00	-0.9018	-0.9941	0.09229	. | .*
1992:09:00	-0.93543	-0.8788	-0.05663	.* | .
1992:10:00	-0.98823	-0.90568	-0.08255	* | .
1992:11:00	-0.96451	-0.95015	-0.01436	. *| .
1992:12:00	-1.01561	-0.93713	-0.07848	* | .
1993:01:00	-0.78458	-0.97673	0.19215	. | . *
1993:02:00	-0.81041	-0.80859	-0.00182	. * .
1993:03:00	-0.82512	-0.82946	0.00433	. * .
1993:04:00	-0.82186	-0.83738	0.01551	. |* .
1993:05:00	-0.80701	-0.83616	0.02915	. |* .
1993:06:00	-0.76273	-0.82631	0.06358	. | *
1993:07:00	-0.90702	-0.79469	-0.11233	*. | .
1993:08:00	-0.81349	-0.89904	0.08555	. | *
1993:09:00	-0.74775	-0.82899	0.08123	. | *
1993:10:00	-0.66674	-0.77585	0.10911	. | .*
1993:11:00	-0.71675	-0.72527	0.00852	. * .
1993:12:00	-0.766	-0.76192	-0.00408	. * .
1994:01:00	-0.74356	-0.79557	0.05201	. |*.
1994:02:00	-0.75951	-0.75505	-0.00446	. * .
1994:03:00	-0.70369	-0.75706	0.05338	. |*.
1994:04:00	-0.78805	-0.72282	-0.06523	* | .
1994:05:00	-0.77442	-0.77738	0.00296	. * .
1994:06:00	-0.80523	-0.76228	-0.04295	.* | .
1994:07:00	-0.89743	-0.78527	-0.11216	*. | .
1994:08:00	-0.83007	-0.84963	0.01957	. |* .
1994:09:00	-0.7975	-0.79897	0.00147	. * .
1994:10:00	-0.83123	-0.77338	-0.05785	.* | .
1994:11:00	-0.68331	-0.74468	0.06137	. |*.
1994:12:00	-0.77391	-0.50754	-0.26637	|* . | .

1995:01:00	-0.35676	-0.57562	0.21885	.	. *
1995:02:00	-0.17188	-0.22686	0.05498	. |*.
1995:03:00	-0.16919	-0.15038	-0.01882	. *| .
1995:04:00	-0.07461	-0.18702	0.1124	.	.*
1995:05:00	-0.07584	-0.11158	0.03575	. |*.
1995:06:00	-0.13711	-0.12548	-0.01163	. * .
1995:07:00	-0.15838	-0.17089	0.0125	. * .
1995:08:00	-0.15308	-0.18536	0.03228	. |*.
1995:09:00	-0.09059	-0.16218	0.0716	.	*
1995:10:00	-0.08837	-0.06909	-0.01927	. *| .
1995:11:00	-0.14631	-0.08018	-0.06612	*	.
1995:12:00	-0.18951	-0.14211	-0.0474	.*| .
1996:01:00	-0.14664	-0.17911	0.03246	. |*.
1996:02:00	-0.18397	-0.1486	-0.03537	. *| .
1996:03:00	-0.14149	-0.189	0.04751	. |*.
1996:04:00	-0.15169	-0.16586	0.01417	. |*.
1996:05:00	-0.20065	-0.17232	-0.02833	. *| .
1996:06:00	-0.18791	-0.20702	0.01912	. |*.
1996:07:00	-0.23566	-0.2068	-0.02886	. *| .
1996:08:00	-0.26868	-0.2431	-0.02558	. *| .
1996:09:00	-0.22581	-0.26113	0.03532	. |*.
1996:10:00	-0.31534	-0.22174	-0.0936	*.	.

Breusch-Godfrey Serial Correlation LM Test:

F-statistic	2.243174	Probability	0.114532
Obs*R-squared	4.586972	Probability	0.100914

Test Equation:
Dependent Variable: RESID
Method: Least Squares
Date: 03/11/08   Time: 11:27

Variable	Coefficient	Std. Error	t-Statistic	Prob.
C	1.229373	2.281716	0.538793	0.5919
LOG(REEXCLO)	0.067427	0.110329	0.611145	0.5433
REXIMLN(-1)	0.066312	0.07323	0.905526	0.3686
LNUSGDP	-0.133946	0.252368	-0.530757	0.5975
RESID(-1)	-0.303043	0.148463	-2.041193	0.0454
RESID(-2)	-0.046458	0.143243	-0.324331	0.7468

R-squared	0.066478	Mean dependent var	-2.58E-16
Adjusted R-squared	-0.007611	S.D. dependent var	0.074624
S.E. of regression	0.074907	Akaike info criterion	-2.262197
Sum squared resid	0.353497	Schwarz criterion	-2.067927
Log likelihood	84.0458	F-statistic	0.89727
Durbin-Watson stat	1.944518	Prob(F-statistic)	0.488564

COVARIANCE MATRIX

	C	REXIMLN(-1)	LNUSGDP	LOG(REEXCL
C	4.855597	-0.00265	0.065411	-0.537999
REXIMLN	-0.00265	0.010115	0.004308	0.000417
LNUSGDP	0.065411	0.004308	0.00364	-0.007134
LOG(REEXCLO)	-0.537999	0.000417	-0.007134	0.059617

White Heteroskedasticity Test:

F-statistic	10.45906	Probability	0
Obs*R-squared	31.29682	Probability	0.000008

Test Equation:
Dependent Variable: RESID^2
Method: Least Squares
Date: 03/11/08   Time: 11:29
Sample: 1991:02 1996:10
Included observations: 69

Variable	Coefficient	Std. Error	t-Statistic	Prob.
C	-0.589239	0.271825	-2.167712	0.034
LOG(REEXCLO)	-0.074604	0.012968	-5.753014	0
(LOG(REEXCLO))^:	0.00413	0.053048	0.077863	0.9382
REXIMLN(-1)	-0.061689	0.021351	-2.889265	0.0053
REXIMLN(-1)^2	-0.014435	0.017969	-0.803329	0.4248
LNUSGDP	0.064249	0.03004	2.138756	0.0363

R-squared	0.453577	Mean dependent var	0.005488
Adjusted R-squared	0.41021	S.D. dependent var	0.011206
S.E. of regression	0.008606	Akaike info criterion	-6.589798
Sum squared resid	0.004666	Schwarz criterion	-6.395528
Log likelihood	233.348	F-statistic	10.45906
Durbin-Watson stat	1.968705	Prob(F-statistic)	0

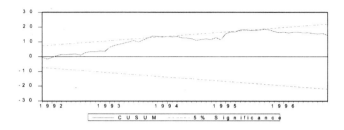

ADF Test Statistic	-4.4435	1%	Critical Value*	-3.5297
		5%	Critical Value	-2.9048
		10%	Critical Value	-2.5896

*MacKinnon critical values for rejection of hypothesis of a unit root.

Augmented Dickey-Fuller Test Equation
Dependent Variable: D(REXIMLNRESIDUAL)
Method: Least Squares
Date: 03/11/08   Time: 11:21
Sample(adjusted): 1991:04 1996:10
Included observations: 67 after adjusting endpoints

Variable	Coefficient	Std. Error	t-Statistic	Prob.
REXIMLNRESIDUA	-1.093923	0.246185	-4.4435	0
D(REXIMLNRESIDU	-0.146671	0.196555	-0.746208	0.4583
D(REXIMLNRESIDU	-0.110394	0.124635	-0.885739	0.3791
C	-0.001798	0.009013	-0.199453	0.8426

R-squared	0.626013	Mean dependent var	-0.00284
Adjusted R-squared	0.608204	S.D. dependent var	0.117806
S.E. of regression	0.073739	Akaike info criterion	-2.318725
Sum squared resid	0.342559	Schwarz criterion	-2.187101
Log likelihood	81.67728	F-statistic	35.15165
Durbin-Watson stat	1.960138	Prob(F-statistic)	0

Bibliography

1. Abiad, Abdul, and Ashoka M. (2003): Financial Reform: What Shakes It? What Shapes It?, IMF Working Paper, Working Paper 03/70, available at: http://www.imf.org/external/pubs/ft/wp/2003/wp0370.pdf downloaded on June 24, 2008.

2. Adams, C, Litan R. and Pomerleano (2000): Managing Financial and Corporate Distress Lessons from Asia.

3. Agemon, P. (2002): Benefits and Costs of International Financial Integration: Theory and Facts, The World Bank, available at: http://www.worldbank.org/wbi/globalizationandmacro/management/GDLN/MENA%20DLC/Papers/Session%205/Agenor-BenefCosts02a.pdf downloaded on March 2Oth, 2008.

4. Alegria, Jorge (2004): El Mercado Mexicano de Derivados, available at: www.mexder.com.mx/inter/info/mexder/avisos/ITESM%20%202%20Septiembre%202004.ppt , downloaded on June, 3rd, 2009.

5. Allen, Roy (2000): Financial Crises and Recession in the Global Economy, 2nd Edition, Edward Elgar Publishing, Cheltenham.

6. Andersen, Palle and White, W. (1996): The Macroeconomic Effects of Financial Sector Reforms: an Overview of Industrial Countries, in OECD Proceedings: Macroeconomic Policy and Structural Reforms, Paris.

7. An, Galina & Iyigun, Murat F. (2004): The Export Technology Content, Learning by doing and Specialization in Foreign Trade, in: Journal of International Economics, Elsevier, vol. 64(2), December, p. 465-483.

8. Angell, Wayne (1992): Cooperative Approaches to Reducing Risks in Financial Markets, in: Edwards, Franklin and Patrick, Hugh (1992): Regulating International Financial Markets: Issues and Policies, Kluwer Academic Publishers, Boston, available at: http://www.mof.go.jp/f-review/r32/r_32_151_186.pdf downloaded on January 2nd, 2009.

9. APEC and Banco de México (2003): 9TH APEC Finance Ministers´ Process: Improving the Allocation of Domestic Saving for Economic Development, available at: www.banxico.org.mx/ downloaded on March 20th, 2008

10. Arestis, Philip (2005): Fiscal Policies in Emerging Markets, Book review, edited by Mario Blejer and Skreb Marko, MIT Press 2002, Cambridge and London: in Journal of Economic Literature, 2005, Vol. 43, p. 187-188.

11. Arndt, Sven, Huemer, A. (2002): Trade, Production Networks and The Exchange Rate, Lowe Institute of Political Economy Claremont McKenna College, available at: http://www.claremontmckenna.edu/econ/papers/WP04-02.pdf , downloaded on Dec. 3rd, 2007.

12. Arnoldi, Jakob (2003): Derivatives: Virtual Values and Real Risks, available at: http://tcs.sagepub.com/cgi/content/abstract/21/6/23 , downloaded on Dec.1, 2009.

13. Arpan, J.S., Kim, D.S. (1973): Export Development, Product Life Cycle and LCDS: the case of Korea, in: Journal of Economic Development, 4 (2), 61– 87.

14. Asian Development Bank (1997): Asia's Growth Prospects Stable at Reduced Level, available at: http://www.adb.org/Documents/News/1997/nr1997019.asp downloaded on March 23rd, 2008.

15. Aspe, Pedro (1993): El Camino Mexicano de la Transformación Económica, Fondo de Cultura Económica, México D.F.

16. Aizenman, Joshua (2005): Financial Liberalizations in Latin-America in The 1990s: Reassessment, in: NBER Working Paper Series, Working Paper 11145.

17. Avilés, Roberto (1994): Obtienen beneficios Grupos Financieros, Grupo Reforma, 04-Nov., México, D.F.

18. Bhagwati, Jagdish (1978): Foreign Trade Regimes and Economic Development: Anatomy and Consequences of Exchange Control Regimes, National Bureau of Economic Research, Cambridge.

19. ---------------------- (1983): International Factor Mobility, Essays in International Economic Theory, Vol. 2, MIT Press, Cambridge.

20. ---------------------- (1984): Why Are Services Cheaper in Poor Countries?," Economic Journal 94, (June), p. 279-286.

21. Balassa, Bela (1964): The Purchasing Power Party Doctrine: A Reappraisal, in: Journal of Political Economy, Nr. 72, December, p. 584-596.

22. ----------------- (1971): The Structure of Protection in Developing Countries. Johns Hopkins University Press, Baltimore.

23. -------------------(1971): The Structure of Protection in Developing Countries, Johns Hopkins University Press, Baltimore.

24. Banco de México (1993): Informe Anual, Dirección de Investigación Económica del Banco de México, México, D.F.

25. -------------------------- (1994): Informe Anual, Dirección de Investigación Económica del Banco de México, México, D.F.

26. -------------------------- (1995): Informe Anual, Dirección de Investigación Económica del Banco de México, México, D.F.

27. ------------------------- (1996): Informe Anual, Dirección de Investigación Económica del Banco de México, México, D.F.

28. ------------------------ (2003): "Implications of Financial Liberalization for the Promotion and Allocation of Domestic Saving: The Case of Mexico" , in: APEC Policy Dialogue on "Improving the Allocation of Domestic Saving for Economic Development, pp. 197-227.

29. ------------------------- (2008): Estadísticas Financieras y Económicas, available at: http://www.banxico.org.mx/tipo/estadísticas/index.html downloaded in 2008.

30. Bank of International Settlements (BIS) (1993): Annual Report, Basle.

31. --(1994): Annual Report, Basle.

32. --(1994b): Prudential supervision of banks' derivatives activities, Basle Committee on Banking Supervision, availa-ble at: http://www.bis.org/publ/bcbs14.pdf?noframes=1 , downloaded on June 19th, 2009.

33. --(1995): Annual Report, Basle.

34. --(1995b): Issues of Measurement Re-lated to Market Size and Macroprudential Risks in Derivatives Markets, Feb-ruary, available at: http://www.bis.org/publ/ecsc05.pdf , downloaded on June 19th, 2009.

35. --(1996): Annual Report, Basle.

36. --(1996b): Quarterly Review, Basle Au-gust.

37. --(1999): 69th Annual Report, Basle.

38. -- (2009), Measuring Financial Innovation and its Impact, Proceedings of the IFC Conference, Basel, 26–27 August 2008, July available at: www.bis.org/ifc/publ/ifcb31.htm downloaded on Octo-ber 20th, 2009.

39. Barro, Robert (1980): A Capital Market in an Equilibrium Business Cycle Model, in: Econometrica, 48 (Sept.), p. 1393-1417.

40. Barro, Robert (1991): Economic Growth in a Cross Section of Countries, in: Quarterly Journal of Economics, 106, p. 407-444.

41. Basle Committee on Banking Supervision and Technical Committee of the In-ternational Organisation of Securities Commissions ("IOSCO") (1995): Public Disclosure of the Trading and Derivative Activities of Banks and Securities

Firms, Joint Report, November 1995, available at: http://riskinstitute.ch/141190.htm downloaded in June 6th, 2009.

42. Bender Bender und Hemmer Hans-Rimbert (Her.). (1999) Verein für Entwicklungsökonomische Forschungsförderung (Eff) E.V. available at http://www.verein-eff.de/proceedings/tagungsband_1999.pdf downloaded on Oct. 12th, 2008.

43. Bertuch-Samuels, Axel and Störmann, Wiebke (1995): Derivative Finanzinstrumente: Nutzen und Risiken, Deutsche Sparkassenverlag GmbH, Stuttgart.

44. Besley, Timothy and Zagha, R. eds. (2005) Development Challenges in the 1990s: Leading Policymakers Speak from Experience, World Bank and Oxford University Press, Washington.

45. Blanco, Gonzalo and Verma, S. (1997): The Financial System in Mexico. Characteristics, Institutions, Instruments and Operations, Captus Press Inc., North York.

46. Bordo, Michael (2006): Sudden Stops, Financial Crises and Original Sin In Emerging Countries: Déjà Vu?, in: NBER Working Papers, Working Paper 12393.

47. Bordo, Michael and Schwartz, Anna (1996): Why Clashes Between Internal and External Stability Goals End in Currency Crises, 1797-1994, in: Open Economies Review, Nr. 7 p.437-468.

48. Botman, Dennis and Cees, Diks (2002): Location of Investors and Capital Flight, Tinbergen Institute Discussion Paper, TI 2002-013/1 available at: http://www.tinbergen.nl/discussionpapers/02013.pdf downloaded on Oct. 14th, 2008.

49. Bouzas, Roberto and Ffrench-Davis, Ricardo (2005): Globalization and Equity: A Latin American Perspective, in: Natalia Dinello and Squire Lyn (2005): Globalization and Equity Perspectives from the Developing World, Edward Elgar Publishing, Cheltenham.

50. Boyer, Russell (2004): Mundell's International Economics: Adaptations and Debates*, University of Western Ontario Warren Young, Bar-Ilan University, Wednesday, May 19, 2004, Document prepared for the conference to honor Michael Mussa, International Monetary Fund, Washington, D.C. available at: http://www.imf.org/external/np/res/seminars/2004/mussa/pdf/boyer.pdf downloaded on Jan. 2nd 2010.

51. Brainard W., Nordhaus W. and Watts H., eds. (1991): Money, Macroeconomics and Economic Policy. Essays in Honor of James Tobin, MIT Press, Cambridge.

52. Buira, Ariel (2003): The Governance of the IMF in a Global Economy. Available via Internet: http://www.g24.org/buiragva.pdf downloaded on December 5th, 2006.

53. Bulir, Alex and Swiston, A. (2005): Private Saving in Mexico—Long-Term Trends and Short-Term Changes, in: International Monetary Fund. Mexico: Selected Issues. October 20th, p. 22-44.

54. Burger, Albert, ed. (1989): U.S. Trade Deficit: Causes, Consequences and Cures, Luwer Academic Publishers, Boston.

55. Burenstam Linder, Staffan (1961): An Essay on Trade and Transformation, Ph.D. Dissertation of the Handelshögskolan Stockholm, Uppsala.

56. Bustillo, Ines and Velloso, Helvia (2000): Bonds Markets for Latin American Debt in the 1990's, Economic Commission for Latin America and the Caribbean Santiago, Serie Coyuntura No. 12, November 2000, available at: http://www.eclac.cl/publicaciones/xml/9/5169/lcl1441i.pdf downloaded on Oct. 31st, 2009.

57. Bracho, Gerardo (2003): ON the Causes of Mexico's Economic Slowdown

58. Cabello, Alejandra (1999): Globalización y Liberalización Financieras y la Bolsa Mexicana de Valores : del Auge a la Crisis. Plaza y Valdes, México D.F.

59. Calvo, Guillermo (1994): "Comment" to Rudiger Dornbusch and Alejandro Werner, "Mexico: Stabilization. Reform and No Growth", in: Brookings Papers on Economic Activity I: 94. Brookings Institution, Washington D.C., p. 298-303.

60. ---------------------- (2000): Betting against the State: Socially Costly Financial Engineering, in Journal of International Economics, Vol. 51, p. p. 5–19.

61. Calvo, Guillermo and Mendoza, Enrique (1996): Petty Crime and Cruel Punishments: Lessons from the Mexican Debacle, The American Economic Review, Vol. 86, No. 2.

62. Cavallo, Domingo (2006): Tratados de Libre Comercio entre la Unión Europea y Centroamérica, la Comunidad Andina y el Merco Sur: Motor para Nuevas Relaciones Biregionales, Speech held at the America Latina, el Continente Olvidado Conference, December 6th , Hamburg.

63. Cavazos, Ricardo H. (2002): The Adjustment Process of the Balance of Goods and Services against Fluctuations of the Real Exchange Rate: An Application of the J-Curve for the case of Mexico, (available at: http://www.american.edu/cas/econ/workingpapers/2006-05.pdf , downloaded on April 12th, 2007.

64. Cárdenas, Enrique (1996): La Política Económica en México 1950-1994, Fondo de Cultura Económica, México.

65. Cespedes, L.; Chang, R. and Velasco, A. (2003): IS-LM-BP in the Pampas, IMF Staff Papers, Vol. 50, Special Issue.

66. Carstens, Agustin and Werner, Alejandro (1999): Mexico's Monetary Policy Framework under a Floating Exchange Rate Regime, Banco de México.

67. Chang Roberto and Velasco, Andrés (1998): Financial Crises in Emerging Markets: A Canonical Model, in: NBER Working Paper Series, Working Paper 6006.

68. --- (1999): Liquidity Crises in Emerging Markets: Theory and Policy, in: NBER Working Paper Series, Working Paper 7272.

69. Charrette, Susan (1993): The Determinants of Capital Flight, in: Money Affairs, Jan-June.

70. Chestnut, Teddy, Joseph A. (2005): The IMF and the Washington Consensus: A Misunderstood and Poorly Implemented Development Strategy, Council on Hemispheric Affairs, July 17th.

71. Cline, William (1995): International Debt Reexamined, Institute for International Economics, Washington.

72. Commonwealth Treasury of Australia (2003): The Role of Financial Liberalisation in the Promotion and Allocation of Domestic Savings in Australia, in: APEC and Banco de México, "Improving the Allocation of Domestic Saving for Economic Development, p. 79-93.

73. Colander, David (2003): Post-Walrasian Macro Policy and the Economics of Muddling Through, Middlebury College Economics Discussion Paper No. 03-22r, Department of Economics, Middlebury College, available at: http://www.middlebury.edu/services/econ/repec/mdl/ancoec/0322R.pdfhttp://www.middlebury.edu/~econ downloaded on January 2nd, 2007.

74. Correa, Eugenia (2001): La Economia Mexicana y los Mercados Financieros Internacionales, in: Información Comercial Espanola, Revista del Ministerio de Economia,available at: http://www.revistasice.com/cmsrevistasICE/pdfs/ICE_795_8799__4CF5AADC832251B5AFDC3082FD240307.pdf downloaded on: July 1st 2009.

75. Cortez, Klender (2004): Dinámica no lineal del tipo de cambio: Aplicación al Mercado Mexicano, Barcelona: Unpublished PhD. Thesis, Universitat Barcelona.

76. Cronin, Patrick (2003): Explaining Free Trade: Mexico 1985-1988, in: Latin American Politics and Society, Winter 2003.

77. Culpeper, Roy (1995): La Reanudación de las Corrientes Privadas de Capital hacia la America Latina, in: Ffrench-Davis, Ricardo and Griffith-Jones,

Stephany, comp. (1995): Las Nuevas Corrientes Financieras hacia la América Latina, Fondo de Cultura Económica, Chile.

78. Dabat, Alejandro, coord. (1994): México y la Globalización, Centro Regional de Investigaciones Interdisciplinaras, Universidad Nacional Autónoma de México, available at: http://www.crim.unam.mx/bibliovirtual/Libros/ downloaded on Sept. 25, 2008.

79. Dabat, Alejandro and Toledo, Alejandro (1999): Internacionalización y Crisis en México, CRIM; México.

80. Das, Dilip (1999): East Asia Export Growth and Prospects, Asia Pacific Press at the Australia University, available at: http:// ncdsnet.anu.edu.au

81. Delamaide, Darrell (1985): The Off-Balance-Sheet Dilemma, in: Institutional Investor, October 1985.

82. DeLong, Bradford and Eichengreen, Barry (2001): Between Meltdown and Moral Hazard: The International Monetary and Financial Policies of the Clinton Administration, in: NBER Working Paper Series, Working Paper 8443.

83. DeLong; Bradford (1997): Managing International Financial Disorder: Lessons [?] From the Peso Crisis, available online at: http://www.j-bradford-delong.net/comments/managing.html downloaded on July 12, 2008.

84. ---------------------- (1998): Helping Countries Prepare for International Capital Flows. USIA Economic Perspectives (August 5th).

85. --------------------- (1999): Financial Crises in the 1890's and 1990's, in: Brookings Papers on Economic Activity (Fall) p..253-279.

86. --------------------- (2000): The Triumph of Monetarism? Journal of Economic Perspectives (Winter).

87. --------------------- (2001): Animal Spirits, Moral Hazard and the Shadow of the Bretton Woods Conference, available at: http://www.j-bradford-delong.net/TotW/Clinton_IEP downloaded on June 2007.

88. Del Villar, R., Backal, Treviño (1997): Experiencia Internacional en la Resolución de Crisis Bancarias, in: Serie de Documentos de Investigación, No. 9708, Banco de México.

89. De Luna, José (2002): Globalisierung und Finanzkrisen: Lehren aus Mexiko und aus Korea, Dissertation am Fachbereich Politische Wissenschaft der Freien Universität Berlin, available at: http://www.diss.fuberlin.de/diss/servlets/MCRFileNodeServlet/FUDISS_derivate_000000000769/ downloaded on Nov. 2, 2009.

90. Demirgüc, Asli and Detragiache, E. (1997): The Determinants of Banking Crises: Evidence for Developing and Development Countries, in: IMF Staff Papers, Vol. 45, No.1., March, International Monetary Fund, Washington,

91. De Vroey (1984): Inflation a Non-monetarist Monetary Interpretation, in: Post-Keynesian Economics, Sawyer, M. (1988) ed., Edward Elgar Publishing Limited, Aldershot.

92. De la Garza, Enrique (2005): Modelos de Producción en el Sector Maquilador: Tecnología, Organización del Trabajo y Relaciones Laborales, in: Contaduría y Administración, Jan-April, N. 215, Universidad Nacional Autónoma de México, México D.F., p. 91-124.

93. De Leon, Adrian (2004): Trade Liberalization and Productivity Growth, Some Lessons from the Mexican Case, Investigaciones Geográficas, UNAM, México pp. 55-66.

94. Deutsche Bundesbank (1993): Bilanzunwirksame Geschäfte deutscher Banken in: Deutsche Bundesbank, Monatsbericht 10, 1993, p. 47-69.

95. Dinello, Natalia and Squire Lyn eds. (2005): Globalization and Equity Perspectives from the Developing World, Edward Elgar Publishing, Cheltenham.

96. Dodd, Randall (2000): The Role of Derivatives in the East Asian Financial Crisis, in: CEPA Working Papers, Working Paper No. 20, November, available at:http://efinance.org.cn/cn/PHDS/The%20Role%20of%20Derivatives%20in%20the%20East%20Asian%20Financial%20Crisis.pdf downloaded on June 12th, 2009.

97. ----------------- (2002): Derivatives Markets: Sources of Vulnerability in U.S. Financial Markets, available at: http://www.financialpolicy.org/fpfspr8.pdf downloaded on June 20th, 2009.

98. Dooley, Michael (2000): A Model of Crisis in Emerging Markets, in: Economic Journal, V. 110, p. 256-272.

99. Dooley, M., Garber and Landau (2007): The Two Crises of International Economics, NBER Working Papers 13197.

100. Dornbusch, Rudiger (1991): Policies to Move From Stabilization to Growth, Proceedings of the World Bank Annual Conference on Development Economics, World Bank, Washington, D.C.

101. _____ (1992): The Case for Trade Liberalization in Developing Countries, The Journal of Economic Perspectives, Vol. 6, No. 1, pp. 69-85 available at: http://links.jstor.org/sici?sici=0895-3309%28199224%296%3A1%3C69%3ATCFTLI%3E2.0.CO%3B2-G downloaded in June 1st, 2010.

102. Dornbusch, Rudiger and Frenkel, J. ed. (1979): International Economic Policy, Theory and Evidence, The Johns Hopkins University Press, Baltimore.

103. Dornbusch, Rüdiger and Werner, A. (1994): Mexico: Stabilization, Reform and No Growth, Brookings Papers on Economic Activity 1994:I, MIT Press, Cambridge.

104. Dornbusch, Rudiger; Goldfajn, I. and Valdes, R. (1995): Currency Crises and Collapses, MIT Press, Cambridge.

105. Dornbusch, Rüdiger (1997): The Folly, the Crash and Beyond: Economic Policies and the Crisis, in: Edwards, Sebastian and Naím, Moisés eds. (1997): The Anatomy of an Emerging-Market-Crash, Carnegie Endowment for International Peace, Washington, D.C.

106. Dussel Peters, Enrique (2001): Has Nafta Contributed To Economic Development In Mexico? , Conference held at: The Center for International Finance and Development, University of Iowa College of Law, March.

107. ------------------------------- (2003): "Ser o no ser Maquila, ¿Es esa la Pregunta?" in: Comercio Exterior, 53 (4), p. 328-336.

108. -------------------------------(2004): Liberalización Comercial en México: 15 Años Después, Conference held at: "State Reform While Democratizing and Integrating: The Political Economy of Change in Mexico after Fox and NAFTA", Universidad de Notre Dame, South Bend/Indiana, U.S., Nov. 2004, available at: http://kellogg.nd.edu/events/pdfs/peters.pdf downloaded on Feb. 4th, 2008.

109. -------------------------------(2005): Economic Opportunities and Challenges Posed by China for Mexico and Central America, Deutsches Institut für Entwicklungspolitik gGmBH, Bonn, available at http://www.dusselpeters.com/dussel-tema-china.html downloaded on May 2008.

110. Dymski, Gary (2002): The International Debt Crisis, September 12 in: University of California of Riverside Economic Paper 2, available at: http://economics.ucr.edu/papers/papers02/02-10.pdf downloaded on June 20th, 2009.

111. Ebrahim-zadeh, Christine (2003): Dutch Disease: Too Much Wealth Managed Unwisely, in: Finance and Development, IMF, available at: http://www.imf.org/external/pubs/ft/fandd/2003/03/ebra.htm downloaded on Jan. 10th. 2008.

112. Edelstein, P. and Morgan, D. (2006): Local or State? Evidence on Bank Market Size Using Branch Prices, in: Economic Policy Review, Federal Reserve Bank of New York. May 2006. Volume 12 Nr. 1.

113. Edwards, Franklin and Patrick, Hugh (1992): Regulating International Financial Markets: Issues and Policies, Kluwer Academic Publishers, Boston.

114. Edwards, Sebastian (1984): The Order of Liberalization of the External Sectors in Developing Countries, Princeton Essays in International Finance, No. 156, Princeton University, Princeton.

115. --------------------------- (1992): Trade Orientation, Distortions and Growth in Developing Countries, in: Journal of Development Economics, 39, (1).

116. --------------------------- (1994): Trade and Industrial Policy Reform in Latin America, in: NBER Working Paper Series, Working Paper 4772.

117. --------------------------- (1996): Why Are Latin America's Savings Rates so Low? An International Comparative Analysis, Journal of Development Economics, Vol. 51, p. 5–44.

118. --------------------------- (1997): The Mexican Peso Crisis. How much did we know? When did we know it? , in: NBER Working Paper Series, Working Paper 6334.

119. --------------------------- (2004): Thirty years of Current Account Imbalances, Current Account Reversals and Sudden Stops, in: NBER Working Paper Series, Working Paper 10276.

120. --------------------------- (2006): Financial Openness, Currency Crises and Output Losses, NBER.

121. El Universal (2009): El Fobaproa Costó Más que Rescate en EU: Zedillo, Jan. 28th, available at: http://www.eluniversal.com.mx/notas/572604.html downloaded on Jan. 10, downloaded on Jan. 10, 2010.

122. Ellis, Howard S. and Metzler, Lloyd (1949): Readings in the Theory of International Trade, The Blakiston Company, Philadelphia.

123. Ernst, Christoph (2005): Trade liberalization, Export Orientation and Employment in Argentina, Brazil and Mexico, Employment Strategy Papers, International Labor Organization 2005-15, Geneve, available at: http://www.ilo.org/public/english/employment/strat/download/esp2005-15.pdf downloaded on September 22nd, 2007.

124. Erturk, Korkut (2001): Overcapacity and the East Asian crisis, in: Journal of Post Keynesian Economics / Winter 2001–2002, Vol. 24, No. 2 253 available at: http://www.econ.utah.edu/~korkut/overcapacity%20and%20the%20east%20asian%20crisis.pdf downloaded on March 25th, 2008.

125. Estay, Jaime (1997): Relaciones Comerciales Externas y Flujos de Inversión Extranjera hacia la Economía Mexicana.

126. Faini, Riccardo; Pritchett, Lant and Clavijo, Fernando (1998): Import Demand in Developing Countries, Policy, Planning, and Research Working Papers 122, The World Bank, November.

127. Farhi, Maryse and Borghi, Roberto Alexandre Zanchetta (2009): Operações com Derivativos Financeiros das Corporações de Economias Emergentes, Estud. av. [online], 2009, vol. 23, n.66 pp. 169-188, available at: http://www.scielo.br/scielo.php?script=sci_arttext&pid=S0103-40142009000200013&lng=en&nrm=iso downloaded on Sept. 16th, 2009.

128. Federal Reserve Bank of Chicago (1996): The Unique Risk of Investments in Emerging Markets, available at: http://www.chicagofed.org/publications/capitalmarketnews/uniquer.pdf downloaded on June 20th, 2009.

129. Feliz, Raul and Welch, John (1993): The Credibility and Performance of Unilateral Target Zones: A Comparison of the Mexican and Chilean Cases, in Dallas Fed Research Papers Nr. 9331, August, available at: http://www.dallasfed.org/research/papers/1993/wp9331.pdf , downloaded on June 27th, 2009.

130. Feldstein, Martin (1999): International Capital Flows, NBER Books, Cambridge.

131. Fernandez-Vega, Carlos (2002): Mexico, S.A, in: La Jornada, 30 de Abril available at: http://www.jornada.unam.mx/2002/04/30/024a1eco.php?origen=opinion.html downloaded on June 27[th,] 2009.

132. Fernandez-Arias, Eduardo (1996): The New Wave of Private Capital Inflows: Push or Pull?, in: Journal of Development Economics, Vol. 48, p. 389-418

133. Fidler, Stephen (1987a): Why Commercial Banks Look for Liberalization, FT June 16, 1987.

134. Fidler, Stephen (1987b): BIS Concerned at Pace of Change, FT, June 17th, 1987.

135. Fischer, Andreas (1999): Die Auswirkungen der Volatilität des Wechselkurses auf den Schweizer Aussenhandel: Schätzungen mit einem Multivariaten Ansatz, Schweizerische Nationalbank, available at: http://www.snb.ch/de/mmr/reference/quartbul_1999_2_ausw/source/quartbul_1999_2_ausw.de.pdf downloaded on Feb. 7th, 2007.

136. Fischer, Stanley (1994): Comment" to Rudiger Dornbusch and Alejandro Werner, "Mexico: Stabilization. Reform and No Growth", in: Brookings Papers on Economic Activity I: 94. Washington D.C.: Brookings Institution. 303-312

137. ------------------ (2002): Financial Crises and Reform of The International Financial System, in: NBER Working Paper Series, Working Paper 9297.

138. Ffrench-Davis, Ricardo (1992): The Return of Private Capital to Latin America: A Word of Caution in 1992 for "Successful" Countries, in: Williamson, S. et al. , Fragile Finance, ed. by J.J. Teunissen, FONDAD, The Hague.

139. ----------------------------- (2000): Reforming the Reforms in Latin America. St. Antony's Series, Oxford.

140.---------------------------- (2005): Comment on John Williamson, in: Besley, Timothy and Zagha, R. eds. (2005) Development Challenges in the 1990s: Leading Policymakers Speak from Experience, World Bank and Oxford University Press, Washington.

141. Ffrench-Davis, Ricardo and Griffith-Jones, Stephany, comp. (1995): Las Nuevas Corrientes Flnancieras hacia la América Latina, Fondo de Cultura Económica, Chile.

142. Fleming, Marcus (1962): Domestic Financial Policies under Fixed and Floating Exchange Rates, in: IMF Staff Papers 9, pp.369-379.

143. Flood, R. and Garber, P. (1984): Collapsing Exchange Rate Regimes: Some Linear Examples, in: Journal of International Economics, Vol. 17, p. 1-13.

144. Folkerts-Landau, David and Steinherr, Alfred (1994): The Wild Beasts of Derivatives: to be Chained Up, Fenced In or Tamed? in: Finance and the International Economy, The Amex Bank Review Prize Essays, Band 8, New York.

145. Förster, Walter (1936): Theorie der Währungsentwertung, Gustav Fischer Verlag, Jena.

146. Fox, Vicente (2002): Informe de Gobierno (State of the Nation Report), Message to the Honorable Congress of the Union from the President of Mexico, at the presentation of his Second State of the Nation Report, Mexico City.

147. Fox, Vicente (2005): Informe de Gobierno (State of the Nation Report), Message to the Honorable Congress of the Union from the President of Mexico, at the presentation of his Second State of the Nation Report, Mexico City.

148. Fox, Vicente (2006): Informe de Gobierno (State of the Nation Report), Message to the Honorable Congress of the Union from the President of Mexico, at the presentation of his Second State of the Nation Report, Mexico City.

149. Frankel, Jeffrey (2004): Contractionary Currency Clashes in Developing Countries, 5th Mundell-Fleming Lecture, IMF Annual Research Conference, Nov. 3.

150. Frankel, Jeffrey and Romer, David (1999): Does Trade Cause Growth, American Economic Review, Vol. 89, No. 3, June.

151. Frankel, Jeffrey and Schmukler, Sergio (1996): Country Fund Discounts, Asymmetric Information And The Mexican Crisis Of 1994: Did Local Residents

Turn Pessimistic Before International Investors? NBER Working Paper Series, Working Paper 5714.

152. Frankel, Jeffrey and Wei, Shang-Jin (2004): Managing Macroeconomic Crises, NBER Working Paper Series, Working Paper 1097.

153. Frenkel, Jacob and Razin, Assaf (1987): The Mundel - Feming Model: A Quarter Century Later, NBER Working Paper Series, Working Paper 2321.

154. Fukao, K., Okubo, T. and Stern, R: (2002): An Econometric Analysis of Trade Diversion under Nafta, Discussion Paper 491, University of Michigan.

155. Gagnon, Joseph and Rose, A. (1995): Dynamic Persistence of Industry Trade Balances: how Pervasive is the Product Cycle? in: Oxford Economic Papers 47 (2), p. 229– 248.

156. Garcia, Francisco, Hernández, Rosa (1997): La Política Económica y la Crisis de México, Centro de Estudios Estrátegicos, ITESM.

157. Garcia, Samuel (1993): Razones de Peso para el Nerviosismo, in: Corto Plazo, El Norte, 5. Noviembre, 1993.

158. Garber, Peter (1998): Derivatives in International Capital Flows, in: NBER Working Paper Series, Working Paper 6623.

159. Garber, Peter (1999) Risks to Lenders and Borrowers in International Capital Markets, Book chapter in: International Capital Flows, 1999, pp 363-420, National Bureau of Economic Research, p. 363-420.

160. Garber, Peter, ed. (1993): The Mexico-U.S. Free Trade Agreement, MIT Press, Cambridge.

161. -----------------, (2000): What you See versus What you Get: Derivatives in International Capital Flows, in: Adams, Litau and Pomerleano (2000), p. 361-383.n

162. Gärtner, Manfred und Lutz, Matthias (2004): Makroökonomik Flexibler und Fester Wechselkurse, 3. Auflage, Springer Verlag, Berlin.

163. Gavin, M. And R. Hausmann (1996): The Roots of Banking Crises: The Macroeconomic Context, in: Working Paper Series No. 318, Inter-American Development Bank, Washington, D.C.

164. General Accounting Office of the U.S. (1996): Mexico's Financial Crisis— Origins, Awareness, Assistance, and Initial Efforts to Recover, February.

165. Gil-Diaz, Francisco and Carstens, A. (1996): Some Hypotheses Related To The Mexican 1994-95 Crisis, Documento de Investigación No.9601, Serie Documentos de Investigación, Banco de México, Paper to be presented at the Annual January ASSA Meetings, January 5-7, San Francisco, California,.

213

166. Gil-Diaz, Francisco (2000): The China Syndrome or the Tequila Crisis, Working Paper No. 77, Center for Research on Economic Development and Policy Reform, Stanford University.

167. Girón, Alicia (2001): Inestabilidad y Crisis Financiera, in: ejournal Universidad Nacional Autónoma de México, available at: http://www.ejournal.unam.mx/pde/pde124/PDE12403.pdf downloaded on July 1st, 2009.

168. Girton, Lance and Roper, Don (1977): A Monetary Model of Exchange Market Pressure Applied to the Postwar Canadian Experience, in: American Economic Review, Vol. 67, p. 537-48.

169. Glick, Reuven and Rose, A. (1998): Contagion and Trade: Why are Currency Crises Regional, in: NBER Working Paper Series, Working Paper 6806.

170. Glaessner, Thomas and Oks, Daniel (1994): NAFTA, Capital Mobility and Mexico's Financial System, Paper presented at the session of "Capital Mobility and Financial Integration in North America", Allied Social Science Associations (ASSA) annual meetings, Boston, January 3-5, The World Bank, available at: http://www-wds.worldbank.org/external/default/WDSContentServer/IW3P/IB/1999/08/15/000178830_98111703524212/Rendered/INDEX/multi_page.txt downloaded on June 27th, 2009.

171. Gonzalez, Hector (1989): Economías de Escala y Concentración Bancaria, El Caso de México, in: Series de Documentos de Investigación, Banco de México, No. 29, Octubre.

172. Gonzales-Anaya, Jose (2002): " Why Have Banks Stopped Lending in Mexico Since the Peso Crisis in 1995. " Center for Research on Economic Development and Policy Reform, Stanford University. Working Paper No. 118.

173. Gonzalez, Sharaida (1994): Encabeza Ganancias la Banca Mexicana, Grupo Reforma, 19.Dic.

174. Griffith-Jones, Stephany (1995): Las corrientes de Fondos Privados Europeos hacia la América Latina, Hechos y Planteamientos, in: Ffrench-Davis, Ricardo and Griffith-Jones, Stephany, comp. (1995): Las Nuevas Corrientes Financieras hacia la América Latina, Fondo de Cultura Económica, Chile.

175. Grossman, Gene, and Helpman, Elhanan (1991): Innovation and Growth in the Global Economy, MIT Press, Cambridge.

176. Großmann, Jochen (1989): Erscheinungsformen und Auswirkungen der Verbriefungstendenz in Bankgewebe, Ph.D. Dissertation University of Erlangen, Verlag Peter Lang, Nürnberg.

177. Guerrero de Lizardi, Carlos (2001): Modelo De Crecimiento Económico Restringido por La Balanza de Pagos: Evidencia para México 1940-2000, available at: http://www.asepelt.org/ficheros/File/Anales/2004%20-%20Leon/comunicaciones/Guerrero.doc downloaded on April 21st, 2009.

178. Gurría Trevino, José Angel (1995): Corrientes de Capital, El caso de México, in: Ffrench-Davis, Ricardo and Griffith-Jones, Stephany, comp. (1995): Las Nuevas Corrientes Financieras hacia la América Latina, Fondo de Cultura Económica, Chile.

179. Hayami, Yujiro and Godo, Y. (2005): Development Economics, From the Poverty to the Wealth of the Nations. Oxford University Press, Oxford.

180. Hale, David (1995): Lessons from the Mexican Peso Crisis of 1995, for International Economic Policy, Preliminary manuscript, Oesterreichische National Bank (September), Vienna.

181. Hale, Galina and Arteta, C. (2006): Currency Crises and Foreign Credit in Emerging Markets: Credit Crunch or Demand Effect? available at: http://www.stanford.edu/group/SITE/Web%20Session%201/hale.pdf downloaded on December 2006.

182. Hamberger, Carl (1992): Geldpolitik bei hoher Kapitalmobilität, in: Köhler, Claus and Pohl, R. Hg. (1992) : Währungspolitische Probleme im integrierten Europa, Duncker & Humblot, Berlin.

183. Harberger, Arnold (1982): The Chilean Economy in the 1970s: Crisis, Stabilization, Liberalization,Reform, in: Karl Brunner and Allan Metzler, eds., Economic Policy in a World of Change, Carnegie-Rochester Conference Series on Public Policy, Vol. 17, North-Holland, Amsterdam.

184. Harberger, Arnold (1985): Lessons for Debtor Country Managers and Policymakers, in; International Debt and the Developing Countries, ed. by Gordon W. Smith and John T. Cuddington, A World Bank Symposium. Washington, D.C.

185. Heath, Jonatan (1995): La Inversión Extranjera de Portafolio, in: Reforma, 15. June 1995.

186. ----------------- (1996): La Inversión de Cartera en México, in: Comercio Exterior, Jan. 1996, Vol. 46, Nr. 1, p. p 34-38.

187. Hellmann, T., Murdock, K., and Stiglitz, J.E (2000): Liberalization, Moral Hazard in Banking and Prudential Regulation: Are Capital Requirements Enough? , in: American Economic Review, 90 (1).

188. Herz, Bernard (1987): Geldpolitik bei finanziellen Innovationen, Fritz Knapp Verlag, Frankfurt, Ph. D. Dissertation, University of Tübingen.

189. Hinshaw, Randall, ed. (1975): Key Issues in International Monetary Reforms. Dekker, New York.

190. Hirsch, S. (1975): The Product Cycle Model of International Trade: A Multi-Country Cross-Section Analysis, Oxford Bulletin of Economics and Statistics 37 (4), 305–317.

191. Hobday, M. (1995): Innovation in East Asia: the Challenge to Japan Edward Elgar Publishing, Aldershot.

192. Hoffmann, Mathias, Sondergaard, Jens, Westelius, N. (2007): The Timing and Magnitude of Exchange Rate Overshooting, Discussion Paper Series 1: Economic Studies, No. 28/2007.

193. Howell, M. (1993): Institutional Investors as a Source of Portfolio Investment in Developing Countries, document presented in the Symposium Portfolio Investment in Developing Countries, organized by the World Bank, Sept. 9 and 10th.

194. Ibarra, Alejandro (1999): Disinflation and the December 1994 Devaluation in Mexico, in: International Review of Applied Economics, Vol. 13, No. 1.

195. Illing, Gerhard (2001): Financial Fragilities, Bubbles and Monetary Policy, Cesifo Working Paper No. 449, April 2001.

196. IMF (1994): International Capital Markets: Development, Prospects and Policy Issues, September 1994, Washington, The International Monetary Fund.

197. --- (1995): International Capital Markets: Development, Prospects and Policy Issues, August 1995, Washington, D.C.

198. --- (1995b): Developments in 1994. Annex I: Factors behind the Financial Crisis in Mexico, June, Washington D.C..

199. --- (1995c): World Economic Outlook, Annex1, June 1995.

200. --- (2002): Global Financial Stability Report. World Economic and Financial Surveys, Washington.

201. --- (2005): Mexico, Selected Issues. October 20th.

202. --- (2005a): Common Criticisms on the IMF: Some Responses, available at: http://ww.imf.org/external/np/exr/ccrit/eng/crans.htm#7 downloaded on March 25th, 2005.

203. --- (2006): Mexico: Financial Sector Assesment Program Update – Technical Note- Derivatives Market –Overview and Potential Vulnerabilities, IMF Country Report No. 07/169, May, available at:

http://www.imf.org/external/pubs/ft/scr/2007/cr07169.pdf , downloaded on Nov. 28, 2009.

204. ---(2009): World Economic Outlook, IMF available at: http://www.imf.org/external/pubs/ft/weo/2009/02/pdf/c4.pdf downloaded on March 2010.

205. Instituto Nacional de Estadística, Geografía e Informática, INEGI (2007): Síntesis Metodológica de la Estadística del Comercio Exterior de México, available at: http://inegi.gob.mx , downloaded on Feb. 4th 2008.

206. -- (2006-9) Banco de Información Económica, available at: http://inegi.gob.mx

207. --
(2009): Producto Interno Bruto en México Durante el Primer Trimestre de 2009, Comunicado Núm. 149/09, 20 de Mayo de 2009, Aguascalientes,

208. --
(2009a): Resultados de la Encuesta Nacional de Ocupación y Empleo, Cifras Durante El Segundo Trimestre de 2009, Comunicado Núm. 217/09, 14 de Agosto de 2009, Aguascalientes,

209. Instituto para la Protección al Ahorro Bancario (2001): Marco legal y normatividad para la Protección al Ahorro, México, Septiembre.

210. Jeanneau, Serge and Tovar, Camilo (2008): Financial Stability Implications of Local Currency Bond Markets: An Overview Of The Risks, in: BIS Papers, No. 36, available at: http://www.bis.org/publ/bppdf/bispap36e.pdf , downloaded on June 23th, 2009.

211. Jeanneau, Serge and Pérez-Verdía, Carlos (2005): Verringerung der Anfälligkeit des Finanzsystems: Die Entwicklung des Inlandsmarktes für Staatsanleihen in Mexiko, BIZ Quartalsbericht, Dezember available online at: http://www.bis.org/publ/qtrpdf/r_qt0512ger_h.pdf downloaded on July, 31st, 2009.

212. Japan's External Trade Organization (1997): White Paper on International Trade, available at: http://www.jetro.go.jp/WHITEPAPER/Trade97/index.html downloaded on March 25th, 2008.

213. Jha, Raghbendra (2003): Macroeconomics for Developing Countries, Routledge, London.

214. Joebges, Heike diss. (2005): Transmissionsmechanismen von Währungskrisen am Beispiel der Tequilakrise (1994/5) und de Asienkrise (1997)

215. Kahler, M.ed.(1998): Capital Inflows, New York, Council on Foreign Relations.

216. Kamin, Steven and Wood, P. (1997): Capital Inflows, Financial Intermediation and Aggregate Demand: Empirical Evidence from Mexico and other Pacific Basin Countries, Board of Governors of the Federal Reserve System, International Finance Discussion Papers, June, Number 583.

217. Kaminski, Graciela (2000): Currency and Banking Crises: The Early Warnings of Distress, George Washington University, available at: http://www.gwu.edu/~clai/working_papers/Kaminsky_Graciela_07-00.pdf downloaded on Oct. 1st, 2008.

218. Kaminski, Graciela and Schmukler, Sergio (2007): Short-Run Pain, Long-Run Gain: Financial Liberalization and Stock Markets Cycles, available at: http://home.gwu.edu/~graciela/HOME-PAGE/RESEARCH-WORK/WORKING-PAPERS/booms-crashes.pdf downloaded on Jan. 3rd, 2010.

219. Kane, Eduard (1992): Government Officials as a Source of Systemic Risks in International Financial Markets, in: Edwards, Franklin and Patrick, Hugh (1992): Regulating International Financial Markets: Issues and Policies, Kluwer Academic Publishers, Boston.

220. Katz, Arnold (2006): An Overview of BEA's Source Data and Estimating Methods for Quarterly GDP, Bureau of Economic Analysis, U.S. Department of Commerce, available at: www.bea.gov/papers/pdf/china_source_data_estimating_methods.pdf downloaded on Feb. 22, 2008.

221. Kaufmann,D., Mehrez, G. and Schmukler (1999): Do Resident Firms Have an Informational Advantage? Policy Research Working Paper, The World Bank, available at: http://www-wds.worldbank.org/external/default/WDSContentServer/IW3P/IB/2000/01/15/000094946_99123006244653/Rendered/PDF/multi_page.pdf downloaded on Oct. 2nd, 2008.

222. Kaufmann, George (1992): Banking and Financial Intermediaries Markets in the U.S. Where to, Where from? , in: Edwards, Franklin and Patrick, Hugh (1992): Regulating International Financial Markets: Issues and Policies, Kluwer Academic Publishers, Boston.

223. Kessler, Timothy, (1999): Global Capital and National Politics: Reforming Mexico's Financial System, Praeger Publishers, Westport.

224. Kiel Institute of World Economics (1995). The Mexican Reform Process: Improving Long-Run Perspectives. Mastering Short-Run Turbulences. Study commissioned by the Mexican-German Chamber of Commerce and Industry, June, Kiel.

225. Kildegaard; Arne (2005): Fundamentals of Real Exchange Rate Determination: What Role in the Peso Crisis? In: El Colegio de México, Centro de Estudios Económicos in its journal Estudios Económicos. Vol. 21, Issue 1, p.

p. 3-22, available at:
http://revistas.colmex.mx/revistas/12/art_12_1124_8531.pdf downloaded on
May 10th. 2009.

226. Killick, Tony ed. (1984): The IMF and Stabilization, Developing Countries
Experiences, Heinemann Educational Books, London.

227. Köhler, Claus and Pohl, R. (1992): Währungspolitische Probleme im Integrierten Europa, Duncker & Humblot, Berlin.

228. Köhler, Wilhelm (1988): Faktorproportionen und Internationaler Handel,
Theorie und empirische Untersuchungen am Beispiel Österreichs, Tübingen:
Möhr.

229. Kravis, Irving and Lipsey, R. (1983): Toward and Explanation of National
Price Levels, Princeton Studies in International Finance 52 (November).

230. Krugman, P. (1979): A Model of Balance of Payment Crises, in: Journal of
Money, Credit and Banking.

231. --------------- (1979 b): A model of innovation, technology transfer, and the
world distribution of income. Journal of Political Economy 87 (2), 253– 266
(April).

232. --------------- (1988): Differences in Income Elasticities and Trends in Real
Exchange Rates, NBER Working Paper Series, Working Paper 2761.

233. --------------- (1990): Rethinking International Trade, MIT Press, Cambridge.

234. --------------- (1991): Geography and Trade, The MIT Press, Cambridge.

235. --------------- (1991b): Target zones and exchange rate dynamics, Quarterly
Journal of Economics, vol. 106, núm. 3, p. 669-682.

236. --------------- (1995): Emerging Market Blues, in: Foreign Affairs, July/August,
New York.

237. --------------- (1996): Pop Internationalism, MIT Press, Cambridge.

238. --------------- (1998): The Role of Geography in Development, Paper prepared for the Annual World Bank Conference on Development Economics,
April , Washington D.C..

239. Krugman, Paul and Helpman, E. (1992): Trade Policy and Market Structure,
MIT Press, Cambridge.

240. -- (1996): Market Structure and Foreign Trade,
MIT Press, Cambridge.

241. Krugman, Paul and Hanson, G. (1993): Mexico-U.S. Free Trade and the Location of Production, in: Garber, Peter, ed. (1993): The Mexico-U.S. Free Trade Agreement, MIT Press, Cambridge.

242. Krugman Paul and Obstfeld, M. (2003). International Economics: Theory and Policy, 6th edition, Adison Wesley, Boston.

243. Krueger, Ann (1978): Foreign Trade Regimes and Economic Development: Liberalization Attempts and Consequences, National Bureau of Economic Research, Cambridge.

244. Krueger, Anne and Tornell, A. (1999): The Role of Bank Reestructuring in Recovering from Crises: Mexico 1995-1998, in: NBER Working Paper Series. Working Paper 7042.

245. Kumhof, Michael (2004): Balance of Payment Crises: The Role of Short Term Debt, Stanford University, February 11, 2004, available at: http://www.stanford.edu/~kumhof/bigbop.pdf , downloaded on April 16th, 2007.

246. La Porta, Rafael, Lopez-de-Silanes, F. (1997): The Benefits of Privatization: Evidence from Mexico, in: NBER Working Paper Series, Working Paper 6215.

247. La Porta, R., Lopez-de-Silanes F and Zamarripa, G. (2003): Related Lending, in: Quarterly Journal of Economics, February, Vol. 118, Iss. 1, p. 231-6.

248. Laffont, J.J. and Tirole J. (1993): A theory of Incentives in Procurement and Regulation. The MIT Press, Cambridge.

249. Lall, S. (1998): Exports of Manufactures by Developing Countries: Emerging Patterns of Trade and Location, in: Oxford Review of Economic Policy 14 (2), p. 54– 73.

250. Lall, S. (2000): The Technological Structure and Performance of Developing Country Manufactured Exports,1985–98, in: Oxford Development Studies 28 (3), p. 337–369.

251. Landell-Mills, J. (1986): The IMF's International Banking Statistics, Washington, DC, IMF.

252. Leamer, Edward (1993): Wage Effects of a U.S. Mexican Free Trade Agreement, in: Garber, Peter, ed. (1993): The Mexico-U.S. Free Trade Agreement, MIT Press, Cambridge.

253. Ledermann, D., Menendez, A., Perry, G. and Stiglitz, J. (2000): Mexico, Five Years after the Crisis, in: Annual Worldbank Conference on Development, Pleskovic, B. and Stern, N. (2000) eds., the World Bank and Oxford University Press. Washington D.C.

254. Ledermann, Daniel; Maloney, W. and Serven, L. (2003): Lessons from Nafta for Latin America and the Caribbean Countries: A Summary of Research Findings, The World Bank, Washington, D.C.

255. Lerner, A (1944): The Economics of Control, Macmillan, New York.

256. Lewis, Marvin and Mizen, P. (2000): Monetary Economics, Oxford University Press, Oxford.

257. Little, Ian; Scitovsky, T. and Scott M. (1970): Industry and Trade in Some Developing Countries, Oxford University Press, Oxford.

258. Lopes, Francisco (1998): The Transmission Mechanism of Monetary Policy, in: a Stabilising Economy: Notes on the Case of Brazil, BIS Policy Papers, available at: http://209.85.129.104/search?q=cache:SJkbEFKoFsoJ:www.bis.org/publ/plcy0 3b.pdf+Transmission+mechanism+of+monetary+policy&hl=de&ct=clnk&cd=4 downloaded on February 23rd, 2007.

259. López, Pablo (2005): Coloquio Predoctoral Latinoamericano, in: Revista Leadership, Administración de Riesgos Financieros, Universidad Nacional Autónoma de México, available at: http://cladea.revistaleadership.com/doctoral/6.PAPER.Pablo%20Lopez-2005%20Final.pdf downloaded on June 15th, 2009.

260. Loyola Alarcón, José Antonio (1995): Desequilibrio Externo y Crisis Económica, Editorial Pac, México.

261. Lustig, Nora (1995): The Mexican Peso Crisis: the Foreseeable and the Surprise, Brookings Institution, available at: http://www.brookings.edu/views/papers/bdp/bdp114/bdp114.pdf downloaded on June 12, 2010.

262. ---------------- (1998): The Remaking of An Economy, The Brookings Institution, Washington, 2nd Ed.

263. Mancera, Miguel (1995): "Don't Blame Monetary Policy", in: The Wall Street Journal (January 31).

264. --------------------- (1997): Problems of Bank Soundness: Mexico's Recent Experience, Prepared for the "Seminar on Banking Soundness and Monetary Policy in a World of Global Capital Markets," IMF, January 28.

265. Mankiw, Gregory (2007): Macroeconomics, 6th edition, Worth Publishers, New York.

266. Manrique, Irma coord. (2000) Arquitectura de la Crisis Financiera, 1ª. Ed. Editorial Porrua, México.

267. Mares, M. (2005): Resoluciones Bancarias a Prueba de Balas. Artículos. Radioformula, January 28th, México, D.F.

268. Marshall, A. (1923): Money, Credit and Commerce, Macmillan, London.

269. Martinez, Lorenza; Sanchez O. and Werner A (2000): Consideraciones sobre la Conducción de la Política Monetaria y el Mecanismo de Transmisión en México, Banco de México.

270. McKinnon, Ronald (1982): The Order of Economic Stabilization: Lessons from Chile and Argentina, Carnegie –Rochester Conference Series on Public Policy 17, Autumn.

271. McKinnon, Ronald and Pill, H. (1995): Credible Liberalizations & International Capital Flows: The Overborrowing Syndrome, The American Economic Review, Vol. 87, No. 2, Papers and Proceedings of the Hundred and Fourth Annual Meeting of the American Economic Association (May, 1997), pp. 189-193.

272. Mc.Cartney Matthew (2004): Export Promotion, The Fallacy of Composition and Declining Terms of Trade (or the Moors Last Sigh), in: Department of Economics Working Papers, University of London.

273. Meigs, James A. (1997): Mexican Monetary Lessons, in: Cato Journal, Vol. 17. No.1. available at: http://www.catoinstitute.org/pubs/journal/cj17n1/cj17n1-4.pdf , downloaded on October 29th 2006.

274. Meltzer, Alan (1996): A Mexican Tragedy, American Enterprise Institute, January Washington D.C.

275. Menkhoff, Lukas (1999): Die Rolle Finanzieller Globalisierung in der Asienkrise, in: Dieter Bender und Hans-Rimbert Hemmer her. (1999) Verein für Entwicklungsökonomische Forschungsförderung (Eff) E.V. available at http://www.verein-eff.de/proceedings/tagungsband_1999.pdf downloaded on Oct. 12th, 2008.

276. Michaely, Michael (1985): The Demand for Protection against Exports of Newly Industrialized Countries, in: Journal of Policy Making 7 (1).

277. Mishkin, Frederic (1991): Asymmetric Information and Financial Crises, a Historical Perspective, in: Financial Markets and Financial Crises, edited by R. Glenn Huber, University of Chicago Press, p. 69-128.

278. Moreno-Brid, Juan Carlos (1999): Mexico's Economic Growth and the Balance of Payments Constraint: a Cointegration analysis, in: International Review of Applied Economics, Vol. 13, No. 2 available under: http://pdfserve.informaworld.com/846882_777306414_713673024.pdf downloaded on Dec. 13. 2008.

279. Moreno Brid, Juan Carlos (2001): Essays on Economic Growth and the Balance of Payments Constraint; with special reference to the case of Mexico, Ph.D. dissertation, Faculty of Economics and Politics, University of Cambridge.

280. --------------------------------- (2006): Exportaciones, Términos de intercambio y Crecimiento Económico de Brasil y México, de 1960 a 2002: un Análisis Comparativo, in: Problemas del Desarrollo, No. 146, julio 2006.

281. --------------------------------- (2006b): Manufactura y TLCAN: un camino de luces y sombras, in: Economía UNAM, No. 008, May, available at: http://www.ejournal.unam.mx/ecu/ecunam8/ecunam0806.pdf downloaded on June 1st, 2008.

282. Morales, H. (1992): Necesario liberar la paridad cambiaría del peso frente al dolar: Friedman; in: El Economista, May 20th.

283. Morera, Carlos (1998): El Capital Financiero en México y la Globalización. ERA, México.

284. Mishkin, F. (1996): The Channels of Monetary Transmission. Lessons for Monetary Policy, in: NBER Working Paper Series, Working Paper 5464.

285. --------------- (1996b): Understanding Financial Crises: A Developing Country Perspective, in: NBER Working Paper Series, Working Paper 5600.

286. --------------- (2001) Monetary Policy. NBER Research Summary. Available at: http://www0.gsb.columbia.edu/faculty/fmishkin/PDFpapers/01NBERRE.pdf downloaded on Nov. 24, 2006.

287. --------------- (2007): Monetary Policy Strategy, MIT Press, Cambridge.

288. Mooslechner, Peter (2003): Finance for Growth, Finance and Growth, Finance or Growth . . . ? Drei Erklärungsansatze zum Konnex zwischen den Finanzmarkten und der Realwirtschaft, in: Berichte und Studien 1/2003, ONB: Wien available at: http://www.oenb.at/de/img/ber_2003_1_tcm14-445.pdf , downloaded on March 20th, 2008.

289. Mundell, Robert (1961): The International Disequilibrium System, in: Kyklos.

290. -------------------- (1962): Capital Mobility and Stabilization Policy under Fixed and Flexible Exchange Rates, in: Canadian Journal of Economic and Political Science, Vol. 29, pp. 475-485.

291. -------------------- (1975): International Monetary Reform: Exchange Rate Issues in: Hinshaw (1975) ed.

292. -------------------- (2002): Notes on the Development of the International Macroeconomic Model, Columbia University Discussion Paper Series, Discussion Paper #:0102-33, New York.

293. Naím, Moisés and Edwards, Sebastian eds. (1998): Mexico 1994: Anatomy of an Emerging-Market Crash,: Carnegie Endowment for International Peace, Washington, D.C.

294. Narayan, S., and Wah, L.Y., (2000): Technological Maturity and Development without Research, in: Development and Change 31, p. 435–457.

295. Negrin, Jose Louis (2000): Mecanismos Para Compartir Informacion Crediticia: Evidencia Internacional y la Experiencia Mexicana, Banco de México, Dirección General de Investigación Económica, Working Paper 2000–05, México, D.F.

296. Neimann, Nancy (2001): States, Banks and Markets: Mexico's Path to Financial Liberalization in Comparative Perspective. Westview, Boulder.

297. Novelo, Federico (1999): La Política Exterior de México en la Era de la Globalización, PhD Thesis, Universidad Autónoma Metropolitana Xochimilco, available at http://www.eumed.net/tesis/fjnu/index.htm downloaded on march 24th, 2008.

298. Nunnenkamp, Peter (1992) Economic Policies and Attractiveness for Foreign Capital:The Experience of Highly Indebted Latin American Countries, Kiel Working Paper No. 539, available at: http://www.econstor.eu/dspace/bitstream/10419/617/1/042680468.pdf downloaded on Jan. 10th, 2010.

299. Obstfeld, M. (1998): The Global Capital Market: Benefactor or Menace. Draft prepared for the Journal of Economic Perspectives, April 27th, Berkeley.

300. ------------------(1994): The Logic of Currency Crises; in: NBER Working Paper Series, Working Paper 4640.

301. ------------------------------------- (2000): The Six Major Puzzles in International Macroeconomics: Is There a Common Cause? in: NBER Working Paper Series, Working Paper 7777.

302. ------------------------------------- (2007): The Unsustainable U.S. Current Account Position Revisited, NBER Working Papers, Working Paper 10869.

303. Obstfeld, M. and Rogoff, K. (1994): The Intertemporal Approach to the Current Account, in: NBER Working Paper Series, Working Paper 4893.

304. Obstfeld, M., Shambaugh, J. and Taylor, A. (2004): The Trilemma in History:Tradeoffs among Exchange Rates, Monetary Policies, and Capital Mobility, available at: http://elsa.berkeley.edu/~obstfeld/ost12.pdf downloaded on June, 14, 2010.

305. OECD (1996): Macroeconomic Policy and Structural Reforms, in: OECD Proceedings, Paris.

306. -------- (1996): Report on a joint meeting of management and trade union experts, OECD Labour / Management Program Government Policies Towards Financial Markets, 6 May 1996, Paris.

307. ------- (2002). Economic Survey: Mexico, Paris.

308. ------- (2006): Economic Policy Reforms: Going for Growth 2006: Structural Policy Indicators and Priorities in OECD Countries.

309. Ötker, Inci and Ceyla Pazarbaşioğlu (1996): Speculative Attacks and Currency Crises: The Mexican Experience, in: Open Economies Review, Vol. 7. P. 535-552.

310. Pätzold, Jürgen (1993): Stabilisierungspolitik, Verlag Paul Haupt, Bern.

311. Pacheco-Lopez, Penelope (2005): The Impact of Trade Liberalisation on Exports, Imports, the Balance of Payments and Growth : the Case of Mexico, Journal of Post Keynesian Economics , Issue: Volume 27, Number 4 /, available at : ftp://ftp.ukc.ac.uk/pub/ejr/RePEc/ukc/ukcedp/0401.pdf downloaded on April 20th, 2009.

312. Pacheco-Lopez, Penelope and Thirlwall, A.P. (2005): Trade Liberalisation, the Income Elasticity of Demand for Imports and Growth in Latin America, University of Kent Research Papers 05/06, available at: http://www.kent.ac.uk/economics/documents/research/papers/2005/0506.pdf downloaded on January 12, 2010.

313. Palazuelos Manso, Enrique (2001): Desequilibrio Externo y Crecimiento E- conomico en Mexico. Una Perspectiva de Largo Plazo, in: Revista ICE; Noviembre-Diciembre, No. 795, available at: http://www.revistasice.com/cmsrevistasICE/pdfs/ICE_795_9- 36__C98B7E7C5470BB04AA6F4AEE4FB5AE0D.pdf downloaded on April 21st, 2009.

314. Palley, Thomas (2009): Re-specifying the Keynesian Income-Expenditure Model to Properly Account for Imports: Implications for Fiscal Policy, Schwarz Center for Economic Policy Analysis (CEPA) Working Paper, February 2009, available at: http://www.cepa.newschool.edu/publications/workingpapers/SCEPA%20Worki ng%20Paper%202009-1.pdf downloaded on Nov. 13th, 2009.

315. Palma, Jose (2006): Growth after Globalisation: a 'Structuralist-Kaldorian' Game of musical chairs? A background paper for the World Economic and Social Survey 2006, Cambridge, available at: http://www.un.org/esa/policy/backgroundpapers/palma_final_paper.pdf downloaded on March 10th, 2008.

316. Partnoy, Frank (1999) F.I.A.S.C.O.: The Inside Story of a Wall Street Trader, Penguin, New York.

317. Perrotini, Ignacio (2003): Integración, Crecimiento y Asimetría Monetaria en el TLC: El Caso de México, Revista Venezolana de Análisis de Coyuntura, Vol IX, No. 1 (ene-jun), p. 253-282, available at: http://redalyc.uaemex.mx/redalyc/pdf/364/36490110.pdf downloaded on April 21st, 2009.

318. Österreichische Gesellschaft für Wirtschaftsraumforschung (1990): Wirtschaftsgeographische Studien, Service Fachverlag, Wien.

319. Perry, George (1991): Goals and Conduct of Stabilization Policy, in Money, Macroeconomics and Economic Policy. Essays in Honor of James Tobin, Brainard, Nordhaus and Watts (eds). Cambridge: MIT Press.

320. Persson, T.; Roland, G. and Tabellini, G. (2003): How Do Electoral Rules Shape Party Structures, Government Coalitions, And Economic Policies? available at: http://www.iies.su.se/~perssont/papers/prt4_21nov03.pdf downloaded on Jan. 24th, 2007.

321. Phelps, Edmund (1990): Seven Schools of Macroeconomic Thought, Oxford University Press, Oxford.

322. -------------------- (1997): A Strategy for Employment and Work: The Failure of Statism, Welfarism and Free Markets, Rivista Italiana degli Economisti, a. II, n. 1, Roma: April. Available at: http://www.columbia.edu/~esp2/strategy.pdf downloaded on Feb. 7th 2007.

323. Phelps, E. and Teck, H. (2005): A Structuralist Model of the Small Open Economy in the Short, Medium and Long Run. Singapore Management University and Columbia University, SMU Economics and Statistics Working Paper Series, May.

324. Pozos, Fernando, ed. (2003): La Vulnerabilidad Laboral del Model Exportador en México, Universidad de Guadalajara, Guadalajara.

325. Prinz, Aloys (1999): Stabilisierungspolitik: Theoretische Grundlagen und strategische Konzepte, Verlag Franz Vahlen, München.

326. Prebisch, Raul (1950): Commercial Policy in the Underdeveloped Countries, American Economic Review, 40, (2).

327. ------------------ (1984): Five Stages in my Thinking on Development, in: Dudley Seers, Pioneers in Development, Oxford University Press, Guadalajara.

328. Puyana, A. And Romero, J. (2006): The Mexican Economy after Two Decades Of Trade Liberalization: Some Macroeconomic and Sectoral Impacts and the Implications for Macroeconomic Policy, Paper presented at the International Development Economics Associates (IDEAS) and United Nations De-

velopment Programme (UNDP) conference on 'Post Liberalisation Constraints on Macroeconomic Policies', Muttukadu, India.

329. Razmi, A. and Blecker, Robert (2004): The Limits to Export-Led Growth: An Empirical Study, American University, Washington, D.C.

330. Ramos, Jorge Luis (2008): Descripción de la Política Económica y el Desarrollo en el Sector Automotriz Mexicano, in: Ensayos, Autorneto, Julio 24, available at: http://autorneto.com/literatura/ensayos/politica-economica-y-desarrollo-2/ downloaded on March, 20th, 2009.

331. Reinhart, Carmen and Vincent: Some Lessons for Policy Makers Dealing with the Mixed Blessings of Capital Inflows, in: Capital Inflows, Kahler, M.ed.(1998), New York, Council on Foreign Relations, pp. 93-128.

332. Reinhart Carmen and Dunaway Steven (1996): Dealing with capital Inflows: Are there any lessons? available at: http://mpra.ub.uni-muenchen.de/13764/1/unu-wider.pdf downloaded on Jan. 14, 2010.

333. Reinhart, Carmen and Rogoff, K. (2004): The Modern History of Exchange Rate Arrangements: A Reinterpretation, in: Quarterly Journal of Economics, Issue 1, p. 1-48.

334. --- (2008): Is the 2007 U.S. Sub-Prime Financial Crisis So Different? An International Historical Comparison, in: NBER Working Paper Series, Working Paper 137261.

335. Reisen, Helmut (1998): Sustainable and Excessive Current Account Deficits, in: OECD Working Paper Series, WP No. 132 available at: http://www.oecd.org/dataoecd/18/39/1922517.pdf downloaded on Jan. 3rd 2010.

336. Reyes, Sandra (2009): Encaminan Cambios para Regular Derivados, in: El Norte, Negocios, 16. Sept 2009.

337. Rivera, Edgar (1994): Reduce personal Banco Probursa, in: El Norte, 17 de Noviembre.

338. Rodríguez, Alejandro (2004): El Papel de la Apertura Comercial en el Crecimiento Económico y la Balanza Comercial de México, 1980-2002.

339. Rogoff, Kenneth (2002): Dornbusch's Overshooting Model after Twenty Five Years, IMF Working Paper, WP02/39, available at: http://www.imf.org/external/pubs/ft/wp/2002/wp0239.pdf downloaded on Feb. 12, 2010.

340. Ros, Jaime: (1995): Mercados Financieros, Flujos De Capital y Tipo De Cambio en México, Economía Mexicana. Nueva Época, vol. IV, núm. 1, 1er. Sem. Available at: http://www.economiamexicana.cide.edu/num_anteriores/IV-1/01_ROS_(5-67).pdf downloaded on June 22nd, 2010.

341. Rubio, Luis (1999): Tres Ensayos: Fobaproa, Privatización y TLC. México: Cal y Arena, Centro de Investigación para el Desarrollo, A. C.

342. Rudek, Winfried (2009): The Possibilities and Limitations of Derivatives Statistics Collected By Central Banks, in: BIS (2009), Measuring Financial Innovation and its Impact, Proceedings of the IFC Conference,Basel, 26–27 August 2008, July available at: www.bis.org/ifc/publ/ifcb31.htm downloaded on October 20th, 2009.

343. Sachs, Jeffrey (1988): Creditor Panics: Causes and Remedies, available at: http://www.cato.org/events/monconf16/sachs.pdf , downloaded on May, 11th, 2009.

344. Sachs, Jeffrey and Radelet, Steven (1998): The Onset of the East Asian Financial Crisis, in: NBER Working Paper Series. Working Paper 6680, Cambridge, MA, August 1998.

345. Sachs, Jeffrey; Tornell, A. and Velasco A. (1995): The Collapse of the Mexican Peso: What Have We Learned? , in: NBER Working Paper Series, Working Paper 5142.

346. --- (1996). The Mexican Peso Crisis: Sudden Death or Death Foretold? , in: NBER Working Paper Series. Working Paper 5563.

347. Sachs, Jeffrey; Tornell A. and Velasco A. (1996a): Financial Crises in Emerging Markets: The Lessons from 1995, in: NBER Working Paper Series, Working Paper 5576.

348. Salinas de Gortari, Carlos: (2000): México un Paso Difícil a la Modernidad, Plaza y Janés Editores, Barcelona.

349. Salomon Brothers (1996): Mexican Bank Reference Guide, March.

350. Samuelson, Paul (1964): Theoretical Notes on Trade Problems, in: Review of Economics and Statistics, May, Nr. 46, p. 145-154.

351. Sánchez, Alfredo coord.; (1997): Crisis y perspectivas de la banca comercial, La Crisis Productiva y Financiera en México. Ed. UAM-A, 1997, pp. 93-112,

352. Sánchez, Alfredo and González, Juan (1998): Reestructuración de la Economía Mexicana Integración a la Economía Mundial y a la Cuenca del Pacífico, UAM Azcapotzalco, México.

353. Sarabia, Ernesto and Orozco, Juan Carlos (2009): Crece más el Gasto Público que el PIB, in: El Norte, Negocios, September 21st.

354. Sarialoglu-Hayali, Ayca (2007): Financial Stability and Financial Crises, The Role of Derivative Instruments in International Financial Crises, available at:

http://www.boeckler.de/pdf/v_2007_10_26_sarialioglu-hayali.pdf
downloaded on May 31st, 2009.

355. Schadler, Susan; Carkovic, M., Bennet A. and Kahn, R. (1993): Recent Experiences with Surges in Capital Inflows. IMF Occasional Paper 108. Washington: IMF.

356. Schatan, C. and Castilleja, L. (2005): The Maquiladora Electronics Industry
and the Environment along Mexico's Northern Border (Montreal, Commission
for Environmental Cooperation. Third North American Symposium on Assessing the Environmental Effects of Trade, 30 November-1 December 2005),
available at: http://www.cec.org/files/pdf/economy/final-schatan-T-
ESymposium05-paper_en.pdf downloaded on Oct. 30th, 2007

357. Schatán, Roberto (2002): "Régimen Tributario de la Industria Maquiladora",
in: Comercio Exterior 52(10), p. 916-926.

358. Shaikh, Anwar (2003): Globalization and the Myth of Free Trade, Paper for
the Conference on Globalization and Free Trade, New School University, New
York. Available at:
http://homepage.newschool.edu/~AShaikh/globalizationmyths.pdftionmyths.pd
f downloaded on July 25th 2007.

359. Shambaugh, Jay (2004): The Effect of Fixed Exchange Rates on Monetary
Policy, In : Quarterly Journal of Economics, Issue 1, p. p. 301-352.

360. Sharma, Shalendra (2001): The Missed Lessons of the Mexican Peso Crisis,
in Challenge, Vol. 44, Number 1 / January-February 2001, p. 56 - 89

361. Schneider, Benu (2003): Resident Capital Outflows: Capital Flight or Normal
Flows? A Statistical Interpretation, Working Paper 195, Overseas Development Institute, London, March 2003, available online at:
http://www.trudeaufoundation.ca/libraryservices/download-
nocache/Library/mo/overseas/workingp/wp195pdf downloaded on Oct. 10th,
2008.

362. --------------------- (2003b): Measuring Capital Flight: Estimates and Interpreta-
tions, Working Paper 194, Overseas Development Institute, London, March
2003, available online at:
http://www.trudeaufoundation.ca/libraryservices/download-
nocache/Library/mo/overseas/workingp/wp194pdf downloaded on Oct. 10th,
2008.

363. Schober, Jochen and Störmann, Wiebke (1995): Implikationen des zuneh-
menden Derivathandels von Kreditinstituten und Nichtbanken aus volkswirt-
schaftliche Sicht, in: Bertuch-Samuels, Axel and Störmann, Wiebke (1995):
Derivative Finanzinstrumente: Nutzen und Risiken, Deutsche Sparkassenverlag GmbH, Stuttgart.

364. Schott, Peter (2004): Across-Product vs. Within Product Specialization in International Trade, in: Quarterly Journal of Economics, Issue 1, p. p. 647-677.

365. Schrader, Klaus, Laaser, C. and Sichelschmidt (2006): Schleswig-Holsteins Wirtschaft im Kräftefeld der Globalisierung, Kieler Discussions Beiträge 434/435, Institut für Weltwirtschaft Kiel.

366. Servén, Luis (1998): Macroeconomic Uncertainty and Private Investment in LDCs: An Empirical Investigation, in: World Bank Policy Research Working Papers, WP No.2035, Washington, D.C.

367. Sidaoui, José (2005): The Mexican Financial System: Reforms and Evolution 1995-2005, in BIS Papers, No. 28, available at: http://www.bis.org/publ/bppdf/bispap28s.pdf downloaded on June 19th, 2009.

368. Siebert, Horst and Lorz, O. (2006): Aussenwirtschaft, 8. Auflage., Lucius & Lucius, Stuttgart.

369. Sinn, Hans-Werner (2007): Die Basar Ökonomie, Ullstein, Berlin.

370. Smith, Gordon and Cuddington, John (1985): A World Bank Symposium. Washington, D.C.

371. Smith, Peter H. (1997): Political Dimensions of the Peso Crisis, in: Naím, Moisés and Edwards, Sebastian eds. (1998): The Anatomy of an Emerging-Market-Crash, Carnegie Endowment for International Peace, Washington, D.C., p. 31-54.

372. Sohn, Chan-Hyun, Lee, Hongshik (2006): Trade Structure, FTA and Economic Growth: Implications to East Asia, Centre for International Trade Studies Working paper 2006-1.

373. Solis, Leopoldo (1998): Crisis Económico Financiera 1994-1995, Fondo de Cultura Económica, México.

374. Solis, Ricardo (1998): La Crisis Bancaria en Mexico: Alcances y Limitaciones Del Fobaproa, in: Villarreal, Diana comp. (1998): Política económica y crisis financiera en México, UAM-X, CSH, 1ª. Ed., México.

375. Solow; Robert (1999): The Labor Market as a Social Institution, Basil Blackwell, Cambridge.

376. Soueid, Mazen (2005): Development of Government Securities and Local Capital Markets in Mexico, in: International Monetary Fund (2005) Selected Issues. October 20, 2005, Mexico, D.F.

377. Soros, George (1995): Soros on Soros, John Wiley & Sons Inc., New York.

378. Steinherr, Alfred (1998): Derivatives the Wild Beast of Finance, John Wiley & Sons, New York.

379. Stiglitz, Joseph (2002): Globalization and its Discontents, London: Allen Lane.

380. Stockman, Alan (1982): The Order of Economic Liberalization: Comment, in: Karl Brunnerand Allan Meltzer, eds., Economic Policy in a World of Change. North-Holland, Amsterdam.

381. Stutz, F. and Warf, B (2005): The World Economy. Upper Saddle River: Pearson Prentice Hall.

382. Tanner, Evan (2001): Exchange Market Pressure and Monetary Policy: Asia and Latin America in the 1990s, IMF Staff Papers Vol. 47, No. 3 available at http://www.imf.org/External/Pubs/FT/staffp/2001/01/pdf/tanner.pdf downloaded on April 9th, 2009.

383. Taussig, F. (1927): International Trade, Macmillan, New York.

384. Thirlwall, Anthony (1979): "The Balance of Payments Constraint as an Explanation of International Growth Rates Differences", in: Banca Nazionale del Lavoro Quarterly Review, Vol.128, pp.45-53.

385. Tirole, J. (1997): The Theory of Industrial Organization, MIT Press, Cambridge.

386. Tobin, James (1996): A Currency Transaction Tax, Why and How, in: Open Economies Review, Band 7, 493-499.

387. Tore, Sten (1961): Household Saving and the Price Level. National Institute of Economic Research, Stockholm.

388. Tornell, A, Westermann, F. and Martinez, L. (2004): NAFTA and Mexico´s less than Stellar Performance, NBER Working Paper Series. Working Paper 10289.

389. Tornell, Aaron and Esquivel, Gerardo (1997): The Political Economy of Mexico's Entry into NAFTA, downloaded on june 12th, 2010 available at: http://www.nber.org/chapters/c8595

390. Torre, Leonardo (1999): Reflexiones sobre la Banca en México, in: Entorno Económico Vol. XXXVII Núm. 222 Sep./Oct., CIE, UANL.

391. Torre, L. and Mendoza, G. (1999): El Programa de Rescate y Reestructuración Bancaria en México, 1995-1998: ¿Èxito o Fracaso?, Documento de Investigación No.. Centro de Análisis y Difusión Económica, Monterrey.

392. Truman, Edwin (1996): The Mexican Peso Crisis, Implications for Finance, Federal Reserve Bulletin March.

393. Umlauf, Steven (1993): An Empirical Study of the Mexican Treasury Bill Auction, in Journal of Financial Economics, Vol. 33, p. 313-340.

394. UNCTAD (1997): Trade and Development Report, Geneve, available at: http://www.unctad.org/en/docs/tdr1997_en.pdf downloaded on April 2nd, 2008.

395. ----------- (1998): Unctad Assesses Effects of Asian Crisis On Developing Countries' Trade, available at: ` http://www.unctad.org/Templates/webflyer.asp?docid=3247&intItemID=2024&lang=1, downloaded on March 25th, 2008.

396. ---------- (1999): Foreign Portfolio Investment (FPI) and Foreign Direct Investment (FDI): Characteristics, Similarities, Complementarities and Differences, Policy Implications and Development Impact, Internet edition, available at: http://www.unctad.org/en/docs/c2em6d2&c1.en.pdf, downloaded on Oct. 13th, 2008.

397. --------- (2002): Trade and Development Report, Geneve, available at: http://www.globalpolicy.org/socecon/trade/unctad/2002/tradedevelopment.pdf downloaded on March 25th, 2008.

398. Universidad Nacional Autónoma de México UNAM (1995): Momento Económico, Mexico, Instituto de Investigaciónes Economicas IIEc, different issues, available at: http://www.iiec.unam.mx/Boletin_electronico/1995/num04/secext.html downloaded on Oct. 10th, 2008.

399. U. S Department of Commerce, Bureau of Economic Analysis: A Guide to the National Income and Product Accounts of the United States, available at: http://www.bea.gov/bea/an/nipaguid.pdf downloaded on Feb. 22nd, 2008.

400. --: Appendixes: A. Additional Information about the NIPA Estimates, available at: http://www.bea.gov/scb/pdf/2008/02%20February/D-Pages/0208appendixa.pdf , downloaded on Feb. 22nd, 2008.

401. --(1993): Survey of Current Business, Reliability and Accuracy of the Quarterly Estimates of GDP: October, available at: http://www.bea.gov/scb/account_articles/national/1093od/maintext.htm, downloaded on Feb. 22nd, 2008.

402. U.S. Department of the Treasury, Federal Reserve Bank of New York, Board of Governors of the Federal Reserve System (2007): Report on U.S. Portfolio Holdings of Foreign Securities as of December 31, 2006, November 2007.

403. Van Wijnbergen, Sweder (1991): The Mexican Debt Deal, in: Economic Policy No. 2 (April) pp. 13-56.

232

404. Van Wincoop, Eric and Marrinan, Jane (1996): Public and Private Savings and Investment, in Economics Working Paper and Business, Working Paper 172, Universitat Pompeu Fabra available at: http://www.econ.upf.edu/docs/papers/downloads/172.pdf downloaded on Dec. 10th, 2008.

405. Vargas, José (1994): El Reendeudamiento Externo de México 1988-1994, in: Dabat, Alejandro, coord., México y la Globalizacióbn, Centro Regional de Investigaciones Interdisciplinaras, Universidad Nacional Autónoma de México, available at: http://www.crim.unam.mx/bibliovirtual/Libros/ downloaded on Sept. 25, 2008.

406. Vazquez, Héctor (1995): Medición del Flujo Efectivo de Divisas de la Balanza Comercial de México, Revista Comercio Exterior,08/01/1995.

407. Vazquez, Ian (1996): The Brady Plan and the Market-based solutions to the Debt Crises, Cato Journal, Vol. 16, No, 2 (Fall) available at: http://www.cato.org/pubs/journal/cj16n2/cj16n2-4.pdf downloaded on July 3rd, 2009.

408. ------------------ (2002): A Retrospective on the Mexican Bailout, in: Cato Journal, Vol.21, No. 3.

409. Vega, Francisco Javier (1999): La Singular Historia del Rescate Bancario Mexicano de 1994 a 1999, y el Relevante Papel del Fobaproa, Biblioteca Plural, México, D.F.

410. Vega, Gustavo (1993): Liberalizcación Económica y Libre Comercio en América del Norte: Consideraciones Políticas Sociales y Culturales, El Colegio de México, México.

411. Vigfusson, R.; Sheets, N. and Gagnon, J. Exchange Rate Pass-Through to Export Prices: Assessing Some Cross-Country Evidence, in: Board of Governors of the Federal Reserve System International Finance Discussion Papers Number 902 September 2007 available at: http://www.federalreserve.gov/pubs/ifdp/2007/902/ifdp902.pdf downloaded on Dec. 3rd, 2007.

412. Villarreal, Diana comp. (1998): Política económica y crisis financiera en México, UAM-X, CSH, 1ª. Ed., México.

413. Villarreal, René (2004): TLCAN,La Experiencia de México Lecciones para Colombia, y América Latina, Hacia una Política de Competitividad Sistémica, Foro Internacional sobre Política de Competitividad para el Sector Productivo Industrial frente a los retos de los Tratados de Libre Comercio.

414. Villavicencio, Daniel ed. (2006): La Emergencia de Dinámicas Institucionales de Apoyo a la Industria Maquiladora, Porrua, México.

415. Voss, S. (2002): Tequila sunrise: A medium-term growth perspective for Mexico, DB Research, February 16th.

416. Walton, Michael (1997): The Maturation of the East Asian Miracle, in: Finance & Development, September, available at: http://www.imf.org/external/pubs/ft/fandd/1997/09/pdf/walton.pdf downloaded on March 24th, 2008.

417. Wacziarg, Roman and Welch, Karen (2008): The World Bank Economic Review, World Bank, available at: http://www.gdsnet.org/classes/OpennessSachsWarnerWelch-Wacziarg2003.pdf downloaded on October 20th, 2009.

418. Wayman, Oliver and Morgan Stanley Research (2008): Outlook for Investment Banking & Capital Market Financials, available at: http://www.oliverwyman.com/de/pdf-files/Oliver_Wyman_-_Morgan_Stanley_-_Outlook_for_Capital_Markets_and_Investment_Banking_-_April_08.pdf downloaded on January 12, 2010.

419. Whitt, Joseph (1996): The Mexican Peso Crisis, in: Economic Review Federal Reserve Bank of Atlanta, January-February, p. p.1-20.

420. Williamson, John (1985): The Exchange Rate System, IIE, Washington D.C.

421. -------------------- (1990): Latin American Adjustment. How Much Has Happened? IIE, Washington, D.C.

422. -------------------- (1999): What Should the Bank Think about the Washington Consensus? , Paper prepared as a background to the World Bank's World Development Report 2000.

423. Willson, Berry; Saunders, A. and Caprio, G. (1998): Mexico's Banking Crisis: Devaluation and Asset Concentration Effects, in NYU Financial Working Papers, No. 98075, November, available at: http://w4.stern.nyu.edu/finance/docs/WP/1998/html/wpa98075.html downloaded on June 27th 2009.

424. World Bank (1997): Global Development Finance, Washington. Volume 1. Analysis and Summaries Tables.

425. World Bank and Centre For Latin American Monetary Studies (2004): Payments and Securities Clearance and Settlement Systems In Mexico, Western Hemisphere Payments and Securities Clearance and Settlement Initiative Mexico, March 2003.

426. Wyand, Charles (1938): The Economics of Consumption, The Macmillan Company, New York.

427. Yam, Joseph (1999): Capital Flows, Hedge Funds and Market Failure: A Hong Kong Perspective, in: Proceedings of Conference Capital Flows and the

International Financial System, Reserve Bank of Australia, available at: http://www.rba.gov.au/publicationsandresearch/Conferences/1999/Yam.pdf downloaded on Nov. 25, 2009.

428. Zhang und Lien (2008): A Survey of Derivatives Markets, in: Emerging Markets Finance and Trade, Vol. 44, Number 2 / March – April, p. 39 – 69.

429. Zedillo, Ernesto (1998): 4. Informe de Gobierno (State of the Nation Report), Message to the Honorable Congress of the Union from the President of Mexico, at the presentation of his Second State of the Nation Report, Mexico City.

430. Zuñiga-Villaseñor, Gerardo (2005): Creditor Rights and Bank Lending in Mexico, mimeo, University of California, Berkeley.

431. Zweifel, P. and Heller (1997): Internationaler Handel: Theorie und Empirie, Physica-Verlag. 3. Auflage, Heidelberg.

Áron Kiss

Essays in Political Economy and International Public Finance

Frankfurt am Main, Berlin, Bern, Bruxelles, New York, Oxford, Wien, 2009.
VIII, 110 pp., num. tab.
Finanzwissenschaftliche Schriften.
Verantwortlicher Herausgeber: Kai A. Konrad. Vol. 119
ISBN 978-3-631-59676-0 · hardback € 27,80*

The essays of the book are contributions to the game theoretic analysis of the State. Two of the essays develop further the analysis of political accountability. Political accountability is the study of how the behavior of politicians is shaped by the prospect of reelections. The essays in this book enrich this field by introducing aspects of coalition government and ideology. A third essay focuses on strategic behavior by states in repeated tax competition. The contribution of this essay is the reevaluation of a lower bound to admissible taxrates as a policy instrument to contain tax competition.

Content: Coalitions and political accountability · Divisive politics and accountability · Minimum taxes and repeated tax competition

*The e-price includes German tax rate. Prices are subject to change without notice

Frankfurt am Main · Berlin · Bern · Bruxelles · New York · Oxford · Wien
Distribution: Verlag Peter Lang AG
Moosstr. 1, CH-2542 Pieterlen
Telefax 00 41 (0) 32 / 376 17 27
E-Mail info@peterlang.com

40 Years of Academic Publishing
Homepage http://www.peterlang.com

Peter Lang · Internationaler Verlag der Wissenschaften